THEN IT FELL APART

THEN IT FELL APART

by Moby

FABER & FABER

First published in the USA in 2019
by Faber & Faber Limited
Bloomsbury House
74–77 Great Russell Street
London WC1B 3DA

Typeset by Faber & Faber Limited
Printed in the UK by CPI Group (UK) Ltd, Croydon CR0 4YY

© Moby, 2019

The right of Moby to be identified as author of this work
has been asserted in accordance with Section 77
of the Copyright, Designs and Patents Act 1988

A CIP record for this book
is available from the British Library

ISBN 978–0–571–34889–3

FSC
www.fsc.org
MIX
Paper from
responsible sources
FSC® C020471

10 9 8 7 6 5 4 3 2 1

CONTENTS

SECTION THREE: In My Dreams I'm Dying All the Time

SECTION FOUR: Then It Fell Apart

PREFACE

In 2016, I published my first memoir, *Porcelain*, covering my weird life in New York City from 1989 to 1999. After finishing the book, rather than go back to therapy, I kept writing. I worked on material that was a logical follow-up, picking up where the first book left off. But I was also writing a traditional autobiography, which started at birth and ended around the time *Porcelain* began.

While in New York in early 2017 I thought, *Why not fold the two together?* With *Then It Fell Apart,* that's what I've tried to do. Hopefully, the dysfunction of my childhood provides context for the escalating horrors of my adult life. Oh, the temporal jumping around between chapters was somewhat inspired by *Slaughterhouse-Five*, but without the genius of Kurt Vonnegut.

As before, I've changed some names and details out of respect for other people, but all the stories in this book actually happened.

Thanks,

Moby

PROLOGUE: NEW YORK CITY (2008)

I wanted to die. But how?

It was 5 a.m., and I'd had fifteen drinks, $200 worth of cocaine, and a handful of Vicodin. After I stumbled home at 4 a.m., depressed and alone, I wandered from room to room in my apartment, sobbing and repeating, "I just want to die."

I calmed myself and considered my options.

I could tie a long rope or extension cord to the edge of the rough wooden fence on my roof and drop twenty or thirty feet down the back of the building, most likely breaking my neck. But I knew that sometimes after a long drop the head could become separated from the body. That seemed unnecessarily grisly for the person who found me.

Or I could get into the pristine white bathtub in my minimalist bathroom with the stainless-steel Kohler faucets and the Calacatta marble floor and cut my wrists and slowly bleed to death.

Or I could take an entire bottle of Vicodin, which, combined with the vodka and the cocaine and pills already in my system, would probably stop my heart.

I was still a WASP from Connecticut, and even though I wanted to die I needed to be polite. So before killing myself I would have to remember to unlock my front door and tape a suicide note by the doorknob. That way anyone coming into my apartment would know what to expect and not be too upset.

Over the last few years my depression had been building, and nights like this were becoming the norm.

I was a lonely alcoholic, and I desperately wanted to love someone and be loved in return. But every time I tried to get close to another human being I had crippling panic attacks that kept me isolated and alone.

I'd had a few successful years of making music, and sold tens of millions of records, but now my career was sputtering. I couldn't find love or success, so I tried to buy happiness. Three years earlier I had spent $6 million in cash on a luxury penthouse apartment on the Upper West Side of Manhattan. It had been my dream home: five stories on the top of an iconic limestone building overlooking Central Park.

Having grown up on food stamps and welfare, I'd assumed that moving to a castle in the sky would bring me happiness. But as soon as I moved into my Upper West Side penthouse I was as sad and anxious as I'd been in my small loft on Mott Street.

I sold the sky castle, moved back downtown, and recommitted myself to debauchery. I put tinfoil over the windows and had weekend-long orgies fueled by alcohol and drugs. But the more I threw myself into degeneracy, the more I ended up filled with self-loathing and loneliness.

The world of fame and success that gave me meaning and legitimacy was being taken away from me. And now the only respite I found from anxiety and depression was an hour or two each night when I was full of vodka and cocaine, looking for someone lonely and desperate enough to go home with me.

Recently I'd considered buying a bar and turning the basement into a light-proof apartment, reasoning that if I lived only at night, I'd find happiness. My plan was to sleep in the basement below the bar, wake up at 6 p.m., have dinner, and start drinking and doing cocaine around 10 p.m. I'd stay up until 8 a.m., take a handful of Xanax and Vicodin, and sleep until 6 p.m. I'd spend the rest of my days or years like an anxious, defeated Nosferatu, until my life finally, mercifully ended.

For decades alcohol and drugs had made me happy. But now I needed more and more alcohol and cocaine to get drunk and high, and my hangovers lasted for days. And when I was hungover, which was almost every day, I couldn't string sentences together or even remember simple words.

I'd vaguely considered getting sober, but the impulse never lasted for more than a few days. I'd even gone to some AA meetings, and while I appreciated the chance to look at beautiful alcoholic women covered in tattoos, I'd decided that institutional sobriety didn't work for me. So I kept drinking, kept buying cocaine, kept trying to stave off hangovers with handfuls of Xanax and Vicodin, and kept wanting to die.

My daily routine had become rote and tautological: after getting out of bed in the late afternoon I would stumble to my bathroom, step into the shower, and as the hot water poured over me I'd say one word over and over: "Fuck."

As in: "Fuck, I'm hungover again." And: "Fuck, I'm sick." And: "Fuck, I'm such an idiot." And: "Fuck, I hate myself."

But maybe tomorrow I wouldn't wake up and say "Fuck" in the shower. Because maybe I would finally be dead.

Which brought me back to the question of how to end my life. Hanging myself or cutting my wrists seemed too violent. And I'd heard that swallowing pills didn't always work – sometimes people just vomited them up and ended up alive, but with severe liver and brain damage.

A few years ago I'd read about elderly people killing themselves by tying plastic bags over their heads and quietly suffocating on their own exhaled CO_2. So, considering all of my options, tying a bag over my head seemed like an easy and painless and polite way to kill myself.

I walked into my kitchen, got on my knees, and found a box of black plastic garbage bags underneath the sink. I took one out of the box and looked around. When I'd bought this apartment in

1995 it had been an empty storage space in a nineteenth-century loft building. But after a year working with a local architect I'd ended up with my first real home. And it had been beautiful, with skylights and tall ceilings, white brick walls, and a kitchen filled with maple cabinets.

I had made most of my albums here, from the ten million-selling *Play* to my most recent record, the hundred thousand-selling *Last Night*.

I'd fallen in and out of love here. I'd had dinners here with my mother and grandmother, both of them now dead. I'd shown Lou Reed around my studio. I'd even sat on the $8,000 dark-green-and-teak Danish modern couch in my living room and played "'Heroes'" on acoustic guitar with David Bowie.

Growing up I'd assumed that if I could release even one small indie record and play shows to a hundred people a night, I would be happy. Now the long, tall wall leading from my front door to the kitchen was covered with hundreds of gold and platinum records, and I was miserable. So after a lifetime of baffling sadness I was declaring defeat.

I'd built this home. This was where I was going to die.

I took a belt out of my closet and got into bed.

I sobbed into my pillow, asking, "Why?"

I felt like I was asking my dead parents, "What did I do wrong? Why didn't you love me? Why did you leave me?"

I put the bag over my head and thought, *This is it, my last memory: crying inside a plastic garbage bag.* I pulled the belt tight over the bag and lay back, resting my head on my pillow. "I'm sorry, God," I whispered, and closed my eyes.

Section One:

Extreme Places I Didn't Know

NEW YORK CITY (1999)

Play had been out for a week and was poised to fail.

It was early May, and I was walking up 4th Avenue from my loft on Mott Street to Union Square, past buildings that 150 years earlier had been New York's fanciest. On my left was the Colonnade, which in the nineteenth century had been a row of townhouses styled to look like the Acropolis, and was now just a few surviving limestone columns, stained gray and black from a century and a half of factory smoke and exhaust.

I was wearing my usual uniform of old jeans and black sneakers; my small hands were balled in the pockets of my thrift-shop army jacket. The late-afternoon sun stretched down the long crosstown blocks, burnishing the old stone buildings.

I had worked on *Play* for the last two years, and it looked like it would be my final album, a flawed and poorly mixed swan song. I was amazed it had been released at all. A year ago I'd lost my record deal with my American label, and even before the release of *Play* most people in the music business had quietly consigned me to the trash heap of has-beens.

Losing my record deal didn't leave me bitter or surprised, because my previous album, *Animal Rights*, had failed in almost every way that an album could fail. It sold poorly, and received almost exclusively terrible reviews. My former American label, Elektra, was the home of Metallica and other artists who sold millions of albums. Objectively it made perfect sense for them to drop me, as all the evidence indicated that my best years were behind me. In the early

1990s I'd been seen as a techno wunderkind, but as the decade progressed I never lived up to the expectations that led to me being signed to a major record label.

I was still signed to Mute Records in England – but they had never dropped any of their artists. And a new label in New York, V2, had agreed to release *Play*, a decision I assumed stemmed from charity or delusion.

I walked past the former location of the Ritz on 11th Street, where I'd seen Depeche Mode's first-ever US show in 1982, when I was sixteen years old. After seeing the band with their synthesizers and new-wave haircuts I'd dreamed of someday playing my own solo show to a few thousand people at the Ritz. But now I was thirty-three, my glory days were behind me, and tonight I was going to perform in the basement of a record store for maybe fifty people. I tucked my head down against an unexpectedly cold wind and walked up 4th Avenue in the shadows.

I'd started working on *Play* in 1997, writing and recording it on old equipment in my small bedroom studio in my loft on Mott Street. Now that the album was released I realized there was nothing about it that augured success. It was poorly mixed, and when it didn't feature my own thin voice it used vocals recorded forty or fifty years earlier by long-dead singers like Bessie Jones and Bill Landford. I assumed that *Play* would soon be forgotten, as 1999 belonged to Britney Spears and Eminem and Limp Bizkit: pop acts who made albums in expensive studios and knew how to write and record songs that sounded huge on the radio.

Not much had worked out for me in the past few years: my mother had died, I was battling near-constant panic attacks, I was guzzling ten or fifteen drinks a night, and I was running out of money. But today I was happy, as I had been allowed to release one final album.

After tonight's show in the basement of the Virgin Megastore in Union Square my band and I were scheduled to do a two-week tour

extreme places i didn't know

of small venues in North America, and then a two-week tour of small venues in Europe. Playing small shows and waking up hungover in parking lots wasn't everyone's idea of glamour, but I was excited to have this one last month on tour. Afterward my career as a professional musician would be over, and I could go back to school or figure out what else I could do with the rest of my life.

For this short tour I'd put together a small band: Scott, a dark, handsome drummer I'd worked with since 1995; Greta, a tall, tattooed bass player with spiky bleached hair; and on keyboards and turntables, Spinbad, a DJ-comedian with a shaved head and a carefully trimmed goatee. I was going to sing some of the songs, but most of the sampled and female vocals were going to be on tape, as I couldn't afford to hire a real singer.

I turned onto 14th Street and walked into the record store, holding a dripping bottle of Poland Spring I'd bought from a pretzel vendor. I took the escalator down to the basement, where my band and crew had already set up our equipment. Even though I barely had a career I still had three managers, and one of them, Marci, was at the bottom of the escalator, badgering the store manager. Marci had exploding curls of red hair, and she was short, fierce, and loyal. The store manager was trying to back away from her.

"Hi, Marci," I said.

"Mo! How are you?"

"Hungover," I told her. "When do we go on?"

"It was supposed to be 5.30, but I think we can push it back to 6?" she said, smiling aggressively at the store manager.

"Okay," he conceded. Everyone eventually conceded in the face of Marci's persistence. "But you guys need to be wrapped up by 6.30."

"Is that okay, Moby?" Marci asked.

"I guess so," I said with a shrug. I walked over to my band and road crew.

"Hey, Mo!" said Dan, my lighting designer. "How are you?"

"Hungover."

Dan was a Brit with a tall green Mohawk. We didn't actually need a lighting designer to play this show under the fluorescent bulbs of a record-store basement, but he had shown up to help carry equipment and lend support. He was hanging out with Steve, a disturbingly tall and attractive sound tech, and J.P., an unfailingly friendly sound man from Manchester who'd started out working with the Happy Mondays.

My new tour manager, Sandy, walked over. "Everything okay, Moby?" he asked.

Sandy was British, a bit taller than me, and handsome – with a full head of blond hair that I envied. He'd been a tour manager for successful British indie-rock bands, and I was surprised that he'd been willing to spend a month overseeing my small, unexceptional tour.

"I'm good, Sandy, how are you?" I asked politely. He was a rock 'n' roll tour manager who lived on a series of tour buses, but he seemed professional and erudite. I wanted him to think well of me.

Other than my band and crew, there were only a handful of people in the basement. Some were wandering around the magazine racks, and a few were watching us set up equipment. I walked onto the small stage, picked up my guitar, and started playing "Stairway to Heaven." The store manager rushed over and remonstrated, "You need to keep it down before you go on."

I looked at him and blushed. "Sure thing," I said, and turned off my guitar.

This wasn't glamorous. But it was something. At the end of the *Animal Rights* tour I'd been playing to twenty-five people a night. If we drew fifty tonight, it would be a 100 percent increase.

I put down my guitar and wandered around the store, looking at the racks of CDs and cassettes and music magazines and books. I picked up a copy of the UK weekly *Melody Maker* to see if they'd reviewed *Play*. They had. They'd given it two stars out of ten, and mostly used the review as an opportunity to malign me personally. My heart sank.

Marci walked up to me. "What are you reading, Mo?"

"*Melody Maker* review."

"How is it?"

I shrugged and handed her the review. She read it and shook her head. "Well, at least the *Spin* review was good!" she said with bright and unwarranted optimism.

I gathered my band, walked back onstage, and picked up my guitar. I tapped on the microphone and surveyed the scene. I'd hoped for fifty people to be at our first show, but in the bright store lights I could see only thirty looking down at us from the balcony.

"Hi," I said cautiously into the mic, "I'm Moby, and this is 'Natural Blues,'" and we started the first show of the *Play* tour. I hoped people were watching us play our instruments, and maybe wouldn't notice that the female vocals were pre-recorded and nobody was actually singing. When the song ended a few people clapped, while the rest of the shoppers went about their business.

We played "Porcelain" and "South Side" and "Why Does My Heart Feel So Bad?" and "Go" and "Bodyrock," and then ended with "Feeling So Real." "Go" and "Feeling So Real" had been European hits, and at various points I'd stood onstage at raves and played them for tens of thousands of people. Now I was in a basement playing them for thirty people who applauded politely while a bunch of commuters looked for Hootie & the Blowfish CDs.

As soon as the show ended the audience dispersed and my band and crew and I started unplugging microphones, packing up the drums, and putting guitars in cases. I smiled. This was my life for the next month, and this was enough.

My father drove into a wall and killed himself.

He and my mother had been living in a basement apartment in Harlem with Jamie, their dog, Charlotte, their cat, three rescued lab rats, and me. One night after a bad fight with my mom, my dad got drunk and drove into the base of a bridge on the New Jersey Turnpike at a hundred miles an hour.

He had grown up in New Jersey, and after college had joined the army as a sharpshooter. He left the army to move to New York City, grew a mustache and let his hair grow long, and became a beatnik. In 1962 he met my mom at Columbia University, where he was getting his master's degree in chemistry and she was working as a receptionist.

My mom was a short, blonde, twenty-year-old WASP from Connecticut, and together they drank wine and smoked pot and listened to Ornette Coleman records and wandered around New York City and fell in love. They loved each other almost as much as they loved being young in New York City at a time when it seemed like the artists and the intellectuals and the radicals were reinventing the world.

They were married in New Jersey, and years later my mom told me that I was conceived in their basement apartment in Harlem while they listened to *A Love Supreme* by John Coltrane.

At first their world felt idyllic, but then the banalities interrupted: rent, groceries, animals who needed to go to the vet. After I was born on September 11, 1965, their soundtrack changed from obscure jazz LPs to a newborn crying in his crib. In the rest of the world the revolution was unfolding and revealing itself, but because of me they were in a basement apartment in Harlem, smoking cigarettes and changing diapers.

So they fought. My father, who was already a heavy drinker, drank more. He'd disappear for days on end, leaving my mother broke and alone in a cold apartment with a wailing newborn. One night she threatened to divorce him and take me away. That night he drove into the base of a bridge and died.

After the funeral my mother drove her 1964 Plymouth to Connecticut with Jamie the dog, Charlotte the cat, the rescued lab rats, and me. We moved into a small apartment in an old, gray, Victorian house next to a prison in Danbury. It had a small kitchen lit by a circular fluorescent bulb, a living/dining room with a thrift-shop couch and an old black table, a bedroom where my mom slept, and a small closet where I slept.

In September 1968, after we'd lived in Danbury for a year, my mom asked me what I wanted for my third birthday. Even more than toys what I wanted was to eat Kaboom cereal. I loved sickly sweet Kaboom, so for my birthday dinner she let me have two bowls of it. After my second bowl I begged for a third, but she said no.

I pleaded – but she remembered the last time I'd eaten too much Kaboom and had vomited up cereal pieces and pink milk on the peeling linoleum kitchen floor. When I realized she was cutting me off from my supply of Kaboom I ran crying to my closet. I curled up on my metal-framed camp bed and cried into my pale green blanket.

Earlier that day my mom had given me a plastic kazoo as my birthday present. I thought that after Kaboom my new kazoo was the greatest thing on the planet. All day I'd carried it with me, even bringing it into the bathtub to see if it would make sounds underwater, which it didn't. So now I put the kazoo in my mouth to see what it would sound like if I cried into it.

I cried loudly into the kazoo, making a buzzing wail, and my mom opened the door to see what I was doing. She started to ask, "What is that sound?" but couldn't finish the sentence because once she saw me crying into the kazoo, she started laughing. And even though I was still miserable after being denied my third bowl of Kaboom, I started laughing too.

I climbed under the blanket to play my favorite game: There's a Lump in the Bed. The game involved me crawling under the blankets and my mom saying, "There's a weird lump in the bed!" She would then push down on me (i.e. the lump). When my mom said, "Is there a weird lump here?" I said from underneath the blanket, speaking through my kazoo, "I'm not a lump, I'm a kazoo!"

I poked my head out of the blanket. She was laughing so hard that she was crying, and had taken off her glasses to wipe her eyes. "Why are you crying?" I asked, still talking through the kazoo.

My mom was pretty, with short blonde hair that got longer and curlier as the 1960s progressed. She'd loved the beatniks. She'd wanted to stay in New York so she could be a painter and hang out with the bohemians in Greenwich Village. But now she was a single mother attending community college and living next to a prison.

Through my kazoo I asked again, "Why are you crying?"

A few months later my mother graduated from the local community college with a degree in English literature. She was a widow in Connecticut, but she longed to be with her people: the beatniks, who had moved to San Francisco en masse and become hippies. For her, the East Coast was the land of dead husbands and conservative parents and apartments next door to prisons. California was the land of Jim Morrison and Jefferson Airplane, with droves of young people migrating west to be reborn next to the endless Pacific.

Her graduation present from her parents was a pair of tickets to San Francisco: one for her, one for me. While we stood at the gate at JFK airport, a United Airlines agent asked me if I'd ever flown before.

extreme places i didn't know

"No," I said breathlessly.

"Well, this is for our first-time flyers," she said, and handed me a big yellow pin with the cartoon image of a grinning and possibly pregnant jumbo jet. We boarded, and I sat in my orange-and-brown middle seat, clutching my new yellow pin. I didn't have many possessions: my kazoo, a few stuffed animals, some Babar books. But now I had a big yellow pin that proved that I'd been on an airplane.

After we took off the ginger ale was free, so I kept drinking it. When I told my mom for the third time in ninety minutes, "Mom, I need to pee," she looked annoyed. I had learned that I had two moms: one was happy and calm and laughed with me when I cried into my kazoo; the other was mad at the world and at me.

"Just pee in your seat if you have to go so bad," she snapped.

I'd never been on an airplane and didn't know what the protocol was. So I peed in my seat and promptly started crying.

"What!?" My mom turned to me. "Why are you crying?"

"I peed in my seat and it's wet."

She sighed and scooped me up. In the bathroom she dried me off and yelled at me, "I didn't mean to really pee in your seat!"

"But you said to."

"I was being facetious," she said, forgetting that as a three-year-old, I didn't know what "facetious" meant.

She took me back to our seats and had me sit on a folded blanket. "Is that okay?" she asked. I couldn't talk without crying again, so I nodded my head.

A flight attendant came over and asked if I wanted to go upstairs to visit the upper deck. Awestruck, I immediately forgot about my wet seat. "There's upstairs?" I asked.

She took my hand and walked me up the metal spiral stairs to the upper deck, where a few businessmen were standing around a bar, smoking cigarettes and drinking brown liquor. "This little guy has never been on a plane before!" the smiling flight attendant announced.

new york city (1965–8)   15

"I've never been on a plane before!" I told the businessmen, to make sure they knew.

"Well, have some peanuts!" one of them said, handing me a packet of airline peanuts. It was silver and blue and looked like the future.

"Can I keep them?"

"Ha! They're yours, sir!" the businessman said, shaking my tiny hand.

The flight attendant took me downstairs and back to my seat. "Mom," I said, "the man gave me peanuts." I held up my airplane peanuts in their shiny wrapper.

"That's great," she said, and went back to reading the in-flight magazine.

I opened my fold-down table and played with my giant yellow jumbo-jet pin and the packet of airplane peanuts from the future.

extreme places i didn't know

3

LONDON, ENGLAND (1999)

I wouldn't normally have looked for vegan food in the King's Cross neighborhood of London, since it was a filthy pit of grease and vice, but I'd finished the soundcheck and I was hungry. I was wearing my daily tour uniform of jeans, a black T-shirt, an old army jacket, and a black New York Yankees cap I had bought at JFK before flying to the UK. Even though it was June, it was cold and raining, and my sneakers were soaked.

The hookers and drug dealers huddled in doorways and underneath bus shelters, smoking cigarettes and staring disconsolately at the wet streets. For most people, King's Cross would've been frightening, but its damp squalor reminded me of Times Square in the 1970s.

A few blocks away from the Scala – the venue where I would be performing in a few hours – I found a vegetarian Indian restaurant. So many things in my life had fallen by the wayside during the 1990s: Christianity, sobriety, fame. But after I became a vegan in 1987 my commitment to veganism had never faltered. I might drink myself to death or even forsake my eternal soul, but I would never do anything that contributed to the suffering of an animal.

I ordered rice and lentils with fried potatoes, and sat on a stool with my styrofoam tray full of greasy food. The restaurant's window was covered with steam on the inside and streaks of rain on the outside. Through the atmospheric chiaroscuro King's Cross looked soft, like a Turner painting. I could see shapes and colors through the steam and rain; a few people hurried past the window like windblown flags.

My four-week *Play* tour was almost over, and it had been more successful than the *Animal Rights* tour I'd done a few years ago. Almost all the venues we'd played had been half-full – this was progress, even if the venues had been tiny. I was excited for tonight's show, because afterward Mute (my European record label) were going to throw a party for me in the bar above the club.

I had been drinking almost every night since the tour started, but hadn't met any women. Every time I drank I hoped I'd meet a beautiful woman who would offer love and validation. But so far on this short tour drinking had delivered only drunkenness.

I knew I would meet someone tonight. How could a musician play a concert in London and then go to a party being thrown for him by his record label and not find someone to kiss at least?

I took my empty tray, still glistening from greasy potatoes, and threw it in the overflowing trash by the door of the restaurant. When I stepped outside the rain had picked up, so I pulled up the hood of my jacket and rushed back to the Scala.

At 10 p.m. we played a seventy-five-minute set for two hundred people, a crowd that half filled the room. During "Next Is the E" I climbed on top of one of the onstage monitors, hoping to strike a rock-star pose, but my sneakers were still damp and I slipped. Luckily the strobes were flashing, and nobody seemed to notice when I fell. The audience clapped politely between songs, and a few people even danced cautiously to some of the older rave tracks, like "Go."

After the show my band and I changed out of our sweaty black stage T-shirts into our black after-show T-shirts. At the party a few fans came up to me as I was ordering shots of vodka and told me that they'd enjoyed the show and that they loved *Play*. This surprised me – I didn't think anyone had heard it. We were performing some songs from the album, but they were slower and more subdued than the older rave songs, so they weren't going over very well. I'd taken "Porcelain" out of the set; it was so quiet that I could sometimes hear people talking over it while we played.

I drank the free vodka and talked with people from the record company, but by 1 a.m. I was drunk and alone in the bar with the bartender and the janitor. The bartender turned off the Blur cassette he was playing and flicked on the harsh overhead lights. "Sorry, mate," he said with what seemed like genuine sympathy, "party's over." I pulled on my army jacket and stumbled down the stairs, out into the rain.

I drunkenly shuffled down the wet sidewalk, looking at shuttered storefronts and feeling sorry for myself. How badly was I failing as a musician that I couldn't even find someone to flirt with at my own after-show party?

Waiting to cross the street I saw a delicate blonde prostitute standing in a bus shelter. She was smoking a cigarette and scanning the street through half-closed eyes. She had long, thin, alabaster legs. An off-white raincoat partially covered her short skirt and yellow halter top. Her bleached-blonde hair was cut short, and she had a little pixie nose.

Over the last few years I'd dated a variety of sex workers, although I'd never paid money for sex. But standing in the rain in King's Cross at 1 a.m. I realized that I could pay this beautiful woman to come back to my hotel room. I was drunk and lonely and wanted to feel another person next to me. Ideally that person would like me and desire me, but I was desperate enough for validation that I would accept being just another customer.

I wanted to talk to her, but as I'd never approached a prostitute I didn't know what to say. I assumed that if I asked "How much?" she'd look at me suspiciously. Her eyes would be hidden, but when she saw my vulnerability she'd soften. Maybe she would even smile at me. We'd go back to my hotel and we'd sit on my bed talking. We'd share our loneliness, and through our mutual brokenness we'd fall in love. She'd see my flaws and inadequacies and love me in spite of them. I'd hold her on my sagging hotel bed and we'd relax, knowing that we were going to save each other.

And finally at dawn we would sleep, safe in each other's arms.

I stood in a phone booth for several minutes, enjoying my fantasy and trying to summon the nerve to approach her. My biggest fear was that she'd reject me. Rationally I knew that prostitutes didn't reject people who were going to pay them. But I still feared that when she looked at me, she'd know that I was an impoverished white-trash kid with attachment issues.

I heard someone say my name, "Moby? What are you doing here?"

I snapped out of my reverie. A group of Mute employees were standing next to me. I said, too quickly, "I was just walking back to my hotel."

They were nonplussed, as I hadn't been walking. I'd been standing. In the shadows at 1 a.m. in King's Cross, staring at a prostitute.

The Mute staffers pretended everything was normal, that standing by yourself in the rain in King's Cross late at night was something that people did. "We're going to meet some people at the bar of your hotel," one of them said awkwardly. "Want to come?"

"Sure," I said, and took one last look at the beautiful prostitute as she leaned into an idling car.

extreme places i didn't know

4

SAN FRANCISCO, CALIFORNIA (1969)

I caught a pigeon.

My mom and her San Francisco friends had gotten high and gone to Golden Gate Park to have a picnic on the grass. They smoked cigarettes and drank wine on a tie-dyed blanket, while I ran through flocks of pigeons, waving my arms, amazed that I could make them fly. I went back to the blanket, exhausted and exhilarated.

"Hey, go catch us a pigeon, Mobes," my mother's friend Jason told me. Jason, like all of my mom's San Francisco friends, had been a preppy kid in Connecticut in the early 1960s. Now he lived near Haight-Ashbury and had a thin brown beard and hair down to his shoulders.

"Okay," I said, and walked back to the pigeons. This time I didn't wave my hands – I just walked up to a stout gray pigeon and picked it up. I returned to Jason and presented the softly cooing bird to him with outstretched arms. "Here," I said.

"Mobes, let it go," my mom said gently.

I was confused. Jason had asked me to catch a pigeon. So I caught a pigeon. And now my mom was telling me to let it go. Adults were confusing.

"Okay," I said, putting the pigeon on the ground. "Bye, pigeon." The pigeon cocked his head at me and then walked back to the flock to rejoin his friends.

"How did you do that?" Jason asked me.

"I picked it up," I said, surprised that I had to explain something so simple.

"Betsy, I think he's magic," breathed Piper, one of the hippie girlfriends.

My mom smiled at me. "I think you're right."

I didn't like San Francisco or all the scary hippies. But I loved standing in the sun with my mom smiling at me and telling me I was magic. "Should I get another pigeon?" I asked.

After Golden Gate Park, we went to an arts and crafts festival. Wherever we went, my mom's friends had the same routine: pile into a Volkswagen, drive somewhere in San Francisco, smoke pot, wander around with other hippies, smoke pot. My mom's friends didn't seem to have jobs, although they complained sometimes about not getting enough money from their parents back in Connecticut.

The arts and crafts fair was in a public square surrounded by scraggly trees, with hippies painting, playing guitar, and dancing to drum circles. It was all chaos to me, so I clutched my mom's leather fringe handbag wherever we went.

In Connecticut my mom had been a short-haired preppy from Darien who smoked pot and listened to Jefferson Airplane records. But since we arrived in San Francisco she'd done everything she could to leave Connecticut behind and fit in with the other hippies. Her blonde hair was now wild and curly. She wore flowing orange batik dresses and faded denim skirts. And even though pot was illegal, she and her friends smoked it openly, the way my grandparents and their friends drank gin and tonics.

"Here you go, Mobes," my mom said, high and smiling. She leaned down and put a small silver peace pin on my overalls.

"What is it?" I asked.

"It's a symbol of peace," Piper said. "Do you like peace?"

I didn't really know what peace was, but I was happy to have another pin. With my pregnant jumbo-jet pin, I now had two.

*

extreme places i didn't know

The next day my mom and her friends decided to drive to the beach to take acid. They found a low-rent day-care center run by hippies, near where we were staying in the Tenderloin. "I'll be back tonight," my mom said as she dropped me off. I watched her get into a VW Bug with her friends and drive away.

The day care was in an old Victorian house, with a small patch of dirt out front. The other kids all knew each other – I assumed they were here every day. I found a Tonka truck with three wheels and pushed it around the dirt, picking up pebbles and garbage, hoping my mom would come back soon. I was three years old and scared, and I didn't know why my mom had left me here alone.

After a few hours I'd made a couple of sandbox friends, but I was still terrified. The day-care workers weren't nice. They smoked cigarettes and smelled like wine, and they watched sullenly from the porch while the kids played in the dirt.

At naptime we went inside, got our mats, and lay down. I fell asleep, hoping that when I woke up my mom would be there.

Some time later I was jostled awake, not by my mom but by one of the day-care workers. He looked like all the other hippies: faded jeans, an R. Crumb T-shirt, long black hair, a thick beard. He held his finger to his lips, making the universal gesture for "Sssh, be quiet." He took my hand and led me to a bathroom in the back of the house. We stepped inside and he locked the door, again holding his finger to his lips.

He pulled down his pants and sat on the toilet lid. "Here," he said, gesturing at his penis, "you can touch it."

I didn't know what to do.

"It's okay," he said. "You have one too. It's okay to touch it." He guided my three-year-old hand to his erect penis. "Now rub it," he said, and leaned back as I tried to do what he told me.

"You can put your mouth on it too," he said.

Afterward he took my head in his hands and stared in my eyes.

"You did good. But you can't tell anyone. Do you hear me?" His grip on my head got harder. "Not ever."

He led me back to my mat, and I lay there, not sleeping, not moving.

My mom and her friends collected me in the early evening.

"Hey, Mobes, sorry we're late," my mom said, walking up to the porch.

I didn't know how to say anything, so I stared at the ground.

"Mobes?" she asked. "Are you okay?"

"He's just tired," one of her friends said. "It's late. Right, little man?"

I felt heavy, like I was about to start sobbing forever.

They put me in the back of the VW Bug, and we headed back to the house where we were staying. "Did you have fun with your new friends?" Jason asked me.

I couldn't say anything.

Jason smiled at me. "Don't worry – we're going back to the beach tomorrow, so you can see all your friends again."

5

NEW YORK CITY (1999)

Suddenly, and surprisingly, my failure of an album wasn't failing.

The four-week tour was over, and I was back home in New York. But something was happening – *Play* was selling more every week, even though it had been out for over a month. When I released *Everything Is Wrong* and *Animal Rights* in 1995 and 1996 they each had their most successful weeks in the seven days after they were released, and then quickly drifted off into obscurity.

But that wasn't happening now. *Play* wasn't disappearing. And, by association, I wasn't disappearing. In fact, I was looking at myself on the corner of Broadway and Houston Street, and I was over fifty feet tall.

Someone from Calvin Klein had approached me after hearing *Play* and asked me to be a part of an ad campaign that featured musicians. Kim Gordon and Jon Spencer were doing it, so it didn't seem like too much of a compromise. Nobody had ever asked me to model clothes before – but now I was looking at myself on a billboard covering the entire face of a building.

The photo shoot took place in a five-thousand-square-foot white-walled loft in Chelsea. The giant space was filled with food and assistants and racks of clothes and klieg lights the size of oil barrels. For my shoot they built a desert set in the corner of the cavernous studio. The wardrobe person put me in dark jeans and a dark denim jacket, making me look like a male prostitute on the outskirts of El Paso.

A few weeks after the photo shoot I was back in New York, walking to my friend Damian's apartment. The sun had set, but the sky was the dark blue that comes the moment before actual night. It was late June, and the air was the same temperature as my skin. The discount jeans stores and nail salons on Broadway had all closed for the night, so I headed down Greene Street through Soho.

When I first moved to New York in 1989 Soho had been a desolate wilderness without streetlights. There were galleries and artists' studios, but for the most part the neighborhood felt as empty as an Edward Hopper painting. Now the galleries were being replaced by boutiques, and I had even heard that Chanel and Prada were planning on opening Soho stores.

I walked west on Grand Street and passed Lucky Strike, a restaurant where I'd DJed in 1990; when I worked there I'd literally been paid in spaghetti and salad. I crossed Canal Street into the emptiness of Tribeca, and walked a few blocks to Damian's studio. Damian, one of my closest friends since the 1980s, had been my roommate when I moved to New York over a decade ago. He was an exceptionally talented painter, but the art world was wary of him, as he was blond and handsome and took pictures with his shirt off. He was also plagued by social anxiety, which made him seem aloof.

When I arrived at his studio he was shirtless and smoking, standing in front of a giant painting of a swimming pool. He put on a polo shirt, turned off the Nine Inch Nails CD he was blasting out, and locked up his studio.

As we walked outdoors the aroma changed from the fresh oil paint in his studio to old pee. A dump truck lumbered by, its thunder amplified in the canyon of tall buildings. I didn't savor the smell of pee or the sound of dump trucks, but they were part of New York, and I loved New York unconditionally. This was the city of my birth, and it felt safe to me, like a walled medieval town.

We started our night at a party on the rooftop of a tall building in Chelsea. I quickly downed three drinks, and with vodka coursing through my veins I gazed up at the Empire State Building, reflecting on how New York City was a gentle paradox. The surface was

extreme places i didn't know

brutal, but its core felt soft and nurturing, whispering that it would never disappoint me.

Damian walked to where I was standing at the edge of the roof.

"What are you doing?" he asked.

"Anthropomorphizing New York."

"Want to go?"

I finished my fourth drink. "Okay."

We left the party and went to a new club on Bleecker Street, where I drank more. At 1 a.m. we realized we weren't going to find anyone to flirt with us, so we headed further south, meeting our friend Fancy at another new bar, on Broome Street.

"You look amazing," I told Fancy. He was wearing a black three-piece suit and carrying a small briefcase filled with playing cards, dark-blue rayon socks, and a flask of whiskey.

"You look so boring," he told me. He pressed his hand on my forehead, checking to see if I was ill. "Are you okay?" For years he and I had gone out five nights a week, both of us wearing thrift-shop suits and drinking compulsively. Tonight I was in jeans and a T-shirt, a sartorial disappointment.

At 2 a.m. Damian headed home. Fancy and I had a few more drinks and walked over to Sway. We always tried to end our nights at Sway: it stayed open very late and was filled with people who were as debauched as we were. We were both drunk when we got there, so we ordered beer. Beer didn't seem like actual alcohol, more like late-night soda for drunks.

When the DJ played an old Smiths record I danced with a beautiful Norwegian woman Fancy had introduced me to. I bought us beers and we found a booth by the corner of the dance floor. "Do you want another drink?" I asked her as we sat down.

"No," she said, looking at her still-full beer. "I haven't finished this one."

"Okay, hold on." I stumbled to the bar and bought two more beers, just so I'd have enough when last call happened.

We talked about Norway, where I'd been a few times, and then I leaned in to kiss her. "No, sorry, I have a boyfriend," she said.

"Oh," I said, suddenly deflating. "Okay."

The music stopped and the lights came on. Abruptly the bar transformed from a mysterious playground to a brightly lit room filled with blinking alcoholics and drug addicts. "I go find my friends now," she said, leaving me alone in my booth.

I scanned the room to see if there were any other women I could flirt with, but everybody already seemed to be paired off or leaving. I finished my beer and said good night to Fancy. I'd had twelve drinks, maybe thirteen, and I was solidly drunk.

I walked home through Soho and returned to the corner of Broadway and Houston Street. I looked up at my billboard again, marveling that there was an image of myself five stories high. I hated the nights when I didn't find anyone to flirt with or validate me – but seeing myself fifty feet tall made me feel better.

The biblical quotation "What does it benefit a man if he gains the world but loses his soul?" came unbidden into my head, sounding more like a judgmental cricket than Christ challenging his disciples. I didn't want to lose my soul, but I liked that *Play* was selling more than the other albums I'd released. Most likely it wasn't going to keep selling, I decided, so I wasn't really in much danger of gaining the world. And anyway, I'd learned years ago that my soul wasn't worth all that much.

Over the years I'd had a complicated relationship with God. In high school I'd been a punk-rock atheist, and then in the late 1980s I'd become a very serious Christian. By the mid-1990s I had shed my formal Christianity, but I still prayed and thought of myself as a good and spiritual person. And even though I was scrambling to pick up every perk that my small amount of fame had to offer, I still valued the idea that I was a spiritual person, and I believed that materialism and worldliness were not in keeping with my values.

I wanted to do the right thing. But I was sad and lonely, and thought more fame could fix that. Maybe people would see me on a billboard and think that I mattered. Or a woman would read about me in a magazine, and then when I met her she would be more inclined to love me.

I knew that countless people had been damaged and destroyed by fame. But I was sure I could figure out a way to succeed where they had failed – to gain the world and still hold onto my paltry soul.

6

AUSTIN, TEXAS (1999)

"Natalie Portman is where?"

"She's at the backstage door."

We had just finished a show in Austin, playing to four hundred and fifty people at a venue that held five hundred. I walked to the backstage door, sure that this was a misunderstanding or a joke, but there was Natalie Portman, patiently waiting. She gazed up at me with black eyes and said, "Hi."

"Hi," I said. As if this were normal, as if we knew each other, as if movie stars randomly showed up after my shows.

I escorted Natalie backstage and got her a bottle of water. I drank a beer, while my band and crew stood around the dressing room, quiet and uncomfortable. We'd never had a movie star backstage before, and none of us knew what to say or do.

"So, did you enjoy the show?" I asked Natalie.

"I loved it!" she said. She was wearing jeans and a white T-shirt; her dark-brown hair was pulled back in a ponytail. "The songs from *Play* were so great." Natalie sat on the black leather couch and smiled at me. My heart stuttered.

I was nervous, so I made small talk. "We're going to New York in a few days," I said. "For the VMAs."

She smiled again and looked straight into my eyes. "I'll be in New York too. Can we meet up?"

This was confusing. I was a bald binge drinker who lived in an apartment that smelled like mildew and old bricks, and Natalie Portman was a beautiful movie star. But here she was in my dressing room, flirting with me.

"Yeah, let's meet up in New York," I said, trying to emanate a degree of confidence that I had never in my entire life actually felt.

"Well, I should go," she said. "Can you walk me to my car?"

A week later I was standing on a mezzanine at Lincoln Center, playing records during the commercial breaks at the MTV Video Music Awards. There were a few thousand people inside the theater, watching Britney Spears and Eminem and Backstreet Boys perform and win awards. But I was by myself in the cavernous lobby, with two turntables and a few records I'd brought from home.

That afternoon a publicist from my record company had asked me if I had any clothes that would stand out on camera. The best I could come up with was a gold lamé Elvis suit I'd bought at the Salvation Army a few years earlier. It was five sizes too big and had never been washed, but when I wore it I shone like a radioactive clown.

After the show Natalie appeared on the balcony where my turntables were set up. She was wearing a perfectly fitted beige dress and looked disconcertingly like Audrey Hepburn. "What do you think of my suit?" I asked, smiling nervously.

"It's interesting," she said. "What are you doing now?"

"I'm playing a late-night show for Donatella Versace," I said. "Do you want to go?"

"You're DJing?"

"No, playing live."

"Okay," she said, putting her arm on my frayed gold lamé sleeve and confidently leading me out of Lincoln Center. I was thirty-three and she was twenty, but this was her world. I was comfortable in dive bars and strip clubs and vegan restaurants, but I knew nothing about award shows and red carpets.

Natalie had a limo and a driver and a security guard waiting for her, and before going to the Versace event we headed over to the VMA after-show party at the Hudson hotel. In the limo we awkwardly discussed our favorite vegetarian restaurants, while her six-foot-five security guard tried to make himself inconspicuous. When we arrived at the party we stepped out of her limo – and into a phalanx of flashes and yelling photographers.

"Natalie! Over here! Natalie!"

"Natalie and Moby! Over here!"

The paparazzi knew my name. I'd never been photographed by paparazzi. No one had ever yelled my name before, unless they were mad at me. I wanted to stand there and soak up the flashes, but Natalie took my hand and led me into the hotel.

I walked to the bar and ordered two vodka and sodas, one for each of us. "Oh, I don't drink," she said, scanning the room – which, in turn, was scanning us.

"Do you mind if I drink?"

"Okay."

A few feet away I saw Joe Perry and Steven Tyler from Aerosmith, both with perfectly styled long hair and bespoke leather rock-star clothes. Joe Perry made eye contact with me. "Hey, are you Moby?" he asked humbly.

"I am, and you're Joe Perry."

"Man, I just want to tell you how much I love your album."

"You do?" Enough people had told me this lately that it no longer surprised me, but it still confused me.

I tried to endear myself to Steven Tyler and told him the story of the first time I kissed someone, when I was eleven years old. For all of seventh grade I'd had a crush on Lizzie Gordon, and at the end of the school year I'd somehow convinced her to listen to records in my bedroom. I wanted to appear sophisticated, so I made us gin and tonics out of my grandparents' liquor cabinet, even though we were just eleven. I owned only three records, so I put on the first Aerosmith album. When "Dream On" began I leaned over and kissed her. Unfortunately I had never kissed anyone romantically and didn't know how it was supposed to be done. I kept my

extreme places i didn't know

mouth closed and kissed her the way people kissed family members at Christmas. The next day she started dating my best friend, Mark Droughtman, because he was cuter than me and knew how to kiss.

I thought that Steven Tyler would find my story charming, but he stared at me blankly and asked, "Are you with Natalie Portman?"

"I guess so," I said.

"She's so hot," he said, and walked away.

I finished my drink and Natalie's too. We headed out for the Versace party, where I was supposed to perform at midnight. As we left, the paparazzi started screaming again: "Natalie!" "Moby!" "Natalie!"

"They're so annoying," Natalie said as we got into her limo.

"Oh, I know," I said, lying. I loved the paparazzi – they knew my name.

We arrived at Donatella Versace's party, where there were even more paparazzi than at the official VMA after-party. This time they yelled my name as often as Natalie's. I'd only had two drinks, but I felt like I'd swallowed a distillery full of joy. I was hand in hand with Natalie Portman; I'd chatted with Aerosmith; paparazzi were shouting for me.

Growing up as a left-wing punk-rocker I had always decried celebrity culture. I'd revered people like Ian MacKaye, of Minor Threat and Fugazi, who had deliberately eschewed fame. Now I found that my own burgeoning fame was like warm amber, encasing me with a sense of worth I'd never felt before. I knew that cool celebrities were supposed to be confident and unaffected by fame, but every drop of attention I received felt like water on a desiccated sponge. My normal existence was flat and filled with doubt, while this new life was magical. And it all sprang from *Play*, a weird little album that I thought was going to be a failure.

I found my band in an office that had been turned into a dressing room, changed into jeans and a T-shirt, and walked onstage in front of Donatella Versace and fifteen hundred of her best friends.

A few songs into the set, as we were playing "Honey," I looked at the side of the stage. Natalie was there, dancing with Madonna and Gwyneth Paltrow. In unison they raised their hands and smiled and cheered. For me.

I wanted to stop the show and patiently explain to the movie stars and the beautiful people that they'd made a mistake. They were celebrating me, but I was a nothing. I was a kid from Connecticut who wore secondhand clothes in the front seat of his mom's car while she cried and tried to figure out where she could borrow money to buy groceries. I was a depressed teenager whose first band had played a show in a suburban backyard to an audience of zero people and one dog. My brief moment of rave fame had come and gone in the early 1990s. Now it was 1999 and I was an insecure has-been, a wilting house plant of a human being. But we kept playing, and the celebrities kept dancing and cheering.

Somehow a door had opened into this glowing, golden world, and Natalie and Gwyneth and Madonna and David Letterman and Elton John were holding it open, smiling and telling me they loved me.

If nineteen-year-old me – the punk-rock philosophy major – could have seen what was going on, he would have been disgusted by my obsequious running-dog pursuit of fame. "Really?" he would have asked. "You're buying into this celebrity bullshit? Don't you know it's all a facile celebration of commerce and mediocrity?"

And I would have said, "But look, there's Natalie Portman, and she's being nice to me."

extreme places i didn't know

7

OLD SAYBROOK, CONNECTICUT (1971)

My mom inched through the traffic on I-95, smoking one cigarette after another. We'd left Darien forty-five minutes ago, and I'd spent the first thirty minutes of the trip checking out every station on the FM radio. My mom's Plymouth was in the shop, so she'd borrowed a Fiat from a friend of hers. The Fiat had FM radio and air-conditioning, and I'd never been in a car with either.

"Can I turn on the air-conditioning?" I asked.

"No, the air-conditioning wastes gas," my mom said, exhaling smoke.

I returned to the FM radio. I didn't know any of the songs, but sitting on the Fiat's fabric seats and turning the knobs I felt like a king. I spun the dial past a rock station.

"Oh, wait, leave it there," my mom said.

"What's this song?"

"Big Brother and the Holding Company."

My mom sang along with Janis Joplin and tapped her fingers on the brown leather steering wheel, her white cigarette looking like a tiny baton. I cracked open my window so I could get some fresh air.

We were driving to her friend Janet's house in Old Saybrook. Janet and my mom had grown up together, and in the late 1960s had become hippies. Now, in this new decade, neither they nor their friends called themselves hippies. I heard them refer to themselves as seekers, travelers, and freaks. But I still thought of them as hippies.

I'd never talked about what happened to me in San Francisco. I only remembered it because I was still afraid of any man with long hair and a beard.

The freeway traffic cleared up after Bridgeport, and we sped along until we arrived in Old Saybrook. I wished I could spend the weekend in the Fiat: it was clean and new and felt safe, while I had been to Janet's dirty old house enough times to be scared of it.

Janet's house was a one-bedroom cottage near the end of a dirt road. The front room had tapestries on the walls, and an old couch covered in thin blankets. Behind that was a kitchen the size of a closet, which led to her bedroom: a porch with thick plastic stapled over the screens. The driveway was just a patch of dirt and gravel. We pulled onto it and parked the Fiat. My mom opened the trunk and produced her overnight bag and a shopping bag with three jugs of dandelion wine that one of her back-to-the-land friends had made for her.

The front door opened and Janet appeared, smiling and high, with long curly hair and flowing purple and yellow robes. "Betsy!" she called, coughing out pot smoke.

"Janet!" my mom said, smiling. "You furry old freak!"

They hugged. Janet handed my mom a joint in a roach clip with a long feather dangling from it.

I followed them inside and looked around Janet's living room. Next to the tapestries on the walls she had taped pictures of Wavy Gravy and Abbie Hoffman and Krishnamurti. Her coffee table was a wooden ship's door on concrete blocks, holding an impressive collection of half-empty bottles of wine and homemade ceramic ashtrays overflowing with cigarette butts.

I'd seen pictures of my mom and Janet when they were younger. Janet had been a horse-riding prep-school girl from Greenwich. Her dad was a senior vice president at Bear Stearns. Then she traded in Izod shirts and khakis for tie-dye and buckskin jackets. Now she sat on her couch with my mom, passing a joint back and forth.

"I brought Tarot cards," my mom said. "We can read each other's fortunes."

"Far out," Janet said, wheezing slightly as she exhaled pot smoke. "Far out."

"Mom, I'm going outside, okay?" I asked.

"Okay," my mom said in a strained voice, speaking without exhaling so the pot smoke would stay in her lungs.

I went through Janet's backyard to get to an old cemetery behind her house. Cemeteries didn't scare me, even though I'd heard that dead people could take your soul if you opened your mouth when you yawned. Whenever I walked through cemeteries I just made sure to yawn with my mouth closed.

I wandered from grave to grave, reading the epitaphs. My uncle Dave did charcoal rubbings of grisly epitaphs, so I wanted to find a good one and tell him about it. He had a really scary one in his art studio that told the story of a man who'd killed his wife and child, and then, after walking into town, shot himself. Disappointingly, most of the epitaphs in the cemetery behind Janet's house were fairly banal: "Rebecca Waltham, beloved mother and wife"; "Thomas Goodkind, rest his soul."

Behind a moss-covered statue of a winged angel I found some wild strawberries. They were hard and not particularly sweet, but I ate a few, as I'd never seen wild strawberries before. I gave up on looking for grisly epitaphs and sat at the feet of the angel, trying to chew on the hard berries while I thought about my grandfather.

Last summer I'd been walking in Darien with my grandfather when he spotted wild raspberries growing by an old barn. We'd eaten handfuls of the fruit and brought the rest back to my grandmother. "She can make jam out of these," my grandfather told me. That seemed like magic: someone I knew could turn raspberries into jam.

There was a tall tree behind the winged angel, so I climbed it, thinking maybe I could see Long Island Sound from the top. I clambered up as high as I could go, my hands getting covered with pine tar, and looked south. Over the water, great shafts of sunlight were cutting through the clouds. And in the distance, I could see Long Island. I stayed at the top of the tree for thirty minutes, watching the light dance on the gray water, taking in the quiet beauty and the calm grandeur. Plus I had nothing else to do.

When the light dimmed and the air got colder I climbed down. I was brave enough for a graveyard on an overcast day, but not at night. I walked along an old stone wall, looking for bugs. I turned over some rocks and saw millipedes and potato bugs, and got back to Janet's house just as night fell.

Janet and my mom and two of Janet's friends were sitting around the makeshift coffee table, flipping over Tarot cards. Their eyes were glassy and they all had sloppy grins from the pot and the dandelion wine. Charlie, a friend of Janet's, was busy pushing pot around on the cover of *Déjà Vu* by Crosby, Stills, Nash & Young. My mom and her friends spent a lot of time using gatefold album sleeves to help separate hemp seeds from the leaves.

"Hey, Mobes!" Janet said, her voice wet. "Where'd you go?"

"Oh, I just walked around," I said, not surprised that nobody seemed to have noticed that I'd been gone for three hours. On these weekends my mom would smoke pot with her friends, and I'd disappear. There were never any kids around, and never any toys, so I'd learned to explore and make up games for myself. Sometimes I'd reenact TV commercials in the woods, and sometimes I'd just wander along streambeds until I found frogs.

"There's soup in the kitchen, if you're hungry," my mom said. I went into the kitchen and fixed myself some soup with bread and butter. There was a small table in the kitchen, so I ate my dinner there and read a copy of *The Whole Earth Catalog*, a hippie bible that I saw in all the houses of my mom's friends. I didn't know what anything in the catalog actually was, but it was something to look at while I ate.

Charlie came in and poured himself a glass of vodka from a bottle above the stove. He looked like all of my mom's male hippie friends: long hair, sideburns, dirty jeans, and an old jacket. "Hey, kid," he said.

"Hi," I said, hoping he'd leave me alone so I could eat and read in peace.

"You're reading? How old are you?"

"Almost five and a half."

"Aren't you small for five?"

I wanted to say, "I'm small because I'm a kid. Plus you're scaring me. Will you leave me alone, please?" But instead I said, "Five and a half. I don't know."

He nodded and sauntered back into the living room, where someone had just put on a Richie Havens album. My mom and her friends listened to music constantly, and I had become proficient in telling the difference between Donovan, the Doors, and Richie Havens. I liked the calm songs, but the louder ones scared me.

I finished my soup and bread and went to the freezer to see if I could find ice cream. Janet might have been an anti-materialistic seeker who rejected Western society and its phony values, but her freezer was full of ice cream. I made myself a bowl of chocolate, vanilla, and strawberry ice cream and poured a glass of orange juice. I'd paged through all of *The Whole Earth Catalog*, so I read *The Farmer's Almanac* instead. It was boring and adult, but I had nothing else to read.

There were other books in the living room, but I didn't want to go in there. When my mom and her friends got drunk and high they stopped being adults. When my mom got high, which was almost every day, she stopped being my mom. She hid her pot-smoking from her parents, but was open about it with everyone else in her life.

I finished my ice cream and put the dish in the sink. It was time for bed, but I didn't know where I was going to sleep. I reluctantly walked back into the living room, which was cloudy from all the smoke. Janet was on the couch, kissing a hippie with extremely long hair. My mom and Charlie were sitting very close to each other, reading each other's Tarot cards. "Mom, where should I sleep?" I asked.

"Oh, you can sleep anywhere," she said, and turned back to Charlie.

I couldn't sleep in Janet's bed, because that was Janet's bed. And I couldn't sleep on the couch – Janet and the hippie were making out there. I couldn't sleep in the Fiat because it was too cold. I took a pillow and an Indian blanket from the edge of the couch and climbed underneath the coffee table. There wasn't much space, but as Charlie said, I was small for a five-year-old.

I looked up at the wooden slab a few inches from my face and pretended I was in a coffin. Was this what people in the cemetery did after they died? Did they stare at the wood a few inches above their face?

The Richie Havens record ended. After a while I fell asleep.

At dawn I woke up and crawled out from under the coffee table. It was cold and the air smelled like cigarettes and damp wool. Two people were curled up on the couch. I could tell they were naked: a bare shoulder and a foot were sticking out from underneath a pile of blankets. I assumed it was Janet, but it mostly looked like naked skin and curly hippie hair.

In Janet's bedroom Charlie was lying on top of the blankets, naked. He was snoring, and I could see my mom next to him.

I knew that none of them were going to be waking up soon, so I quietly made myself a bowl of ice cream for breakfast. The house smelled strange and I didn't want to have to talk to any of the hungover hippies if they woke up, so I got the keys from my mom's purse and took my ice cream to the borrowed Fiat.

I sat on the clean fabric seats to eat my breakfast and turned on the radio and found a station where the newscaster sounded like my grandfather.

extreme places i didn't know

8

BOSTON, MASSACHUSETTS (1999)

I couldn't sleep because I couldn't stop panicking.

I'd had an amazing night with Natalie in Cambridge, Massachusetts, and at 3 a.m. had returned to my hotel room. I was leaving for the airport in a few hours to fly to the UK, but I was sweaty and wide-eyed with fear, and couldn't sleep.

Whenever I tried to date someone seriously the panic showed up: sleeplessness, muscle tightness, sweating, and galloping, unrelenting thoughts. Before I dropped out of college in 1984 I'd been in relationships for months at a time without problems. But now I usually started panicking after a first date.

I was highly strung, and I stressed out about other things – work, housing, money – but nothing triggered my panic attacks more than getting close to a woman I cared about. I understood the hereditary utility for any species in learning how to panic in the face of real threats, like lions or fire, but I was baffled as to why I panicked in the face of affection and warmth.

For all my life I'd wanted nothing more than to love and be loved. But whenever I found someone to love the panic intervened, screaming at me until I retreated to my solitary world. Some very deep part of my brain was protecting me vigilantly and wanted me to be alone. As soon as I did the panic's bidding and ended whatever relationship I was in, the panic abated.

This tautology of panic had been going on for years now. I held onto the increasingly naive hope that someday I'd meet a perfect, kind woman, and with her I'd finally break the cycle.

Earlier in the night we'd played an outdoor show for a Boston radio station. Our small four-week tour had turned into a five-month one, and there were even plans to follow our upcoming European concerts with shows in Australia, New Zealand, and Japan. Then 1999 would be over and the strange success of *Play* would come to a close.

After tonight's show I'd changed out of my sweaty clothes in the dressing room with my band and crew. "Not sure what you losers are doing now, but I'm going on a date," I announced.

"With a human?" asked Dan.

"Yup," I said, trying to restrain a smug grin.

"No," Steve declared, realizing where I was going.

"Yup," I said, smiling wider.

"Natalie?" Scott asked.

"Yup," I said, walking to the door.

I left the dressing room to a mournful backstage chorus of "Fuck you."

I took a taxi to Cambridge to meet Natalie. We held hands and wandered around Harvard, kissing under the centuries-old oak trees. At midnight she brought me to her dorm room and we lay down next to each other on her small bed. After she fell asleep I carefully extracted myself from her arms and took a taxi back to my hotel. And I started panicking.

I tried to assuage the panic with logic, telling myself that it was unwarranted, as I'd only been on a few dates with Natalie. But the panic was unmollified. It wanted one thing: for me to be alone. When I was single I was safe, according to the deep, broken neural mechanism that harbored the panic.

On some level I understood that my brain was trying to protect me, but unfortunately it categorized emotional intimacy in the same synaptic bunker as fleeing a burning building or being chased by a bear.

The sun was rising over Logan airport, so I got out of bed. I went to the bathroom and looked at myself in the mirror: bald, skinny, exhausted, sad.

One night, years earlier, after another relationship failed because of panic, my frustration and anger boiled over until I started punching myself in the face. I hit myself once. Then again. Then again, very hard, making myself fall backward onto the floor. For a second it felt good and even justified – I had punched myself in my worthless face. Then I was scared, because I didn't know if I was sane. Sane people generally didn't punch themselves in the face until they fell down. And sane people didn't find themselves panicking in hotel rooms because they'd gone on a few pleasant dates with a kind, beautiful, vegetarian movie star.

I had an hour before I had to go to the airport, and I knew from experience that I wasn't going to be able to sleep, so I found a pen and some hotel stationery to write about my panic, and maybe understand it better. I wrote: "why am i panicking? 1. i'm scared."

And that was all I could think of. I knew there was more. The panic had its own origin story, but it was hidden from me. I crumpled up the paper and threw it in the trash.

9

PARIS, FRANCE (1999)

I could never figure out why I was popular in some countries but not others – if I knew, I would have been more consistently successful around the world. I'd had sporadic bouts of success in Germany and the UK, but for the nine years I'd been making records I'd never had much of a career in France. Which was why my managers and I were surprised when an iconic French music magazine, *Les Inrockuptibles*, invited me to play a small concert for them near the Moulin Rouge. Apparently they liked *Play* and had even given it a good review.

We played the concert, the lovely French audience clapped and were very polite, and after the show I went to meet my friend Lorraine, who lived in Paris. She was a tall, dark-haired fashion stylist from London who had briefly dated a friend of mine in New York. I told myself I couldn't stay out too late: I had a 9 a.m. flight from Paris to Bangkok, and then on to New Zealand.

Play had gone gold in New Zealand. I'd never had a gold record before. My manager explained that because the population of New Zealand was so small, a gold record there meant that you'd sold six thousand albums, as opposed to the five hundred thousand you needed to get a gold record in the States. Nevertheless, the New Zealand record company had sent me my first gold record, and nobody could take that shiny framed disc away from me.

I took a cab from the venue. It dropped me off near the Hotel de Ville, and I walked a few blocks to the address Lorraine had given me. I walked in circles for a while, because the address was for the Louvre itself, and I couldn't imagine a bar being in the Louvre. But finally I opened a heavy door, revealing a bar with high ceilings, brass chandeliers, and red-and-gold wallpaper, all inside France's most famous museum.

Lorraine and some of her friends were in a booth. "You found it!" she said, kissing both of my cheeks. I felt absurdly cosmopolitan: I was in the Louvre with glamorous fashionistas after playing a concert in Paris and before flying to Asia. We drank wine, and then vodka, and then pear Armagnac.

At 2 a.m. I declared responsibly, "I should go. I have to fly to New Zealand in a few hours."

"No," Lorraine's friend Mandy said drunkenly. She exhaled a plume of cigarette smoke. "Don't go." Mandy was gamine, with dyed red hair and golden aviator-frame eyeglasses. Originally from Long Island, she was living in Paris doing something fashion-related.

If I went back to the airport hotel where I was staying, I could get a few hours of sleep before the twenty-six-hour journey to New Zealand. But I was in Paris. And after seven or eight drinks I was slightly drunk. And a beautiful elf had just let me know that she didn't want me to leave.

"Okay, but what should we do?" I asked, trusting to fate and a drunk woman I'd just met.

Five minutes later Mandy and I said goodbye to Lorraine and her friends and got a cab to take us to her apartment building near the Arc de Triomphe. As we drove I told Mandy the strange history of the Egyptian obelisk near the Tuileries Garden. She listened and nodded, but seemed bored.

At her apartment building we took a tiny nineteenth-century elevator up to the fourth floor. As it wheezed upward I asked her if she'd listened to WLIR when she was growing up on Long Island.

"DRE," she slurred. "WDRE."

WLIR had been the new-wave station I had grown up listening to. Its signal had been strong enough to make its way across Long Island Sound to Connecticut. In the mid-1980s it was the only commercial new-wave station in or near New York. When I was in high school it had been magical to turn on the radio in my mom's Chevette and hear the Cure and Echo & the Bunnymen as I drove past the houses of girls I had crushes on. And then in 1987 the station had changed its call letters to WDRE.

"So you grew up listening to WDRE?" I asked, trying to get to know the person I was probably going to have sex with.

"Sssshhh," she said, quieting me while dropping her keys on the cement floor. "I live here with this family, and they're asleep . . ."

The apartment was dark and smelled like cigarettes and dust. "You live with a family?" I asked.

Mandy looked annoyed. "They're there." She pointed past a living room. "We're there." She pointed down a short hallway off the kitchen. She got a bottle of red wine from the filthy kitchen and we stumbled through the dark apartment to her bedroom.

When she opened the door to her bedroom a nervous Chihuahua growled at me. But when I sat down on the bed he jumped on my lap and looked at me with plaintive eyes.

"You like dogs?" she asked.

"I love dogs."

"He's George."

I wanted to tell her about my deceased grandmother's dachshund, also named George, but Mandy started kissing me. As we moved to the bed she spilled the bottle of wine. We took off our clothes and had sex on the damp, wine-stained sheets, while her dog paced and whined around us. After sex we passed out.

I woke up an hour later, panicking and disoriented. I flipped open Mandy's cell phone: it was 4 a.m. Mandy was passed out and snoring. George was lying half on the pillow and half on Mandy's head, still staring sadly at me.

I gathered my clothes, got dressed, and tried to wake Mandy up. "Mandy, I have to go to New Zealand now." I shook her shoulder gently. She kept snoring. "Hey, hi, I have to go now."

George growled in his tiny Chihuahua throat and glared at me.

I found a pen and a piece of paper and wrote a little "Thank you, I hope I can see you again" note, along with my email address, and put it underneath the empty bottle of wine. "Okay, good night," I said to George, and pulled her bedroom door closed.

I walked through the filthy kitchen to the front door of the apartment, which was locked on the inside and wouldn't open without a key. I returned to Mandy's bedroom. "Hey, wake up, Mandy," I said, jostling her shoulder a bit harder. "I need to get out. I'm locked in."

She had passed out, and kept snoring. George barked at me.

I found her ring of keys, went back to the door, and tried each one. None of them worked. I went back to her room and turned on all the lights. "Mandy, come on, wake up!" I said loudly, starting to panic. "I'm locked in and I need to go to New Zealand."

She kept snoring. George looked confused.

I inspected the window to see if I could climb out, but we were on the fourth floor and there was no fire escape. I went back to the door, hoping that maybe I had missed some way out, and heard the sweet sound of someone opening the door from the other side. A giant of a man in black motorcycle leathers walked in, smoking a cigarette and carrying a black helmet under his arm.

"Oh, thank you," I said. "Do you speak English?"

He stopped and looked at me quizzically, but said nothing. I decided this wasn't the moment to be effusive.

"Well, thanks," I said, and headed for the door.

He said quietly and in heavily accented English, "You fuck Mandy?"

"Um."

He threw me against the wall of the kitchen and put his left hand around my throat. "You fuck my girlfriend?" he growled, forming a fist with his right hand.

"I have to go to the airport," I tried to say through my squeezed trachea. And then I squeaked, "*Je suis désolé.*"

The leather-clad giant let go of my throat and stood there, his right hand still in the air. Then his hulking shoulders slumped. He stared at the floor and shook his head. "Get the fuck out of my apartment, you fucking American," he told me.

I ran down the four flights of stairs, out the front of the building, and onto an empty Parisian street.

I calmed down, shaken by fear and guilt, and walked two blocks to the Champs-Élysées, where I hailed a cab. "Sofitel at Charles de Gaulle, *s'il vous plaît*," I said to the African driver.

We sped out of Paris on empty streets, as the sky streaked blue and gray with the dawn. As we got close to my hotel, "Why Does My Heart Feel So Bad?" came on the radio. I'd never heard any of the songs from *Play* on the radio before. I was surprised – even though I'd mixed it on an old, cheap console in my bedroom, it didn't sound terrible.

"Can you turn it up?" I asked the driver.

"*Cette chanson?*" he asked, in lilting African-accented French.

"*Oui, monsieur, cette chanson,*" I said. The clouds at the airport turned pink with the dawn.

10

DARIEN, CONNECTICUT (1972)

My mom was stirring a pot of ravioli with one hand and holding a Winston cigarette with the other. I wouldn't be eating with her tonight – I was going to a sleepover at my friend Scudder's house. "I'm going to wait outside for Scudder's dad," I told her.

"It's cold and raining. Don't you want to wait inside?"

"No, I'm okay. Bye!" I said, and shut the door behind me.

A few months earlier we had moved into an apartment on Noroton Avenue, just down the street from the volunteer fire department and around the corner from Darien's one block of sub-sidized public housing. Our home was a converted garage, with a small bedroom by the front door, a bathroom with a vinyl shower stall, a small orange kitchen, and a flight of stairs that led to another small bedroom and a storage room where we watched TV.

Before living here we'd lived a few miles away with my grandpar-ents in their white, seven-bedroom colonial house, surrounded by tall trees and sprawling lawns. But my mom had wanted her inde-pendence, so she moved us to this garage apartment – even though she couldn't really afford the $85 a month rent.

My mom and I were poor, but when we'd lived with my grand-parents I could invite friends over and pretend that I was normal and lived in a normal house. But now we lived in a cold garage apartment and all our furniture came from the Salvation Army or Goodwill. The couch in our living room was so old that bits of foam rubber would fall out onto the floor when I sat down.

I'd learned I was poor in nursery school in Darien. A little blond boy walked up to me and told me, matter-of-factly, "You're poor." I didn't like being poor, especially not in one of the wealthiest towns in the US, and I didn't like not being able to invite my friends over. The only friend who had visited my new house was Robert Downey Jr. – he and his family lived in a small house too.

I wanted to invite my best friend, Bobby Miller, to come to my house and play, but he and his family lived in an eight-bedroom house overlooking a river lined by ferns and birch trees. By Darien standards he and his family were middle class, as Bobby's dad was only a senior vice president at IBM.

One of my other friends, Phil, lived in a brick mansion at the end of a long winding driveway. I'd overheard my grandfather talking about Phil's dad: he had inherited a few hundred million dollars and now ran a bank. Then there was Grant, who lived on ten acres and whose dad worked at Lazard Frères. And Dave, who lived in an old stone mansion and whose dad was an executive at General Electric. On and on, an endless sea of blond, wealthy parents and their blond, beautiful children.

They played tennis. They skied. They were good at lacrosse and field hockey. They knew what Bermuda was. They went to Switzerland for holidays. I had never left the US, but I had gone to a wedding in Nebraska once.

Tonight I'd been invited to a sleepover at my friend Scudder's house. I didn't want Scudder, or his dad, or anyone at all, to know that I lived in a garage apartment. So when I gave Scudder my address, I told him that I lived at the one nice house on my street, a quarter-mile away.

Scudder's dad was picking me up at 7 p.m., so I left our garage apartment at 6.45. I was wearing Lee jeans and a Yale sweatshirt my mom had bought at the Darien Community Center thrift shop. I always tried to pick clothes that I thought would make me look normal and not poor. My sneakers came from a basket at the supermarket: the kind checkout lady had let us use food stamps to buy them. They had four stripes, but I'd removed a stripe on each shoe

extreme places i didn't know

with a razor, hoping to make them look like Adidas. Over my outfit I had my one new piece of clothing, a blue down jacket that my grandparents had given me for Christmas.

I walked to the one nice house on our street and stood under a tree by the driveway, hoping that anyone who drove by either wouldn't see me or would think that I lived there. After a few minutes Scudder's dad pulled up in a brand-new Mercedes.

"Hey, pal," he said. "You didn't have to wait out in the rain."

"Oh," I said, stumped, "I wanted to get some fresh air." I'd heard someone say that on TV, and thought it sounded grown-up.

"Fresh air? It's raining, buddy."

"Well, my mom smokes in the kitchen," I said, thinking quickly.

He winced as I sat wetly on the leather seat of his new German car. "Your jacket's soaked. How long have you been out here?"

"Just a couple of minutes," I lied.

Thankfully he changed the subject. "I hope you're hungry. Mrs. Baldwin is making meatloaf."

"Oh, great, I love meatloaf."

Scudder's dad lit a cigarette, and for the rest of the trip we talked about the Yankees. They were my favorite baseball team, and the catcher, Thurman Munson, was my favorite player. I also liked Sparky Lyle, but since he was a pitcher he didn't get to play as often. Last summer my grandfather had even taken me to Yankee Stadium to see a game. I made sure to work this into my conversation with Scudder's dad, asking him, "Have you seen the Yankees in person?" It seemed like a normal question.

After fifteen minutes we came to Old Cobbler Road, where Scudder and his family lived. Darien had been a town since the sixteenth century, and one way of measuring status was by how old your street was. Old Cobbler Road was a private road with a hand-carved wooden street sign, letting all visitors know that it predated the American Revolution, a war that some Darien residents probably still saw as an affront.

We drove past two stone gates and parked. When we got out of the car a golden retriever and a black Labrador ran up to us, happy and barking. They jumped up and licked my face. "Morgan! Stanley!" Scudder's dad yelled good-naturedly. "Calm down!"

The kitchen was warm and smelled like meatloaf and cigarette smoke. "Hi, Mrs. Baldwin," I said, carefully shaking her hand.

"I wish all of Scudder's friends were so polite!" she said with a smile. "Scudder's in the den."

I'd been to Scudder's house before, so I walked down the carpeted hallway to the den. The walls were covered with framed photos of Scudder and his family: on their sailboat, in the mountains, in Europe, under a giant Christmas tree. In the den, Scudder and his two older brothers were watching *Bowling for Dollars*. "Hey, Scudder," I said.

"Hey, Moby," Scudder replied, not looking away from the TV.

Scudder and I had known each other since kindergarten, but this was the first time we were having a sleepover. I was the only fatherless poor kid most of my friends knew, and sometimes I thought I was invited to birthday parties and sleepovers as a form of local charity. I didn't mind, so long as I got to spend time in warm houses with carpets.

Scudder's brothers didn't acknowledge me. They were big kids, in junior high school. They were tall and good at sports, so I knew not to address them or make eye contact.

The den was the family's casual recreation room, with dark wood paneling, board games on the shelves, and two pinball machines. I'd gone exploring the last time I'd visited, so I knew that the house also had a family room, a formal living room, a formal dining room, a sun room, a large office, and a greenhouse behind the pool and tennis court. There were six bedrooms at the top of the front stairs and two maids' rooms you could get to from a second staircase off the kitchen. Outside, the landscape lights were on. I could see the pool, surrounded by flagstones and covered for the winter.

"I can't wait for summer," I said.

Scudder and his brothers glared at me, annoyed that anybody would be talking to them while they watched TV. This carpeted privilege was their world, and it was all that I longed for. Indoor heating. A pool. But most of all, a sense of belonging. They looked like everyone else at school and lived like everyone else lived. Their parents owned the world, and the world bent to their will. That we lived in the same town was just a strange fluke of real estate and Protestant heredity.

In the eighteenth century I would have been a stable boy, occasionally invited up to the manor house, but afraid of his own shadow and only comfortable with the horses and dogs. When I went to my friends' houses I was always careful to be polite, to sit quietly, and to not draw attention to myself. My greatest fear was that someone would look too closely and see me for who I was.

Scudder's mom called down the hall: dinner was ready. I jumped up, but Scudder and his brothers ignored her. She called again.

"Shouldn't we go get dinner?" I asked.

They ignored me, still absorbed by *Bowling for Dollars*. Scudder's mom came down the hall and turned off the TV. "Mom!" Scudder and his brothers complained in unison.

"Dinner's ready, you little men," she announced.

Scudder's brothers weren't little men; they were tall, terrifying, thirteen-year-old beasts. If I had called them "little men," they would have casually ripped me limb from limb.

We walked down the hall wordlessly and sat at the table in the kitchen. The formal dining room was for holidays and parties, while this country-style kitchen table was for everyday family dinners. Scudder's mom served the food, while Scudder and his brothers went to the fridge and poured Cokes for themselves.

Coke. Beyond the pool and the tennis court and the second set of stairs, this was the greatest luxury I'd seen: bottles of soda in the fridge. My mom and I had milk and orange juice in our fridge, but we watered everything down to make it last longer. "May I have a glass of Coke, Mrs. Baldwin?" I asked.

She smiled at me. "Of course, Moby. Help yourself."

"Why are you so polite?" one of Scudder's brothers blurted. "It's weird."

"I think it's nice," she said. "Clearly your mother has raised you well."

I wanted to say, "I'm not polite, Mrs. Baldwin – I'm terrified." I wanted to stay here and to pretend that I belonged. Being polite seemed like the safest route to not being thrown out.

I filled a glass with Coke and small slices of ice that came from the front of the refrigerator. I took a sip. The bubbles hit my nose and smelled like roses and fruit.

extreme places i didn't know

11

MINNEAPOLIS, MINNESOTA (2000)

"*Play* is number one in the UK!"

I was wearing a yellow rain slicker and talking to my European manager, Eric, on a pay phone outside a drugstore in Minneapolis.

Eric lived in London. Once *Play* had started doing well I called him at the same time every Sunday to find out what my UK chart position was. As *Play* had been number three in the charts the previous week, I was eager to find out its new position. I couldn't believe what Eric had told me, so I asked again, "Really?"

"Really!" he yelled into the phone from six thousand miles away. "You're number one!"

I was in Minneapolis, opening up for the band Bush on an "MTV Campus Invasion" tour. The tour had been strange: Bush's alt-rock fans weren't always keen to hear electronic music played by me and my motley band (a drummer, a bass player, and a DJ). The audiences weren't necessarily hostile, but they did seem confused. Even though *Play* was selling well I hadn't received any royalty checks, and I still couldn't afford to hire a real singer. Without a female singer half of the songs in our setlist required vocal samples on tape. So when we played "Why Does My Heart Feel So Bad?" and "Natural Blues," the microphone in the center of the stage stood there, lonely and unused.

Play had been released ten months ago and had gone from selling three thousand copies a week worldwide to a hundred thousand copies a week worldwide. It was now one of the best-selling records in the world, and a top-ten record in over twenty countries. Eric had told me that in the past two months, *Play* had sold more than all of my previous albums combined.

"Plus 'Southside' is number one at modern-rock radio, and *Spin* wants you to be on the cover," Eric reminded me over the phone. "Isn't that good?"

I agreed – that was good.

I couldn't admit it to anyone, but I loved talking to the press and seeing myself in magazines. I knew that cool musicians didn't care about press attention, or at least they were good at pretending they didn't. But I cared. Whenever I was at home in New York I had a Friday ritual of going to the Soho News store on the corner of Prince Street and Lafayette and looking for myself in their well-stocked racks of magazines. Each time I saw my name or picture in print I felt like I had been legitimized.

The more attention I got, the more I wanted. The more I got of *everything*, the more I wanted. I wanted more touring and more press and more alcohol and more invitations to celebrity parties and more one-night stands. My life was perfect, and I wanted it to go on exactly as it was.

I still prayed every morning, and sometimes I even cautiously asked for God's will to be done. But I really only wanted God's will to be done if God's will involved me being famous.

For a few weeks I had tried to be Natalie's boyfriend, but it hadn't worked out. I thought that I was going to have to tell her that my panic was too egregious for me to be in a real relationship, but one night on the phone she informed me that she'd met somebody else. She'd assumed that I'd be sad or angry, but I was relieved that I'd never have to tell her how damaged I was.

Since then I'd fallen hard for two other women, and would have been happy to be in a monogamous relationship with either of them – except that even making plans to go on a second date made me panic. So I'd given up trying to date seriously, and had embraced being a promiscuous drunk on tour. It wasn't the

extreme places i didn't know

most spiritually or ethically sound behavior, but at least I wasn't panicking.

Even though we'd been broken up for a while, Natalie and I were still friends. A month ago, when I had been on tour in Australia, she'd come to my show in Melbourne and had brought along the cast of the *Star Wars* prequels. In the middle of the show I looked at the side of the stage: Natalie was dancing with Ewan McGregor and the actors who played Jar Jar Binks and young Darth Vader.

Darth Vader dancing with Obi-Wan, I thought, as I yelled out the chorus for "Bodyrock."

After the show I drank champagne and vodka in my dressing room with Ewan McGregor. After a few drinks I decided that he and I should go out and drink more, but that I should be naked. Sandy, my tour manager, urged me, "Moby, at least put on a towel."

So I went out in downtown Melbourne wearing a towel. No shoes. No clothes. Just a towel.

Ewan and I stumbled from bar to bar, getting drunker and drunker. At the end of the night we ended up in a subterranean bar filled with Australian celebrities. I'd had ten or fifteen drinks, so I went to the bathroom to pee, and found myself standing at a urinal next to Russell Crowe. He zipped up his pants, and then pushed me against the wall of the bathroom and started screaming at me.

"Uh, we've never met," I tried to say. "Why are you yelling at me?"

He never told me, but he kept me pinned against the wall while he shouted and screamed. After a minute he lost interest, cursed a few times, and stumbled out of the bathroom.

I went back to the bar and told Ewan, "Russell Crowe just yelled at me."

"Fuck, mate," he said. "I wouldn't worry about it. He yells at everyone."

I hung up the pay phone in Minneapolis and stood in the rain, trying to comprehend what Eric had told me: I had a number-one album in the UK. England was where the rave scene had started. It was where the Clash had started. It was the land of Joy Division and Monty Python and Bertrand Russell and William Blake and John Lydon.

I'd grown up obsessed with the UK, and for a few weeks in high school I'd even tried to pass myself off as British. I imitated the accents I'd heard on *Fawlty Towers* and *Monty Python's Flying Circus* and told people that I was related to Terry Hall, the singer in the Specials. It didn't work out – my accent made me sound like a sub-par Dick van Dyke in *Mary Poppins*. And most of the people in my high school had known me since kindergarten and were confused as to why I was suddenly pretending to be British.

I had a few hours before showtime, so I walked back to the Holiday Inn to make dinner in the bathroom of my hotel room. I'd bought groceries the day before at a health-food store in Wisconsin. Now I took some tofu pups out of their package and put them in a plastic bag in the sink. I then filled the sink with hot water to let the pups warm up. After a few minutes the water cooled off, so I drained the sink and filled it with hot water again. After ten minutes I had tofu pups that were as warm as a lawn on a summer day.

I didn't have a knife, so I used the subscription card from a copy of *In Minneapolis* magazine to spread mustard on two pieces of bread. I put my tofu pups and bread on a hand towel, and ate them while watching an old episode of *The Simpsons* and drinking day-old carrot juice.

There was nothing glamorous about dinner in a Holiday Inn across the street from a bus station, but I had a number-one album in the UK, which made lukewarm Holiday Inn tofu pups the most wonderful meal I'd ever eaten.

12

SOMERSET, ENGLAND (2000)

Before I started playing them in the early 1990s, the only festival I'd ever attended was the 1974 Westport Connecticut Clam Bake. It was a small seafood and music festival: bluegrass bands played on a plywood stage while a few hundred people sat on the grass, drinking beer and eating clams. My mom was dating a banjo player in one of the bluegrass bands, and he let me sit on the side of the stage while his band, the Nutmeg Riders, played a medley of Earl Scruggs songs.

But now I was performing "Porcelain" and watching a sunset brush the sky with pastel streaks, while a hundred thousand people sang along. I was at Glastonbury, the biggest festival in the UK, and arguably the biggest and most iconic festival in the world. And when "Porcelain" ended the crowd cheered: not just typical festival applause, but an overwhelming roar that sounded like love.

I'd played Glastonbury once before, in 1997, doing an afternoon set in a muddy tent for a thousand soggy ravers. This year, however, Glastonbury was warm and dry and overflowing with joy. Before our show I'd walked over to a campsite run by Joe Strummer from the Clash and Bez from the Happy Mondays. I'd loved the Clash in high school; Joe Strummer was, along with Leonard Cohen, Lou Reed, and David Bowie, one of my few living musical heroes. Joe and Bez gave me some poitín – homemade liquor that they had brewed in somebody's kitchen – and then we danced to dancehall reggae, playing on a boombox sitting on a bale of hay.

Now Joe was standing at the side of the stage with Liam Gallagher, dancing and singing along with the unfathomably large crowd in front of me. I'd assumed that Liam would hate me and my music, but the few times I'd met him he had been surprisingly friendly. One time at a festival in France he'd even paid me his highest compliment, snapping his fingers and saying "Tune, mate" while listening to "Natural Blues."

The sun finally sank beneath the horizon as we ended our set with "Feeling So Real." The air was soft. The light was soft. And even though the sun was gone the clouds were still pink and gray and baby blue.

After the show my band and crew and Joe and Bez and some new friends we'd made backstage all came back to my generic but large hotel suite, a few minutes away from the festival. Joe's boombox came with us; someone put on a drum-and-bass CD, while the table in my living room was quickly covered with hash and vodka bottles and lines of cocaine. The air in my suite soon became hazy from cigarettes and hash.

One of Joe's friends offered me a line. Cocaine had always scared me – it seemed like the drug that people did right before their careers ended. I politely said, "No, thank you."

"No worries, mate," he said, and snorted a line the size of my pinkie. "More for me."

Ecstasy didn't scare me, so I took a few pills and washed them down with vodka. When someone put on a hip-hop mix CD I found myself dancing to a Jay-Z track with Becks, an Irish publicist who worked for one of the bigger music magazines. We started touching each other's faces and kissing, so before the song ended I took her hand and led her into my bedroom.

With every month that *Play* sold more and I appeared on more magazine covers, it became easier and easier for me to be promiscuous. I'd spent years going out and drinking enough to work up the courage to talk to women I found attractive. I was still drinking just as much, but now more often than not the women were approaching me.

To keep myself from feeling creepy and ethically compromised

I told myself I was looking for love – but since my crippling panic attacks kept me from having actual relationships, I kept looking for love in the arms of whoever was charitable enough to be with me for a night. Tonight that was Becks from Ireland.

Usually Irish women were reserved, but once I closed the door to my bedroom Becks undid her shirt and stepped out of her pants. She was roughly my height, with short blonde hair and a sprinkling of freckles on her nose. We had both taken ecstasy earlier; her pupils were as wide as planets. "Do you fancy me?" she asked, standing naked in front of me.

"Of course," I said, pulling off my own clothes. "I think you're beautiful."

We fell onto my bed and started having sex.

The door to my suite opened and Scott, my drummer, walked in. "Moby, do you—" he said, and stopped when he saw Becks and me in bed together.

"Go away, Scott," I said.

"Go away, Scott," Becks echoed.

"Sorry!" Scott said, and drunkenly backed out of the room.

I looked at Becks, naked and beautiful underneath me. "Hold on," I told her. I got out of bed and ripped a mirror off a wall. It wasn't a Herculean feat of strength, as it was a cheap mirror held to the wall with a few drywall screws.

I got back in bed and positioned the mirror, and we resumed having sex. "Having sex with you looked so beautiful," I told her. "I wanted you to see what I saw."

"Oh, that's amazing," she said, looking at our bodies reflected in the mirror.

We spent the next few hours having sex and looking into each other's eyes, and by the time we were done it was late and most of the people at the party had left. Someone in the living room put on *London Calling*, but Joe Strummer, who apparently was still there, yelled, "Oh, fuck no!"

Becks and I wrapped ourselves in the stiff polyester bedspread and spooned. My head was spinning from vodka and ecstasy and sex, not to mention a hundred thousand people showering me with love and approval at Glastonbury earlier. Through the door I could hear the David Bowie ballad "Wild Is the Wind."

I sat up and said to Becks, "Come with me."

We put on fluffy bathrobes, and I walked her out to the living room. The party had dwindled to four people, including Pablo, my new percussionist.

While the remaining party stragglers drank the last of the vodka and snorted the last of the coke, I took Becks's hand and we slow-danced to "Wild Is the Wind."

A few years earlier I'd drunkenly sung this song to a woman in a hotel parking lot in Germany, but hearing David Bowie singing it was much better. The song ended and the four degenerates in my hotel suite clapped. I looked at Becks. As she stood in the smoke-filled living room, surrounded by empty vodka bottles and beer cans and cocaine detritus, she had tears on her cheeks.

"Thank you," she said. "That was beautiful. I've never slow-danced with anyone before."

"Really?" I walked her back to the bedroom. "I love slow dancing. I even collect slow-dancing songs."

"What?" She wrinkled her nose.

"Yup." I paused, not sure if I should reveal my most shameful secret. "Even Celine Dion."

Becks looked at me, smiling but concerned. "Celine Dion?"

"A few years ago my friend Fancy and I had a party where we played nothing but slow-dance songs. Everyone got drunk and slow-danced and made out on the dance floor. The highlight was a room full of hipsters drunkenly singing 'My Heart Will Go On.'"

We lay back down in bed and wrapped ourselves in the bedspread again. The sun was up now, shining through the inadequate curtains.

"Excluding Celine Dion, what was your favorite slow-dance song?" she asked.

"'I Only Have Eyes for You' by the Flamingos," I said without hesitation. "The best romantic slow-dance song ever written."

We quietly held each other. She said, "I can't believe I had sex with someone who likes Celine Dion."

I laughed. "Okay, I lied. I made the whole thing up."

"No, you didn't."

"No," I said, "I didn't. But have you heard 'My Heart Will Go On' recently? It's really good."

"You should stop now."

"Okay, you're right."

I lay there, smiling and spooning beautiful Becks. As I was falling asleep I heard "Golden Years" playing in the other room.

"Can I tell you something?" I asked.

"Please," she said, sleepily.

"David Bowie's my neighbor."

"What?" Becks asked, suddenly awake.

"He moved in across the street from me. We're going to be best friends."

She touched my face, looked in my eyes, and asked, "Who are you?"

Through the door I heard Bowie singing that these were my golden years, and that I was going to remain unscathed. All I wanted, with every cell in my body, was for him to be right.

13

DARIEN, CONNECTICUT (1972)

Furman, my mom's new boyfriend, was getting high with my mom before taking me to the Indian Guides Labor Day pancake breakfast.

I'd joined the Indian Guides the year before, in first grade, along with all my friends. It was the first step toward becoming a Cub Scout, and my friends and I very much wanted to be Cub Scouts.

The Indian Guides didn't do very much. In May we had marched in a Memorial Day parade wearing headdresses and feathers, and once a month we met in someone's living room to eat spaghetti and listen to different dads talk to us about camping and tying knots.

Today's pancake breakfast was at my friend Jeff's house. His dad, like all of my friends' dads, worked on Wall Street, had gone to an Ivy League school, played golf, and did his best to look like it was 1952 and that the 1960s had never happened.

Furman looked like the 1960s had never ended. He was six foot two, had black hair down to the middle of his back, and a full black beard. For the Indian Guides' pancake breakfast he had decided to wear leather pants and a fringe vest over his hairy naked chest.

I wanted my grandfather to take me. He was thirty years older than my friends' dads, but he worked on Wall Street and looked like a clean-shaven army colonel. But when my mom told me that Furman was taking me to the pancake breakfast I said nothing. When my mom made up her mind about something I knew not to question it. Both of us were happier when I did what she said.

Before we left, Furman and my mom smoked pot in her bedroom, while I played on the staircase with my Matchbox cars. I knew to be quiet and patient when grown-ups were drunk and high, and grown-ups were always drunk and high.

The weekend before, Furman had taken me and my mom on his friend's boat to one of the little islands off the coast of Connecticut, in Long Island Sound. Furman was in a Connecticut motorcycle gang, the Charter Oaks, and the borrowed boat was full of bearded gang members. When we got to the island I left the adults and wandered off to play by myself. After an hour of walking around and exploring the ruins of an old house at the center of the island I was hungry and bored and I wanted to go home. I worked up my courage, walked into the middle of the bearded gang members, and asked my mom and Furman when we could leave.

"Chill out, man, we're havin' fun," Furman said, smiling at me with boozy, lupine teeth.

I went back to walking around the little island by myself, crying in the woods while the adults smoked pot and drank cheap beer and listened to the James Gang on a portable eight-track player.

Today, after my mom and Furman were done smoking pot, she dressed me up as a little Indian, with my own fringe vest and a headband with feathers in it.

"I don't think the other kids are dressing up, Mom," I complained.

"But it's Indian Guides," she said, putting an extra seagull feather in my headband.

Furman and I left my grandparents' house and cut silently through some of the backyards between their house and Jeff's. We were stepping over a Revolutionary War-era stone wall when Furman stumbled and fell. "Fuck!" he yelled, falling heavily into some leaves and mud.

I looked around, hoping nobody was nearby to hear him swear. He'd said a bad word that you weren't supposed to say, even though I heard my mom's friends say it a lot when they were high or talking about politics. Furman had torn a small hole in his leather pants, and he was furious. "Fuck this," he said.

darien, connecticut (1972)   65

I gaped at him, not sure what to do with this gigantic, angry grown-up.

"What the fuck are you looking at?" he barked at me.

"I don't know," I said.

It was early September, and I had been in a good mood because in a few days I was going to turn seven. I was hoping that for my birthday my grandparents and mom would take me to the restaurant at Old McDonald's Farm, on the border of Darien and Norwalk. Old McDonald's Farm was my favorite place in the world. They served root beer in frosted mugs, and while you waited for your food to come out you could go to the petting zoo and feed corn to the chickens. They even had a nine-hole miniature golf course; I was hoping that my grandfather and I could play before my birthday dinner. Assuming that I made it to my birthday and Furman didn't strangle me in this copse behind Jeff's house.

Normally when my mom and her friends got high they were happy and smiling, if distracted. But Furman was not happy and smiling. He stormed off, muttering to himself.

At Jeff's house the Indian Guide dads were gathered around a long metal pancake grill, set up between the pool and the tennis court. Jeff's dad, our Indian Guide troop leader, saw Furman in his leather fringe vest and said good-naturedly, "Hey, a real Indian's here!"

Furman stopped short and said, clearly and simply, "Fuck. You." He turned and walked away, down the driveway and then down the street, leaving me alone. There was an awkward silence. All the fathers and the other Indian Guides looked at me. Nobody except me was dressed up in feathers; everyone else was wearing shorts and polo shirts.

I recognized the look of embarrassment and pity I was getting from the dads. They felt sorry for me because I was poor and father-less, but I could tell they wished I'd had the decency to stay home. Whenever I showed up in their clean, manicured world I brought the stain of poverty with me.

extreme places i didn't know

I stood on the patio in my vest and headdress and started to cry. I was so ashamed.

One of the fathers walked over with a paper plate full of food. He guided me to a picnic table with a checkered vinyl tablecloth and parked me on the bench. I sat there, crying. My friends Terry and John came over. They were brothers, part of the only Catholic family in the neighborhood. "What's wrong?" Terry asked.

I was six years old, my dad was dead, my mom was a hippie, I was poor, and I'd just been unceremoniously dumped in a suburban backyard by a stoned, furious motorcycle gang member. But I couldn't say any of that. I kept crying onto my pancakes and sausages.

14

NEW YORK CITY (2000)

Singing "Oh babe" felt awkward. But I'd been working on this song for a while and I couldn't think of anything else to sing in the chorus. And this "Oh babe" wasn't sweet or a sensual come-on; it was desperate. I had already recorded myself singing "Oh babe, then it fell apart," but now I was rattling my brain, looking for a better phrase than "Oh babe."

I tried singing "Oh lady." No.

How about "Oh maybe"? No.

"Oh now"? No.

"Babe" was kind of trite, and overused in the rock-music lexicon, but it sounded better than any of the other words I was trying out.

I had one week at home between a tour of Europe and a tour of Australia, and was spending as much of that time as I could recording new music. *Play* had pushed me into the strange pantheon of famous globe-trotting musicians, but my little studio on Mott Street was unchanged. It had originally been designed as a bedroom, but I used it as a place to work on music because, unlike the rest of the loft, it was air-conditioned and quiet. My actual "bedroom" was a storage space under a small flight of stairs. Barely big enough for my bed, it felt like a mid-century, blond-wood version of Harry Potter's bedroom on Privet Drive.

The rest of my loft hadn't changed much since I moved in in 1995. My off-white couch was on its last legs – literally, since it had collapsed under the weight of some friends who had drunkenly danced on it a month ago. Two of the legs had snapped, and I was

extreme places i didn't know

currently propping it up with piles of books and some pieces of wood I'd found in the hallway. The couch also had red stains on the upholstery because a friend and his girlfriend had had sex on it while she was menstruating. I'd turned the cushions over, but there were still some bloody handprints on the back.

In my tiny studio I had equipment scattered everywhere and tapes heaped in random piles. My little gray mixing desk was on top of a wobbly table, which I couldn't lean on because I'd built it out of chipped plywood from a dumpster and it gave me splinters. My keyboards were held up by milk crates; even as a vegan, I had to appreciate their sturdy utility. Plus milk crates were free (if you took them without asking). And they were perfect for storing and transporting vinyl, propping up musical equipment, and using as chairs when you ran out of places to sit. I had borrowed these particular milk crates in the late 1980s from the Stop & Shop near my grandmother's house in Norwalk, Connecticut – although most likely I wouldn't be bringing them back.

Earlier that day my friend Lee had come by for lunch. "So this is where millionaire musicians work?" he asked, taking in the squalor of the studio. "You know, I think you can afford something a little nicer."

He was right, but I loved my little studio.

This new song was sounding like it could have been an outtake from *Exile on Main St.* Or rather, I hoped it sounded like it could have been an outtake from *Exile on Main St.*

I'd been working on the song for a couple of hours, and so far all I had was a slightly shouty chorus and some loud guitars. I added programmed drums, but they held the song back with their rigidity. So I dug through my drum-sample library and found a few breakbeats. They had a looseness the song needed, so I looped them and erased the programmed drums.

Now I had some guitars, a chorus, and some breakbeats, but I needed a verse. A trick I'd learned from listening to Neil Young records was: "When in doubt, use the same chords in the verse that you've used in the chorus, just play them quieter." So I tried a verse that used the same chord progression as the chorus, but more restrained. And it worked.

I turned on the same cheap SM58 microphone I'd used for the past decade and sang, "Extreme ways are back again," with no idea where the line had come from. In the mid-1980s I'd taken a community college course on the history of surrealism, and learned that Marcel Duchamp and the other surrealists hadn't been weird for the sake of being weird, they had been trying to access the subconscious through automatic creative processes. I followed their lead whenever possible, writing and recording music without too much planning and thought, letting my subconscious express itself without interference. I wanted my music to be visceral, not academic. It was fun to think about music, but it was far more powerful to have a spontaneous, emotional reaction to it. So I had to be willing to be spontaneous and emotional when I was writing music, even if it didn't always work out.

"Extreme ways are back again" sounded like a celebration of the shiny lunacy that my life had become. But the underlying chords were dark and sad, making the lyrics also sound like a warning. I wrote some more lyrics for the verses, added some string orchestration, laid down a simple bassline inspired by Bill Wyman, and the song was done.

Except it wasn't. The song sounded fine when I played it back, but it was basic. I hated the word "hook," and deliberately crafting an attention-grabbing element felt crass and mercenary, but I knew the song needed something distinctive. I turned on an old synth and played some analog melodies against the track. They all sounded gratuitous and tacked-on.

Then I remembered my Yamaha sampler, which took years off my life when I had to reboot it in front of an angry audience at my first-ever live show, in 1990 at the Palladium in New York City. It had some remarkable violin samples, which I hoped might provide an interesting hook in an otherwise straightforward song.

I turned on the sampler, inserted the startup disk, and then spent five minutes loading the string samples. No wonder I hated this piece of equipment: it was the slowest, most awkward piece of gear I'd ever owned. I still couldn't believe that I had gone through this laborious process in front of two thousand booing audience members at my first show.

While the last samples were slowly loading, I walked down the hall to the bathroom. My hallway was filling up with framed gold and platinum records. Before *Play* I'd never received a single one. And now *Play* had gone gold or platinum in twenty-five different countries, so more framed awards were arriving every week. I didn't know what to do with them, so they were stacked on top of each other and leaning against the wall in my long hallway.

When I returned to the studio the samples had finally loaded. I experimented with them over the opening of the song, but they didn't work. I switched to another bank of string samples and tried bending the pitch, starting at the root note of the song and going up to thirds and sevenths and octaves. And suddenly everything clicked. With the right pitch, the strings sounded shrill and menacing, like angry wraiths.

I added this shrill hook to the song and listened to the playback. The new orchestration and the pitch-bending strings turned a basic rock song into something sadder and more powerful. It felt finished.

Then I had a thought: Why not add one more bit of conventional songcraft? There was room for a pre-chorus: the space between the verse and the chorus where I could add a misleading pause, creating a sense of reticence. "I would stand in line for this, there's always room in life for this," I sang over descending guitar chords.

I leaned back in my rickety chair and listened to the song from start to finish. My baffling fame made me happier than I'd ever been, as did the alcohol and the drugs and the debauched promiscuity.

But no party or platinum record gave me as much pleasure as the moment when a song came together.

Making a new piece of music was wonderful, but often I'd lose myself in the work for hours and not be consciously aware of what I was doing. It was this moment – stopping and listening when a song was done – that was the greatest part. Not just of my job, but of my life.

15

NEW YORK CITY (2000)

"Moby, do you know Mick?"

I was washing down my second hit of ecstasy with a glass of champagne when Richard Branson introduced me to Mick Jagger.

"No," I said, swallowing. "We've never met." I held out my hand. Mick took it, eyeing me warily. He was wearing a pink silk shirt and a dark-blue blazer, and he was Mick Jagger. The most iconic rock star the world had ever produced was standing inches away from me, in the flesh, giving me a dead-fish handshake.

"Moby's made an amazing album, *Play*," Branson told Mick. "Do you know it?"

"Oh, I've heard it," Mick said flatly, dropping my hand and looking away from me. I stood there awkwardly, not sure if I was allowed to talk to Mick Jagger as an equal or if I had been summoned to Richard Branson's couch as a bald novelty musician with a hit record.

"Well, I'm going to get back to the party," I finally said. "Nice to meet you, Mick." But he had already moved on and was busy flirting with Sophie Dahl, who was next to him on the couch. Sophie was a tall, gorgeous Amazon with platinum hair, most famous for being the granddaughter of Roald Dahl, who'd written one of my favorite books from when I was in kindergarten, *James and the Giant Peach*. She was about a foot taller and forty years younger than Mick, but he was undaunted and she seemed smitten.

My label, V2, had rented an old bank and were throwing a party for the Black Crowes. I'd brought a few friends up to the

VIP balcony, where we drank bottles of free champagne and took ecstasy. I'd been a heavy drinker for a few years, but lately I'd been downing ten or fifteen drinks every night and taking ecstasy whenever I could get my hands on it. I'd even invented what I called my "rock star cocktail": two or three hits of ecstasy, a bottle of champagne, and a bottle of vodka. If the MDMA and champagne and vodka were mixed correctly, everything balanced in my brain, and for a few hours the human condition seemed gentle and sublime. I stumbled to the bar and asked the bartender for another bottle of Veuve Clicquot.

"The whole bottle?" he asked.

"It's okay," I assured him, obnoxiously. "My album's paying for this party."

He handed me the bottle as I spotted the most beautiful woman I had ever seen. She was standing by herself underneath an exposed Edison bulb, and had long, straight, blonde hair. She was wearing a beige fringe jacket and looked as though she'd stepped out of Laurel Canyon in 1968. Even though it was midnight, her hair was touched by the sun and I knew that she would sound like birds.

I walked over to her, emboldened by fame, champagne, and drugs. "Hi," I said. "You're the most beautiful woman on the planet."

She smiled. "And you're Moby, and you're high."

"Those are true things."

"Do you have any more E?" she asked.

"No," I said, suddenly sad. Then I brightened. "But my friend Michael does." I took her hand and led her past Mick Jagger and Richard Branson and Goldie Hawn and Kurt Russell and Kate Hudson and a coterie of models and record-company employees until I found the drug dealer, Michael.

"Michael, this is—" I paused. "I don't know your name."

"Lauren," she said.

"Lauren, and she's the most beautiful woman on the planet. Do you have any more E?"

He laughed and handed me four hits of E. "Here you go, drunky."

I handed an E to Lauren and took another myself. We swallowed them with champagne. "How many Es have you had tonight?" Lauren asked.

"More than two?" I said, trying to keep my head and eyes from vibrating. She smiled and kissed me. I kissed her back. "Do you want to go to Sway?" I asked her.

"I want to go with you," she said, both forthright and demure. She took my hand and led me out of the party.

When we stepped out on Lafayette Street the paparazzi started taking my picture and yelling my name. "Moby!" somebody shouted over the staccato rhythm of flashbulbs. "Is that your girlfriend?"

"I hope so!" I yelled as we got into a taxi. Once the door shut the world got very quiet.

"Spring and Greenwich," Lauren told the cabbie.

A Creedence Clearwater song came on the radio. "Ah!" I yelled. "Turn it up! Please!" The cab driver laughed and played "Proud Mary" loudly as he swerved onto Prince Street.

"Proud Mary" was the first song I ever loved; one of my earliest memories was refusing to leave the car because "Proud Mary" was on the radio. I called it "Rolling on the River" until I was eleven years old, when some older, cooler kid ridiculed me for not knowing it was called "Proud Mary."

I rolled down the window. "Feel the air!" I yelled, happily. Lauren laughed and held my hand. I rolled up the window and got serious. "Lauren, you are so beautiful," I said, and kissed her. "But why doesn't God let us feel like this all the time?"

"What do you mean?"

"I mean that an omnipotent God could give us any resting neurochemical state, so why doesn't he let us feel like this from the time we're born until the moment we die?"

"Are you always like this on E?" she asked.

"Like?"

"Philosophical in taxis."

"I love taxis," I declared earnestly, and we kissed some more.

We pulled up at Sway, my favorite degenerate drug-fueled bar in New York City. Which was high praise, as there were a lot of degenerate drug-fueled bars in New York City. There was a line in front, but a doorman spotted me and whisked us inside. "Bono's here," he said, leading us through the crush of people. "Let me take you to him."

"Bono?" Lauren said. "I've never met Bono."

"He's amazing, I love him," I said, slurring and grinding my teeth. The back room was a bit quieter than the rest of the bar, and ringed with low benches covered in stained and cigarette-burned Moroccan fabrics.

Bono was sitting with some friends, and was dressed all in black and was wearing his lavender sunglasses. "Moby!" he yelled, jumping up. We hugged. "Get this man some champagne!" he told the doorman. "And his lovely lady as well!"

Bono introduced me to Michael Stipe. "I know Michael!" I said, and hugged him. I'd loved Michael since first hearing "So. Central Rain" on college radio in the 1980s; in recent months we'd become late-night celebrity friends. Then Bono introduced me to Salman Rushdie, who smiled at me from behind his professorial glasses. For some reason I never imagined Salman Rushdie smiling. Or hanging out in bars. I became solemn. "It's an honor to meet you, sir," I said. "I think you're lovely!"

He laughed, and said, "Why, thank you. You're lovely too."

Our champagne bottle arrived as the DJ played a Buzzcocks song. Bono and I got up and started dancing to "Paradise."

"Oh irony," Bono said, smiling at me. Bono and I had both been principled punk-rockers in our youth. He had possibly held onto more of his principles than I had, but I understood exactly what he meant. The irony was as potent as the alcohol: two former punk-rock kids drinking $300 bottles of champagne in the belly of the beast and singing along to an old punk-rock song called "Paradise."

At 5 a.m. the owners emptied out the club, but they let ten or fifteen of us stay in the back with new bottles of champagne. I poured Lauren another glass. "The exquisite corpse drinks the new wine," I told her, slurring the 's's.

"What?" she asked. I was about to explain the origins of surrealist automatic writing, but my synapses were too busy enjoying the alcohol and drugs that I had flooded them with.

"You know," Bono said to me as the sun started poking through the heavy curtains, "I really loved that *Animal Rights* album."

"Really?" I said. I was having a hard time seeing Bono. My eyes had taken on a drug-fueled life of their own. "Wow. No one loved *Animal Rights*."

"Well, I loved it. And I love you."

"I love you too."

Lauren leaned in. "Can we go back to my house?" she whispered in my ear.

"You have a house?" I asked, my eyes spinning like tiny drug-fueled carousels.

"Well, my apartment."

"Okay, let's go."

As we got up, Bono said, "Take care of this man, Lauren."

We walked through the empty bar and stepped out into dawn on Spring Street. We took a cab to Lauren's midtown apartment. As we got in the freight elevator, she warned me, "I have a big dog."

"I love big dogs!" I said, too loudly, my voice echoing off the metal walls of the elevator. She just smiled.

When she opened her door a hundred-pound Rottweiler galloped out to meet us. I squatted in front of him and he jumped on me, knocking me to the floor. He licked my face enthusiastically. "He hates people," I said, rolling around in the hallway with the dog.

Lauren laughed. "He's not bright, but he's sweet."

"Ha, like me! What's his name?"

"Bocce."

"Baci, like kiss?"

"No, Bocce, like ball."

Lauren held the door open, and Bocce and I ran around her apartment. He and I were playing tug-of-war with an old piece of saliva-soaked rope when Lauren said, "Okay, Bocce, I have to take this nice man to bed now."

"Where does Bocce sleep?" I asked.

"Usually in bed, but tonight he'll sleep on the floor."

"I'm sorry, Bocce," I said, sincerely, looking into his eyes. "Please forgive me."

Lauren closed her curtains – black, light-proof – and we took off our clothes in the dark. We got into bed and had sweet sex, fueled by champagne and ecstasy, while Bocce snored and snuffled on the floor. Afterward, Lauren said, "Do you want some Xanax? It'll help you sleep after the E."

"Okay," I said. "I've never had Xanax."

"I take mine with Vicodin – do you want some?"

"Sure."

She handed me an orange pill and a white pill. I washed them down with warm champagne from a bottle she had on her bedside table. "Now close your eyes," she said. So I did.

When I opened them it was twelve hours later: 9 p.m. The Xanax and Vicodin had done their job. Bocce was still snoring, as was Lauren. I fumbled for a light, and discovered that I had spent the night in a black four-poster bed. Looped over the post closest to me were a few dozen tour laminates and backstage passes, mainly from hard-rock and heavy-metal bands. I flicked through them: Monster Magnet, Soundgarden, Jane's Addiction.

Lauren woke up. "Good morning," she said sweetly.

"It's 9 p.m."

"Like I said, good morning."

"Monster Magnet?" I asked, holding up the band's laminate.

"Oh, you found my collection."

I laughed. "So I'm not special?"

She smiled sweetly and pulled me close to her. "Oh, honey, you're special."

16

DARIEN, CONNECTICUT (1973)

I was about to get hit. My mom had never hit me before, but she'd never been this mad at me before.

We were standing on the cracked driveway outside our garage apartment and her hand was raised. "That was twenty dollars!" she was yelling. "You almost lost twenty dollars!"

Her hand hovered, and wavered, and she lowered it. "I told myself I'd never hit you," she said to me and to herself, "so I won't hit you."

"I'm sorry," I said quietly.

She grabbed my shoulders. "But never, ever do that again. That's twenty dollars! That's our food money for the month."

"I'm sorry," I said again, scared and trying not to cry.

We had been out running errands. When we parked I had grabbed her purse from the front seat of our Plymouth and somehow let two $10 bills fall into the patchy snow on the driveway. When my mom couldn't find the $20 in her purse she frantically searched our small apartment, looking for the money. After fifteen minutes she went back to the car and found the two $10 bills sitting by the passenger door, already damp from the wet snow. Her relief at finding the money became anger, her face flushed red, and she raised her hand. But she didn't hit me.

We walked back into the house and she lit a cigarette. Her fingers trembled – not from the cold, but from the fear of possibly losing $20. My mom had lost her secretarial job a month ago, right before Christmas, and she hadn't found a new one. We were broke, and could only pay for rent and food with money she borrowed from my grandparents.

Late on Sunday nights, when I was supposed to be asleep, I'd hear her on the phone with her parents: "Mom, I think I need to borrow some money."

My grandmother would ask about work.

"I know. I'm looking every day, Mom," she'd say. "There just aren't any jobs."

We walked into the kitchen and she put the damp bills on the counter to dry out. The old gas heater had gone out, so she lit it with a wooden kitchen match. Its grill turned orange when it warmed up, and it was the only source of heat in the house. After it warmed up the kitchen we'd keep the doors to our bedrooms open and hope that the heat would circulate there. Sometimes when it was really cold our cats, Pakka and Racer, would sleep on the heater all day long.

I sat down at our black kitchen table to do my spelling and math homework. I liked doing homework, but it made me anxious, as I always assumed I was making mistakes. I had a desk in my bedroom: the plywood desk my grandfather had built for my mom when she was in school. The desk still had "I HATE JENNY WILLIAMS!!" carved into it from when my mom was a junior at Darien High School. But I didn't work at my desk during the winter because my bedroom was too cold.

As my mom smoked another cigarette and put away the groceries, she calmed down. "Oh, Pike is coming over later to watch TV," she told me.

I liked Pike. My mom had dated a few different men, and Pike was my favorite. Like some of her other boyfriends, he was in a motorcycle gang and had a leather jacket, but unlike some of the others, he had a job and was nice to me. I didn't know why my mom kept dating motorcycle gang members, but in 1970s suburban

Connecticut they might have been the only men she met who didn't work on Wall Street.

"Can I watch *M*A*S*H*?" I asked my mom after dinner. It was eight o'clock, which was usually my bedtime. But *M*A*S*H* was on at eight, and I loved *M*A*S*H*.

We were in the storage room, where we kept our couch and our small black-and-white TV. It was the coldest room in the house, as it was upstairs and far away from the gas heater in the kitchen. My mom and Pike were underneath a blanket on our brown foam-rubber couch, while I was curled up with the cats on a big stuffed secondhand armchair.

"Okay, you can stay up for *M*A*S*H*," my mom said, smiling at me. She and Pike were high.

"You've got good taste, Mobes," a heavy-lidded Pike said.

"I like *M*A*S*H*," I said.

"Who's your favorite?" he asked.

I considered. "I think Hawkeye. But I like Colonel Blake too. Oh, and Radar."

M*A*S*H started and we stopped talking. It was an understood rule: don't talk when the TV is on, except during the commercials. We would loudly ridicule the commercials, especially the low-budget ones with local salesmen in bad polyester suits, but as soon as the show started everyone knew to be quiet. My placid grandmother, who never raised her voice and spent her days volunteering at the Noroton Presbyterian Church, would bark "Shut up!" with the faintest trace of her old Scottish accent if you dared talk during her favorite show, *60 Minutes*.

I basked in the black-and-white glow, while Pike and my mom smoked pot. Luckily *M*A*S*H* was on channel 2, which came in pretty clearly. We had a wire coat hanger as an antenna, and it worked well for channels 2 and 7. Channels 4 and 5 were okay if you moved the hanger, but 9 and 11 barely came in. At the far end of the dial, channel 13 was just a sea of fog and snow.

When *M*A*S*H* ended I said good night and went downstairs to brush my teeth. I got into bed under a pile of blankets and looked up at my O. J. Simpson and Franco Harris posters. My grandparents had given me the posters for Christmas, and I felt so proud and normal when I looked at them. They were new, and they were the same posters my friends had in their bedrooms. If I squinted when I looked at them, I could pretend that I lived in a normal house. I wanted to make my bedroom look nicer, but so far I just had my mom's old plywood desk, my two posters, and a single mattress on the floor. I turned the light off and fell asleep. And I dreamed.

I had a recurring dream where I was in an old Victorian house that sat under a gray sky in a field of sunflowers. There were other people in the house, but I was the only one who knew that one of the hallways led to a different, darker dimension. In this other dimension there was an entity that could kill me, so when I stepped into it I had to be quiet so that he wouldn't know that I was there. I could feel the presence of this being, but I was safe as long as he didn't see or hear me.

In the dream I stepped out of the shadow dimension and back into a field of tall sunflowers. A little boy ran by me, screaming and on fire. He was half in our dimension and half in the other – and in the other dimension he was being destroyed by the entity. I knew that if I stumbled into the other dimension, I'd end up torn to pieces like him.

I woke up sweating and shaking with fear. I got out of bed and ran upstairs: I needed to tell my mom that I'd had my nightmare again.

There was a candle burning low in my mom's room and the air smelled like pot smoke. "Mom, I had a terrible dream," I said.

My mom and Pike were having sex. "Go back to bed!" my mom yelled.

I froze. I was scared of everything. I was scared of my dark room and the terrible dream, and I was scared of this dark room where my mom and Pike were having sex.

darien, connecticut (1973)   83

"Moby! Go back to bed!" my mom yelled again.

I reluctantly went downstairs. Pakka, the orange tabby we'd rescued a year ago, was on my bed, purring and waiting for me. Racer, the smaller calico we'd rescued a few months later, came into the room, stretched, and lay down next to Pakka.

I shut the door and got into bed with the cats, who curled up next to me. With my door shut the room would get cold, and I'd wake up shivering in the morning. But with the door shut I knew the cats wouldn't leave me.

17

NEW YORK CITY (2000)

I had finally learned the hierarchical taxonomy of limousines.

Back in 1995 I'd gone on tour as the opening act for the Red Hot Chili Peppers and the Flaming Lips. We'd played a few European arenas big enough for the headlining Chili Peppers to drive their limos into the venue and get out right next to the stage. I'd never seen such a thing – it seemed like the absurd and awe-inspiring height of rock-star decadence.

And now, almost every night, I was being chauffeured and dropped backstage in different limos in different parts of the world: prom-night stretch limos in the Midwest, black-window captain-of-industry limos in New York, armor-plated limos in South America, compact Mercedes limos in Germany and eastern Europe. The elegant Mercedes limos were my favorite, as they made me feel like a jaded CIA agent or the president of a discreet Swiss bank.

The tour for *Play*, which was originally supposed to be four weeks long, was now entering its eighteenth month. We were doing what Barry, one of my three managers, called "a victory lap," going to cities we'd already visited multiple times, but now playing cavernous arenas instead of small clubs.

I loved being famous, so I was doing as many print and TV and radio interviews as I could. A recurring question from journalists was about Herman Melville being an ancestor of mine. I'd spent so much time talking about *Moby-Dick* that I felt like a scholar, even though I'd never actually finished the book. I'd decided that the novel was an allegory wherein Moby Dick (the whale) represented the vast and unknowable forces of the universe, while Captain Ahab represented fearful, petty humans, trying to conquer that which was unconquerable, and being destroyed in the process. I would invariably finish my *Moby-Dick* answer by glibly saying, "Of course, I'd much rather be named after the vast and unknowable forces of nature than Captain Ahab." I never admitted that the only foundation for my hermeneutics was heredity.

And now I'd found rock stardom, my own domesticated pet white whale. But my little whale wasn't destroying me; instead, it smiled at me while I rode happily on its back, more like a friendly pony than a malevolent force of nature. I decided that it was my karma to have a benign relationship with fame, my own Moby Dick, and not end up lashed to the whale with harpoons and knotted rope.

We finished our European "victory lap" with a sold-out show at Wembley Arena in London, and then flew to New York to play three sold-out shows at the Hammerstein Ballroom. After the last concert John Lydon, David Bowie, and Kyle MacLachlan came backstage. I'd grown up obsessed with the music of John Lydon and David Bowie, and Kyle MacLachlan had been Special Agent Dale Cooper, the star of *Twin Peaks*.

John Lydon and his wife humbly thanked me for the tickets. Kyle MacLachlan graciously thanked me for the show. And David Bowie asked me when I was free to get coffee in our neighborhood. Sharing bottled water and polite conversation with three of my heroes was staggering, but it felt wrong. I was supposed to be a teenage fan in the suburbs, a supplicant worshiping my heroes from afar. I was supposed to be reading interviews with John Lydon and David Bowie in British music magazines, and videotaping *Twin Peaks* to watch in somebody's basement rec room. But I now lived in a world where I casually pretended to be the equal of my heroes. My hope was that if I pretended long enough, I might at some point stop feeling like an impostor.

After New York I flew to Los Angeles for the final show of the victory lap: a concert at the Greek Theater. The Greek wasn't huge – it held only five thousand people – but it was one of the most beautiful outdoor venues in the world, and it seemed like a perfect way to bring the curtain down on a bafflingly long and wonderful tour. The tickets for the Greek show sold out in less than a day, so my managers raised the possibility of moving to a bigger venue. But I wanted to finish the tour with one night in an iconic Los Angeles venue surrounded by pine trees.

At the Greek we ran through the songs from *Play* and a bunch of my older rave tracks. At one point, while we were playing "Porcelain," I looked in the front row and made eye contact with Christina Ricci, who was singing along. I'd met her a few times in New York, saying hello in bars, but we'd never been close.

After the show Christina came backstage. Everything about her was beautiful. With her perfectly straight, short black hair she looked like a voluptuous Louise Brooks, come to life in the twenty-first century. I offered her champagne, and as I was uncorking the bottle Morrissey walked in. With his trademark swoosh of dark hair he looked like a glamorous Mexican film star. I'd never met him, and I was immediately nervous in his presence, as I'd been a huge fan of the Smiths and his solo albums.

Often when I met my heroes I was stumped. I wanted to be a fan and gush and tell them how much I loved their work. But I also wanted to be cool, and so would pretend to be unfazed by meeting them. I didn't know what to say to Morrissey, so I offered him champagne. He declined, brusquely asked me to consider producing his next album, and after a polite handshake left.

"Was that Morrissey?" I asked Christina after the door closed.

She laughed. "I think it was."

After two bottles of champagne Christina and I got into my black stretch movie-star limo and went bar-hopping in Hollywood. When the bars closed at 2 a.m. we headed west, meeting up with photographer David LaChapelle at the Standard hotel, where I was staying. The hotel bar was still serving alcohol, so we crowded into a vinyl booth with David and his coterie of degenerates and beautiful freaks. Being around him always felt like stepping into an early John Waters movie.

"Moby," David said, "meet Holly."

"Hi," I said, smiling drunkenly at a blonde and aging – but still beautiful – drag queen.

"Moby," David said, as if explaining a profound truth to a simpleton, "this is Holly from 'Walk on the Wild Side.'"

"Oh," I said, taken aback. "Can I kiss you?"

"Of course, darling," she said, in a hoarse rasp reminiscent of Marianne Faithfull.

I leaned over and kissed Holly. I was straight, but I knew that if you're in a booth at 3 a.m. drinking champagne with Holly from "Walk on the Wild Side," you kiss her. And not a chaste peck on the cheek, but an open-mouthed kiss. You can't kiss Holly the way you would your great-aunt.

David slammed down a shot of tequila and yelled, "Let's go to the disco!"

"There's a disco?" I asked.

He took my hand and Christina's and walked us through the Standard's kitchen to a door that led to a dark private club, hidden deep within the bowels of the hotel.

As we stepped into the disco the first person I saw was Joe Strummer. I hadn't seen him since Glastonbury, so I ran up to him and hugged him.

"Joe!" I yelled.

"Moby!" he yelled.

We wrapped our arms around each other and started dancing to a Donna Summer track.

"I love you, Joe!" I yelled drunkenly.

"I love you, Moby!" he yelled back, just as drunkenly.

Christina joined us, followed by David and Holly. We all held onto each other and danced wildly to the looping synths and otherworldly beauty of "I Feel Love."

We drank more. We danced more. And at 5 a.m., after hugging everyone one last time, Christina and I left the club and went up to my room. My room wasn't terribly fancy, but on the balcony you could see the dark Pacific Ocean, far in the distance. We opened another bottle of champagne and sat on the balcony's mid-century chairs, basking in the warm night air and gazing at the endless lights of Los Angeles. The sun started to come up, just a thin rose-colored sliver on the eastern horizon. I put my champagne glass down and kissed Christina.

As the sky turned pink we sat on my balcony kissing, talking, and drinking champagne. LA was usually a loud city of twenty million people, but at dawn it was so quiet I could hear birds.

I was with a smart, beautiful movie star, and I was closing the book on the greatest eighteen months of my life. The realization came to me as slowly and gently as the dawn: this was actually my life.

"Do you think things will calm down now that your tour is over?" Christina asked me.

I smiled and took a slug of champagne from the bottle. "Oh, I hope not."

Section Two:

We Are All Made of Stars

18

DARIEN, CONNECTICUT (1973)

I hated Watergate. I didn't really know what it was, just that it involved men in suits in Washington, DC, taking up television time that was supposed to be dedicated to cartoons.

It was summer vacation, and I was hot and bored and alone. My friends spent their summers swimming and sailing and playing tennis, or going to their beach houses on Nantucket or Fishers Island. Every morning I turned on the TV, hoping to see Woody Woodpecker or Bugs Bunny or some other cartoon sociopath, and instead got a broadcast of men smoking cigarettes and mumbling in a Senate hearing room somewhere in Washington. TV was my life, and Watergate was stealing it from me.

Luckily the Watergate hearings happened during business hours, so I still had Saturday-morning cartoons, late-afternoon movies on channel 9, and Norman Lear sitcoms like *All in the Family* at night, while my mom and I silently ate dinner in front of the television.

We had moved out of the garage apartment on Noroton Avenue and were staying with my grandparents until we moved to Stratford, Connecticut, in August. I hadn't seen our new house in Stratford, and my mom hadn't told me why we were leaving Darien. One morning a few weeks earlier she'd mentioned it while she made coffee: "Oh, we're moving to Stratford."

"Will I go to school there?" I asked.

"Yes," she said, and lit a cigarette.

Now that Watergate had stolen daytime TV from me, I had to find other things to do at my grandparents' house to fill the long, hot afternoons. My uncle Joseph had given me a musty wooden box filled with his childhood coin collection, so I set it up on my grandmother's porch and invented a game called "Bank." I arranged the coins in his collection by place of origin and denomination, and pretended to make loans from one country to another. Greece would loan money to the US, the Ukraine would loan money to Japan, South Korea would loan money to Mexico. I wondered if this was basically what my grandfather did when he went to work on Wall Street.

It passed the time. I sat in a painted wicker chair, pushing coins around on an old card table while bumblebees flew idly into the porch's screens – but without television I was very bored. Occasionally I'd get up and turn on the TV, hoping that maybe the loves of my life had returned: Droopy Dog, Wile E. Coyote, Heckle and Jeckle. But they hadn't.

One morning I set up my Matchbox cars so they would jump over piles of coins from the coin collection. My grandmother was at her volunteer job at the Noroton Presbyterian Church, so as usual I was home alone. But sometimes I liked being left alone: I could go through adult things, like closets and bookshelves, without having to explain myself.

Everything about adults was a mystery, from their alcohol and their drugs to their clothes and their books. Most fascinating to me were the objects my mom and my grandparents had stashed in the backs of their closets and forgotten about: old calendars, worn-out shoes, empty bottles of shampoo. I would turn on the fifteen-watt bulb inside a closet and sit there, playing with these discarded things that once had a purpose.

Just as I knocked over a tower of Greek drachmas with a Matchbox car, the doorbell rang. I looked through a window: my mom's new boyfriend, Pete, was standing on the front step. His black Triumph motorcycle was in the driveway. I opened the door.

"Hi, Pete."

"Hey, Mobes, is your mom home? I wanted to see if she wanted to go for a ride."

Pete was wearing a leather jacket, but he was beardless and had shorter hair than my mom's other boyfriends. They'd been dating for only a month, but he smiled at me and seemed nice, so I liked him.

"No, she's at work," I told him. After a long stretch of unemployment my mom had found another secretarial job. She hated being a secretary, but it was the only work she could find.

Pete put on his mirrored sunglasses and looked at me. I could see myself in the lenses. "You want to go for a ride and visit your mom?" he asked.

I thought for a second. I had spent the last six weeks playing with my coins and Matchbox cars – maybe I could leave them alone for a few hours? Plus I'd never been on a motorcycle before.

I nodded eagerly. "Okay." I hopped on the motorcycle behind Pete. He kick-started the bike, which made a sound louder than anything I'd ever heard. He put the motorcycle in gear, pulled out of the driveway, and zoomed down a suburban road underneath pines and oaks.

"You okay?" he yelled back at me.

My arms were around his waist, my face was pressed into the back of his black motorcycle jacket, and the wind roared in my ears. I'd been on speedboats, and I'd ridden my bicycle really fast downhill, but I'd never felt speed like this. "I'm okay!" I yelled back. It was a hot day, so I was wearing my standard summer gear: shorts, a T-shirt with a frog on it, green flip-flops. The air was like little whips of fire on my skin.

Pete parked at the Baskin-Robbins on Post Road. "Should we get some ice cream?" he asked.

"Yeah!" I said, amazed at what my day had become. Every summer day was the same: wake up, have breakfast, turn on the TV, turn off the TV because of Watergate, play with coins, ride my bike, play with Matchbox cars, wonder what Stratford was going to be like, eat dinner in front of the TV, sleep. But now I was a seven-year-old who rode on the back of motorcycles and went to Baskin-Robbins.

We walked in and I immediately smelled the frozen cardboard and cold sugar. Carvel was my favorite – their ice cream was soft like cake frosting – but Baskin-Robbins was still ice cream, so I had no complaints. "What do you want, Moby?" Pete asked.

"Bubblegum," I said decisively, standing on tiptoes so I could peer through the glass at the brown cardboard tubs of ice cream.

"Bubblegum?"

"He means bubblegum ice cream," explained the bored teenager in the Neil Young and Crazy Horse T-shirt behind the counter. Bubblegum ice cream was an unexpected miracle: it was pink and contained pieces of pink bubblegum. It shouldn't have existed, but it did. And I loved it.

Pete bought our ice creams and we ate them next to the dumpster behind the store. "You want to go visit your mom?" Pete said, tossing the rest of his cone into the garbage and lighting a cigarette.

"Sure!" I said, hurriedly eating the last bits of my cone and trying not to swallow too much soggy napkin.

Pete kick-started his bike. I could see other people in the parking lot looking at us. I was adjacent to power – a powerful machine and a powerful man. Pete wasn't clean-cut like my friends' dads, and he worked at an auto-body shop, not Bear Stearns. But despite the tough exterior, he was kind. My mom liked him, and so did I.

Now and then I fantasized about having a dad and living in a real house. Pete probably wouldn't be able to buy me new Izod shirts or get us a house on Fishers Island, but of all the men my mom had dated since my dad died, he was one of the only ones I hoped she'd marry.

I clung tightly to Pete's waist as he pulled out of the parking lot. "Let's go the long way!" he yelled.

"Okay!" I yelled back. The wind hit my face like a barrage of baby slaps. When Pete accelerated the wind became so fierce it turned my

we are all made of stars

shorts and T-shirt into violent, snapping flags. We headed down Tokeneke Road and through the winding roads near the beach. Trees passed by like we were zooming through a blurry green tunnel.

I moved my leg and immediately felt searing pain that quickly blossomed into spectacular, raging agony. Pete sensed something and pulled over. I didn't want to cry. I didn't even want Pete to know I was in pain. I didn't want to screw this day up. But I'd pressed my leg against the exhaust pipe and now I had a bright-red burn, about the size of a fist, blossoming on my small, exposed calf.

"Oh shit," Pete said, looking horrified. "We need to get you to your mom."

I nodded, blinking back tears. I'd never even imagined pain like this was possible. I wanted to will it away and return to the bliss of motorcycles and ice cream and tunnels of blurred trees.

We pulled up to my mom's office. Pete looked panicked. "Mobes, tell your mom I'm sorry. Really, I'm sorry." He pulled the visor down over his helmet and rode away. The roar of his motorcycle faded in my ears, leaving a silence that slowly filled with cicadas and the other grating noises of summer.

I'd never been to my mom's new office, but she had pointed it out to me after she got the job. The company had a weird, hyphenated name I couldn't quite remember, just like the other places where my mom had worked as a secretary: Perkin-Bowes, or maybe Pitney-Elmer.

I stepped into the office, which was brightly lit and fully air-conditioned. Phones were ringing and Xerox machines were whirring, and my mom was sitting at the front desk. She was wearing a secondhand beige suit and had pulled her long curly hair back in an attempt to make her look less like a hippie who dated motorcycle gang members.

"Moby?" she said, confused, as I stepped inside and finally started crying.

"I'm sorry, Mom, it was my fault," I cried. "I burned myself. I'm sorry, I'm sorry."

19

SAN BERNARDINO COUNTY, CALIFORNIA (2001)

In my dressing room at an amphitheater in the desert outside LA I was teaching New Order how to play a Joy Division song. "Fuckin' hell," Peter Hook said. "We haven't played this one since Ian was alive."

I'd organized an outdoor summer tour called Area:One, and for the last six weeks I'd traveled around North America with Outkast, the Roots, New Order, Incubus, and a host of DJs, including Carl Cox and Paul Oakenfold. I was the headliner, but I was also the tour promoter. The idea for a weird twenty-first-century version of the Rolling Thunder Revue, with dance music and hip-hop and rock music, had come to me in a bar at 5 a.m. last February.

The rest of the world had huge music festivals, but Lollapalooza had ended a few years earlier, and apart from a new event called Coachella there weren't any eclectic music festivals in the US. I explained my idea for a traveling festival to my managers; we then approached a production company that was eager to work with me after the success of *Play*. We made a list of bands and DJs we wanted on the lineup – and to my surprise the majority said "Yes" when we made offers to them.

For me the strangest thing about Area:One was being on tour with Peter Hook and Stephen Morris and Barney Sumner. I'd grown up loving New Order and Joy Division, so it was disconcerting that my heroes were one of my opening acts. It was also unsettling that I almost thought of them as friends.

A few days before, at our show just outside San Francisco, I'd worked up my nerve and walked into New Order's dressing room to ask what seemed like a potentially awkward question: "Should we play a Joy Division song together on the last night of the tour?"

The old suburban goth in me expected them to say, "No, Moby, the past is sacrosanct and we shan't revisit it." But the members of New Order opened up some cans of Coors Lite and said, "Sure, why not?"

It didn't take me long to teach them "New Dawn Fades": not only had they written the song, it had just four chords. After we rehearsed it with an acoustic guitar, Hooky looked at me kindly, like an older brother. "Moby," he said, "Ian would be proud."

I smiled and pretended this was a small moment; ostensibly the guys in New Order and I were peers. But growing up in Connecticut I had been almost cripplingly obsessed with Joy Division. My high-school yearbook quote had even been the last lovelorn stanza from "Love Will Tear Us Apart." I'd spent hours listening to Joy Division cassettes on my Walkman, as I rode my bike around Darien to stare longingly at the houses of the girls I had crushes on. Ian Curtis had died before I discovered the band, but I'd felt more of a connection to him than I did to most of my friends and family members.

I left New Order's dressing room and walked down the hall. I'd hoped that Christina Ricci was going to come to the show, but so far I hadn't seen her. We'd tried dating for a few weeks the previous autumn, but it hadn't worked out due to distance and my panic attacks. Outside my own dressing room I found John Taylor (from Duran Duran) and Charlize Theron, sitting at a plastic picnic table.

I'd known Charlize since the mid-1990s, when she dated a friend of mine, and I'd met John recently. They were both very tall and they looked slightly awkward, like hyper-attractive praying mantises, folded into two of the small plastic chairs next to the picnic table.

"Hi, Charlize. Hi, John," I said. "Do you want to come inside?"

"Andy Dick's in there," Charlize said, picking her words carefully. "It's not nice."

I opened the door to my dressing room and looked inside. Andy Dick was perched on a table with his pants down around his ankles, squatting over a vegan end-of-tour cake that my managers had given me. A group of his friends were standing around the table and chanting, "Poop! Poop! Poop!"

"I'm trying!" he yelled, his sweaty blond curls pasted against his head.

"Poop! Poop! Poop!" they shouted.

"What are you doing?" I asked.

"Andy's trying to poop on your cake," my friend Lee said.

Lee and I had grown up together in Connecticut, and he had been one of my first roommates in New York in the late 1980s. He and his wife and some of their friends had flown to LA for the last show of the tour.

"Oh, okay," I said, only mildly annoyed that now I wouldn't be able to eat my vegan cake.

I grabbed a beer for myself and some water for Charlize and John, and walked outside, being sure to shut the door behind me.

"So Andy Dick is trying to poop on my cake," I informed them.

"That's disgusting," Charlize said.

"Well, yup."

I'd never organized a festival before, but Area:One had been a success. The weather had been perfect, the bands and DJs had all gotten along, and every show had sold out. It felt right to end this perfect tour by playing to twenty thousand people in the California desert, as I'd come to love Los Angeles. When I'd first started visiting LA in the early 1990s I'd assumed that I wouldn't like it. My friends in New York had told me that it was the land of rapacious agents and vapid actors. But the more time I spent in LA, the more I found it to be a welcoming town of mountains, mid-century houses, and sunny vegan restaurants.

At 10 p.m. I walked onstage, starting my set with "Bodyrock" and playing for ninety minutes. Then, before the first encore, I told the crowd, "I can't believe I'm going to say this, but I'm going to sing a Joy Division song with Joy Division." Peter and Barney came onstage. Stephen sat at the drum kit. And Billy Corgan and John Frusciante, who were as obsessed with Joy Division as I was, came onstage and were handed guitars. I counted off – "One, two, three, four" – and we all started playing "New Dawn Fades."

It was rushed and imperfect – nobody onstage had rehearsed the song more than once. But it was magical because I was singing a Joy Division song with Joy Division. During the second verse I sang as high and loud as I could, similar to a live version I'd heard on a bootleg cassette of a 1978 Joy Division concert. When I finished the verse, Peter Hook looked at me and smiled. He had tears in his eyes.

New Order, Billy Corgan and John Frusciante left the stage and, as I'd done at almost every show since 1995, I finished the show with "Feeling So Real." I remembered one of the first times I played the song, at a small rave outside Washington, DC. I'd been full of joy and optimism then, as I was now. Unfortunately the optimism I felt in 1995 was followed by losing my American record deal, battling unrelenting panic attacks, going broke, and watching my mother waste away and die from cancer.

But now, as I screamed joyfully over the top of "Feeling So Real" for tens of thousands of dancing people, I felt redeemed. *Play* had sold over ten million copies, and I'd gone from being a failure to a legitimate rock star. This world was mine. I was going to hold onto it and never let anyone or anything take it away from me.

When I walked offstage my roadie, Kevin, handed me a cold, expensive bottle of champagne. He smiled and said, "You've got a guest."

Standing by a rack of guitars was Katie, whom I'd been trading emails with since we met a few months earlier in France. She was originally from San Francisco, but was working on her master's degree in Lyons, where I'd played a show. We'd never kissed, or even held hands, but through our constant emailing I felt like I knew her. Katie looked like a beautiful blonde surfer, even though she'd never been on a surfboard. She'd grown up near the beach in California, but had spent her childhood reading books and staying away from the ocean.

I ran over to her and gave her a sweaty hug. "I flew here to see you!" she said.

"From France?"

Katie laughed. "I don't like you *that* much. From San Jose."

We walked backstage so I could introduce her to my friends. My life was surreal, but I was getting used to it: I was headlining a festival I'd organized, singing a Joy Division song with Joy Division, and being met after the show by a smart, beautiful woman I'd last seen in Europe.

I walked into my dressing room with Katie and said, "Hey, everybody, this is—"

But nobody was paying attention. They were all looking at Andy Dick, who had his pants down around his ankles again. Instead of trying to poop on my cake he was now peeing into a champagne bottle.

"Is that Andy Dick?" Katie asked me.

"Yup," I said.

Andy noticed me. "Moby!" he said, handing me the bottle he'd been peeing in. "Have some champagne!"

Lee told him, "Andy, it doesn't work if he sees you pissing in the bottle."

"Oops," Andy said. "Do you want some cake?"

20

STRATFORD, CONNECTICUT (1974)

"What's an orgy?"

I was sitting in the back of my mom's Plymouth, while she and her friend Russ sat in front, smoking cigarettes and talking. Russ had mentioned something about an "orgy." I had never heard the word before, so I wanted to know what it meant.

Last August we had moved twenty miles up the Connecticut coast from Darien to Stratford. My mom's friend Cathy had found our house in Stratford, a run-down three-story clapboard building from the 1930s, and talked my mom and some of her other hippie friends into renting it with her. In December Russ had moved in. He was a tall, thin jewelry designer from Vermont, with a red pony-tail that went all the way down to his waist. He made jewelry in our garage and sold drugs out of our kitchen.

Russ snickered and turned to look at me in the backseat. "Little man, an orgy is when a bunch of grown-ups have a really nice party. Maybe when you're grown up you can have orgies."

My mom gave him an angry look. "Russ . . ." she said, warning him.

"What?" He had a broad grin. "You want to have orgies when you're grown up, right, Mobes?"

"I don't know," I said, still not sure what an orgy was.

My mom and Russ had just been at the unemployment office in Bridgeport, picking up their unemployment checks and seeing if there was any work. Russ didn't really need a job, as he was a drug dealer, but he liked getting his monthly check from the government.

My mom, on the other hand, had lost her last secretarial job and desperately needed work.

Before we headed to the grocery store we dropped Russ off at our house. The house was falling apart and smelled like mildew, which is why the rent was cheap. I didn't like the house, I didn't like Stratford, and I didn't like the rotating cast of gang members and hippies who came through our kitchen to buy drugs from Russ. But although my mom liked to talk to me about art and books and spirituality, she never asked me for my opinions on where we lived, and I'd learned to keep them to myself.

Cathy and my mom had gone to Darien High School together, and Cathy had been a preppy debutante before she became a hippie. I'd seen a picture of her from the early 1960s, in her white gown on the steps of the Waldorf-Astoria. Now she had wild, black hair and looked like Grace Slick from Jefferson Airplane.

I thought that Russ was Cathy's boyfriend – he slept in her room most of the time – but I wasn't sure. A few times I'd seen him sneaking in and out of my mom's room.

One time I asked my mom about it. She told me, "Oh, Russ is giving me massages to help with my headaches." I didn't know that my mom had headaches, but I was glad that Russ was contributing something to the house other than illegal hash and mediocre jewelry.

After dropping off Russ, my mom and I went to Cumberland Farms grocery store. It was February and the sky was dark and low; a light snow had turned into a cold drizzle. We walked through the fluorescent-lit supermarket aisles and filled up our basket: milk, bread, cereal, orange juice, a pack of cigarettes, and a can of Chef Boyardee ravioli. We got to the cash register and the bored teenage clerk rang it up. "Nine dollars and twenty cents," he said.

My mom looked in her wallet and froze, her face turning red with anger and embarrassment. "I only have eight dollars," she said, her voice tight. "Mobes, we need to put something back."

She reached for the cigarettes, but I said, "It's okay, Mom. I'll put the ravioli and bread back." I hated that she smoked, but I knew that when she didn't she was miserable and angry. We needed food, but she needed cigarettes more.

After I returned the items to the shelves she angrily asked the clerk, "Is that enough?"

He rang up the milk, cereal, orange juice, and cigarettes. "Yup," he said, still indifferent.

In the car my mom lit a cigarette with shaking hands. I knew not to talk to her when she was this angry and ashamed, so I sat in my seat and looked through the rain-streaked windows. I wanted to turn on the radio, but instead I sat as still and quiet as I could.

When we got home she went upstairs. I put the meager supply of groceries away and poured myself a glass of diluted orange juice. When we moved to Stratford we started adding even more water to our milk and orange juice, to make them last longer. The results had tasted strange at first, but now when I had undiluted milk or orange juice at a friend's house they tasted heavy and syrupy.

I drank my juice in the kitchen while reading an article on *The Six Million Dollar Man* in the *Dynamite* magazine my friend Ron had given me. Then I went upstairs to do homework. My new bedroom was slightly bigger than my old one, but it looked about the same, with a single mattress on the floor and a homemade plywood desk by the window. Before we moved to Stratford I had carefully rolled up my Franco Harris and O. J. Simpson posters. When we arrived the first thing I did was hang them on the wall over my bed. Even though they were getting older, I still felt proud every time I looked at them.

This year I was going to Birdseye Elementary School, about a mile from our house. It was very different from Royle Elementary, the school I'd attended from kindergarten through third grade. Royle was clean and well-funded; Birdseye was dirty and falling apart. The Royle student body was exclusively white, while Birdseye's was

90 percent black and Latino. But after a couple of weeks I made a gaggle of new friends and enjoyed school as much as I ever had. In some ways I was happier, for while none of my new black and Latino friends were as poor as I was, they were almost all struggling and middle class, which meant I felt less shame about using food stamps and wearing secondhand clothes.

I still couldn't invite most of my new friends to my house, though. Not because we were poor, but because Russ was selling drugs out of the kitchen.

My English homework was to write a report on the state of Oregon, but when I sat down at my desk I realized that I needed to go to the library to consult the encyclopedia. I loved libraries, especially in the winter. They were warm, clean, and safe.

Normally I would have walked to the library, as it was only a half-mile away, but it was getting darker outside and the rain had picked up. I walked to my mom's room to ask for a ride. Before I knocked on her door, I hesitated. I could hear her crying. I foolishly knocked anyway, regretting it even as I did it.

From inside her room, my mom screamed, "What?"

I wanted to run away but I asked my question: "Mom, can I get a ride to the library?"

"Go away!" she yelled, sobbing. "Leave me alone!"

I walked back to my room as quietly as I could. I shut the door and went into my closet to listen to the radio. Whoever lived here before me had put a small bench in there, which I thought was exotic – I had never seen a bench in a closet before. It wasn't an especially comfortable bench, but I liked sitting in the closet with the door closed and listening to the radio in the dark. The closet smelled like old wood, and being in there reminded me of sitting in the closets in my grandparents' house.

I turned on the radio my aunts and uncles had given me for my most recent birthday, and I was in luck: Casey Kasem's *American Top 40* was on. I loved Kasem, a deep-voiced radio DJ who was also the voice of Shaggy on *Scooby-Doo*. He introduced a Cat Stevens song, and I started to calm down. My mom had a Cat Stevens record, and even though he had long hair and a beard, he didn't seem too scary.

Listening to the radio made me feel a little better, but I was still mad at myself. I felt stupid: I knew better than to ask my mom for something when she was upset. I shouldn't have bothered her, so her yelling at me was my fault. My job was to keep my mom from getting upset. When she was upset it was the end of the world and I'd failed.

I sat in the dark closet, listening to the radio and wondering when it would be okay for me to go back outside.

21

NEW YORK CITY (2001)

It was my birthday, and it was only 8.50 a.m. So why was my phone ringing?

I had gone out the night before with Bruce Willis and Ben Stiller and gotten drunk at a Fashion Week party. At 3 a.m., before leaving Lot 61, a bar in Chelsea, I considered trying to find someone to come home with me. But I suppressed that impulse and staggered home alone. After spending time with Katie in Los Angeles and realizing how much I liked her, I was thinking about finally working through my panic attacks and trying to have a real relationship. I had booked a car to take me to JFK later in the afternoon: Katie was flying from San Francisco to New York to stay with me for a while, and I wanted to pick her up at the airport.

Katie and I were still getting to know each other through daily emails and phone calls. I was happy – and surprised – that so far I didn't feel crippled by panic, the way I usually did when I tried to date someone.

The phone eventually stopped ringing. I rolled over and tried to go back to sleep. Then it started ringing again. Fuck. It was probably a telemarketer or a wrong number – nobody I knew would call me this early, especially not on my birthday. After five rings it stopped, and I rolled onto my other side.

And then it immediately started ringing again. I wanted to keep ignoring it, but on the off-chance it was an important call I got out of bed, ran across the concrete floor of my loft, and picked up the phone. "Hello?" I said, hungover and expecting to hear a telemarketer asking me to change my long-distance service.

"Moby!" It was Damian, one of my oldest friends, and he was screaming. "Go up on your roof!"

"Damian? What?"

"Go up on your roof!" he repeated, his voice desperate and panicky. "The World Trade Center's been hit!"

"What?"

"Go up on your roof!"

I was walking up the stairs to my roof, a towel around my waist, when I heard the sound.

I found out later that the first plane had hit the North Tower while I was asleep. At first people assumed it was a horrifying mistake: a plane had gone off course and accidentally flown into the building. And now everyone in lower Manhattan was on their roofs to see what was happening. The sound I heard as I walked up to my roof was made by the thousands of people on the roofs around me gasping, and then screaming, as they saw the second plane approaching the World Trade Center. As I stepped onto the roof I heard the sound as it hit the South Tower.

After the first plane hit there was horror, but still innocence. People assumed what they'd seen was a terrible, terrible accident. When tens of thousands of people on the rooftops saw the second plane hit, however, they wailed not just with sorrow for the dead, but with the realization that what they were seeing was intentional.

My brain shut down, unable to make sense of what was in front of me. This was my roof, with its gray wooden deck and the weather-damaged table where I ate my pancakes and read *The New Yorker*. There was the outdoor shower I'd never hooked up. There were the small planters where I was trying to grow lavender and peppermint. And there, less than a mile away, were both towers of the World Trade Center, crowned with fire.

I'd seen the Twin Towers dozens of times every day, these calm, stoic sentinels at the base of Manhattan. I remembered visiting my grandfather's office in the Woolworth Building when the World Trade Center was just a construction site: two huge holes in the bedrock of lower Manhattan. As the towers grew they blocked my grandfather's windows, and his secretary dryly noted, "There goes my view."

And now these impossibly huge buildings were on fire.

Skyscrapers weren't supposed to burn, especially not on cloudless, beautiful days. None of it seemed real. The billowing orange flames looked like special effects. But they weren't, and thousands of people were dying half a mile away from me.

Damian was still on the phone. "Moby, what's happening?" he screamed. Then he started sobbing. I'd known Damian since the late 1980s, and I'd never even seen him get choked up. And now he was standing on Church Street in Tribeca, watching bodies falling from the towers and crying uncontrollably into his phone.

The streets below me were full of sirens – the police, the fire department, the National Guard, every emergency vehicle in New York – all headed south to the World Trade Center.

"Damian, I have to find out what's going on," I said. He was still crying, and I felt bad leaving him, but I needed to do something, anything. I couldn't just stand around and helplessly watch Armageddon. "Are you going to be okay, Damian?" I asked, but his phone had gone dead.

I went downstairs, threw on my clothes from the night before, and turned on my TV, radio, and computer. I checked every news site and flipped through all the channels. Everybody was telling me what was happening, but not why or who was responsible. I wanted new information, and I didn't need CNN to show me images that I could see from my roof.

As I compulsively flicked from channel to channel and site to site I heard a new sound. I had thought the earlier sound, of the plane hitting the South Tower, had been the worst thing I would ever hear in my life. This new sound was louder, deeper, and much worse.

we are all made of stars

I ran up to my roof and saw just one remaining tower, surrounded by an apocalypse of smoke and dust. Where was the other tower? The tower where I'd taken my grandmother for her birthday lunch the year before she died? The tower that had held thousands of people this morning?

"No," I said quietly. "No. No."

I fell silent and watched a plume of ash and smoke rise, billowing into the clear blue sky.

I had no way to process what I was seeing. Hundred-story-tall buildings didn't collapse on beautiful days. Unimaginable numbers of people didn't take the subway to work and end up dead. On the rooftops around me nobody was screaming now. They were sobbing, or like me had been struck mute.

I'd had simple hopes for today, my birthday. I'd pick Katie up at the airport, and after dinner at Angelica's Kitchen we'd go to a few Fashion Week parties. We'd drink vodka and take some ecstasy, and then have sex on my roof.

But now the world had ended.

I looked at the expanding horror of fire and smoke and dust. How many people had just died? "No," I kept saying to myself, listening to the screaming sirens and watching the monstrous cloud engulf lower Manhattan.

"No."

22

NEW YORK CITY (2001)

A month after 9/11 everyone in New York was still grieving. The fires at the World Trade Center were still burning, the streets were still full of police and military, and every fence and empty wall was covered with pictures of the thousands who had died. Most of my friends had settled on drunkenness as the only practical way of processing the unprocessable.

I was going out six or seven nights a week, and had accepted that every night someone – maybe me – was going to start sobbing.

The world had lost its mind, and it looked like the New York I knew and loved had suffered a fatal blow. Stores and restaurants were closing, businesses were going bankrupt, and people were leaving the city in droves. My relationship with Katie had ended before it really started: she didn't want to move to New York, and I didn't want to leave the city of my birth. Towering New York, the city that had given me and the world so much, was vulnerable for the first time in its history. I didn't want to anthropomorphize New York and say that it needed me, but I wasn't going to leave the city I loved when it was broken.

But I didn't know how to process my sorrow. I was traumatized, but as I hadn't lost anyone on 9/11 I didn't feel like I had the right to grieve fully. So, like many other New Yorkers, I drank more, took more drugs, and went home with anyone who would have me.

One night I'd been at the Mercer hotel bar, getting drunk and hoping someone would take me up to her room, when a man named Larry introduced himself and asked me if I wanted to take a helicopter ride to Staten Island.

I'd been told never to get in cars with strangers, but no one had ever said anything about staying out of helicopters. "Of course," I said to this random person. "When?"

"Tomorrow, 3 p.m. Be at the heliport at 27th Street and the West Side Highway."

The next day I woke up at 2 p.m., had a quick breakfast, and took a taxi to the heliport. Larry met me and escorted me into a small waiting area, where he introduced me to the other people who'd be flying with us to Staten Island. There were three Cirque du Soleil performers, a club promoter I vaguely recognized, two stern older men in dark suits who looked like organized-crime figures, and a former runner-up in the Miss USA pageant.

"We're taking two helicopters," Larry told us. "We'll have dinner in Staten Island at my friend's house, and then the helicopters will take us back."

I was happily confused: acrobats and mob bosses taking helicopters to Staten Island, which was only a thirty-minute drive away?

"Does any of this make sense to you?" I asked the former runner-up in the Miss USA pageant.

"Absolutely not," she said. "Oh, my name's Clarice."

"Moby," I said, shaking her hand and feeling like I had an ally during whatever was about to happen.

We flew down the Hudson River. I didn't want to look at the spot where the Twin Towers had been, but I had to. Seeing their ruins, piles of rubble over a hundred feet tall, brought back the torrent of anger and hopelessness I'd been trying to mute with vodka and ecstasy. I didn't know if I'd ever wake up and not feel the steel weight of grief on my chest.

Mercifully we pulled away from lower Manhattan and landed a few minutes later on Staten Island, on the lawn of a new mansion next to the Atlantic Ocean. A small man named Steven met us. He was in his late forties, about five foot ten, and was wearing a black suit with no tie. His thinning red hair was combed straight back. "Thank you all for coming," he said politely, as we stepped out of the wind of the helicopter rotors and the Atlantic Ocean and into his living room, with its floor of gold-veined marble. There were a few butlers holding silver trays and champagne glasses, so I started drinking.

"This is your house?" Clarice asked him.

"Yes," he said, and grinned. "Would you like a tour?"

"Of course."

The men who looked like mob bosses left through a side door, but the rest of us walked across the marble floor, our feet echoing in the cavernous space. "Let me tell you a story," Steven said as we left the living room and came to an entrance hall centered around a giant jade tiger standing on a plinth. He then led us up a marble staircase that looked like it had been imported to Staten Island from an MTV video shoot in antebellum Georgia.

"I always wanted to be a pharmacist," Steven said, "so I went to pharmacy college in the 1970s. My dad had been a pharmacist in Queens, and I wanted to have a fancy pharmacy in Manhattan on 5th Avenue and sell upscale stuff, like Aramis." He slowly led us through a warren of bedrooms and sitting rooms, all with panoramic windows facing the Atlantic Ocean. "After I graduated from college, I borrowed some money and opened my pharmacy, but nobody came in. After a couple of months I was sweating, 'cause the guys I borrowed money from were going to take my thumbs if I couldn't pay them back."

Clarice and I looked at each other, suddenly understanding why the men we'd flown out with looked like organized-crime bosses.

"So I was scared, and I needed to do something to drum up business. I found some old dolls in the basement of the pharmacy, and a friend of mine who did set design on Broadway put them in

we are all made of stars

the store window and made it look nice." He interrupted himself. "Oh," he said, "this is my bedroom."

Steven opened a door onto a sprawling room with wall-to-wall pink carpeting. The bed was on a podium, looking at a raised jacuzzi that was in front of a wall of glass with a spectacular view of the ocean.

"The jacuzzi's carpeted," Clarice whispered to me.

"People started coming to my store," Steven said, "but only to buy the dolls in the window. After a few days I ran out of dolls and I couldn't afford to buy more. I went to a garment factory in Queens and paid some ladies to make dolls for me out of old scraps. I put them in the window and people loved them." He led us to a small sitting room, smiled proudly, and pointed at two dolls sitting on the couch. "And that's how I helped invent the Cabbage Patch doll."

We were all stunned into silence. "I sold it to Coleco for a ton of money and started producing movies with my friend Steven Seagal, who lives next door."

"Is Steven Seagal here?" one of the Cirque performers asked.

"No. He sends his regrets, but he's in Russia with Putin."

Clarice and I looked meaningfully at each other. I wasn't sure whether we were really at a gold-veined marble mansion in Staten Island with the man who'd had a hand in inventing the Cabbage Patch doll, or in the desert overdosing on mescaline.

"And now, let's eat!" Steven said, leading us down a back staircase to the kitchen, where his mom was making dinner. We all sat at a long table in the kitchen, while servants brought us platters of Italian food that his mom had prepared.

"Hey, did you see the news about the Russian guy they found on the pier?" the club promoter asked, as bowls of salad were replaced with bowls of spaghetti.

"No, what happened?" I asked.

"He was tied to some wood and had a bullet hole in his forehead."

One of the mob bosses, who hadn't spoken up to that point,

dabbed his mouth with a napkin and said quietly, "He shouldn't have been on Staten Island."

"I need to drink more," I said to Clarice, increasingly sure that we weren't on mescaline, but not sure we were going to get out alive.

We had dessert, and after digestifs in an oak-paneled library we flew back to Manhattan. "Thank you, Larry," I said, after we landed. "That was the strangest thing I've ever experienced."

"What are you guys doing now?" he asked. "Want to go to a party?"

I was supposed to meet my friends Lee and Dale, so I asked if they could join us.

"Sure!" he said. He gave me the address of a restaurant on Park Avenue and 20th Street, which I texted to them. Larry, Clarice, and I took a taxi across town to the restaurant. Lee and Dale were waiting outside – it was a party for a wealthy real-estate developer and security was strict, so they weren't allowed in without us.

On Staten Island I'd had three glasses of champagne, three glasses of red wine with dinner, a shot of vodka before dessert, and an Armagnac digestif, so I was well on my way to getting drunk. Lee and Dale had been drinking since the middle of the day, so they were even more liquored up than I was.

"Hey!" I said, once we were inside the party. "This is where I met David Bowie!"

Clarice's eyes widened. "You met David Bowie?"

"Actually, now he's my neighbor. We wave at each other from our balconies."

"What?"

"Come over later and I'll show you," I told her.

She smiled inscrutably.

"Dale," I said, once we had ordered drinks, "tell Clarice about 'knob touch.'"

"First off, you're beautiful," he told her.

"She's a Miss USA runner-up," I said, proud of my new friend.

"Okay," Dale continued, "'knob touch' is when you take your penis out of your pants at a party and brush it up against someone."

"Eww," Clarice said, grimacing. "And that's sexy?"

"No, no," he said seriously, "it's not sexual, it's just stupid and funny. You only knob-touch their clothes, and the person you knob-touch can't know they've been knob-touched."

Clarice turned to me. "Have you done this?"

"No," I admitted.

The party wasn't that exciting. It was mainly full of businessmen and real-estate developers, most notably Donald Trump, who was standing a few yards away from us at the bottom of a staircase, talking loudly to some other guests.

"Moby, go knob-touch Donald Trump," Lee said.

"Really?" I asked. "Should I?"

Donald Trump was a mid-level real-estate developer and tabloid-newspaper staple whose career had recently been resuscitated by a reality-TV show.

"Yeah," Dale said.

"Yeah," Clarice said, mischievously.

"Shit," I said, realizing I now had to knob-touch Donald Trump. I drank a shot of vodka to brace myself, pulled my flaccid penis out of my pants, and casually walked past Trump, trying to brush the edge of his jacket with my penis. Luckily he didn't seem to notice or even twitch.

I walked back to my friends and ordered another drink. "Did you do it?" Clarice asked.

"I think so. I think I knob-touched Donald Trump."

After a few more drinks I asked Clarice, "Do you want to come to my house and see David Bowie's balcony?"

"That's a pretty good pickup line. Okay."

We got in a cab and headed down Broadway, stopping at my local deli to buy beer. The afternoon of September 11 it had been filled with people silently stocking up on water and food. Nobody knew the extent of what had happened or how bad it might get. The man standing in line in front of me was covered in gray dust from the towers. His head was bowed and he was crying quietly.

A month later the deli was brightly lit at 1 a.m. and felt almost normal. Clarice and I brought a six-pack of Sierra Nevada up to my roof and I pointed out David Bowie's balcony across the street. A mile away and to the left of Bowie's apartment was the gaping hole where the Twin Towers had been.

Clarice took my hand and pointed. "That's where we were." I realized she was right – you could see Staten Island through the space where the World Trade Center had been.

"Do you think you'll stay in New York?" I asked.

She wrinkled her nose. "I think so. And you?"

This was the city of my birth, the city where you could meet a beautiful woman and take her to your roof to look at David Bowie's apartment, and also the city where strangers took you on helicopter rides to Staten Island and then watched as you surreptitiously knob-touched Donald Trump.

"I don't know what would ever make me leave," I said.

STRATFORD, CONNECTICUT (1975)

After school my friend Ron and I went to play in the ruins of an abandoned mansion.

Ron was one of my best friends in Stratford. Everyone called him J.J., because he was black and skinny and looked like a younger version of Jimmie Walker, who played J.J. in *Good Times*. The girls all loved him because he was handsome and tall for a fifth-grader, but he wasn't interested in girls. He didn't know he was gay, because none of us knew what gay was. We just knew that he didn't like girls.

We wandered around the ruins, balancing on the stone foundations and imagining what the rooms looked like before the house burned down.

"When I get rich I'm going to buy this, and this is where I'm going to put the pool table," Ron said, standing in a weed-covered lot by the crumbling foundations.

I said, "No, when I get rich I'm going to buy this and get married to Francie" – the girl who lived next door, whom I had a huge crush on – "and we'll live here." I picked up a chunk of concrete and threw it in the direction of the crumbling fireplace.

After we were done pretending we owned the ruined mansion we ran around in the woods for a while and found some waterlogged porn magazines. I tried to pry the pages apart with a stick, but the magazines were just a soggy mess. We did see some pictures of naked women with black mounds of pubic hair.

"Eww," Ron said, and turned away. I stared at the pictures, with my heart in my throat. Porn was rare and illicit and usually hidden. But here it was, soggy and damaged and still powerful. I wanted to take the magazine home with me and hide it so I could look at sodden images of breasts and pubic hair whenever I wanted, but Ron wisely told me to leave it where we'd found it.

We walked back to my house. On the way Ron looked down a storm drain for some reason. "There's five dollars in there!" he yelled.

"What?" Yes, there was a $5 bill sitting at the bottom of the drain.

"How do we get it?" he asked, more excited than I'd ever seen him.

"Let's lift," I said. We clutched the wet, slimy metal of the drain. "One, two, three, *pull!*" I said, but for all our efforts nothing happened.

"Is there another way down there?" Ron asked. We looked around for some other magical sewer entrance nearby, but unsurprisingly there wasn't one.

"Let's find a stick," I suggested. We searched by the side of the road and found a long, thin stick. We put a dollop of mud on the end of it, and I lowered it slowly into the drain. On the first try the bill stuck to the stick. As I pulled it up, Ron grabbed it.

"I have five dollars!" Ron yelled, his eyes wide. We stared at the bill. It was wet and dirty from the sewer mud, but still beautiful. "I'll give you a dollar, 'cause you helped me get it," Ron said earnestly.

"That seems fair," I said, as that seemed a responsible, adult thing to say in the presence of so much money.

I'd held $5 bills before: for my birthday the previous year my grandmother in New Jersey had sent me a card with a new $5 bill in it. But this was even more remarkable: it was money that had been handed to us by the benevolent gods of the storm drain.

"Why did you look in that storm drain?" I asked Ron, happy but confused.

"I don't know!" he shouted.

We ran back to my house.

"I found five dollars, Betsy!" Ron yelled, as soon as we got inside. (My mom the hippie wanted my friends to call her by her first name.)

"Can we go to Bradlees?" I asked.

Bradlees was the lowest of low-rent department stores. Macy's and Bloomingdale's were at the top of the ladder, but we couldn't afford to shop at either one of them. J. C. Penney's was a step down, but still too fancy for us. Caldor was the poorer stepchild to J. C. Penney's, but even it was too aspirational for us. On the very bottom rung of the department-store hierarchy was Bradlees, and that was where we did most of our shopping. Bradlees smelled like fried food and polyester, and it was invariably filled with new immigrants, white-trash families from Connecticut, and crying toddlers in pee-stained shorts.

We got into my mom's Plymouth and drove the two miles to Bradlees. "I'm giving Moby a dollar," Ron explained, "because he was there when I found the five dollars."

My mom smiled. "That's very nice of you, Ron. What are you going to buy, Moby?"

"'Convoy,'" I said without a second's hesitation.

I had heard the song "Convoy" on the radio and fallen in love. It was about trucks and CB radios, and it was the greatest song I'd ever heard. I had no idea what a bear in the air or a Kenworth were, but everything about the world of "Convoy" seemed exotic.

Ron took the $5 bill out of his pocket and showed it to me again. Looking once more at Abraham Lincoln's face, I said for the twentieth time, "I can't believe you found five dollars."

We parked next to a huge pile of melting gray snow. Ron and I ran to the front of Bradlees, yelling for my mom to catch up.

"Come on, Mom!"

"Hurry, Betsy!"

She laughed and followed us across the wet parking lot. We knew Bradlees like it was our second home, so Ron ran off looking for candy and T-shirts, while I walked over to the record section. There were vinyl albums from Elton John and Bob Seger and the Eagles, but I had come for one thing only, and it was there in the singles section: C. W. McCall's "Convoy."

I picked it up carefully. Just a simple piece of vinyl in a simple paper sleeve, but it was going to be my first record. I walked back to the front of the store and waited for Ron to show up and give me the dollar I needed to buy the seven-inch single.

He soon showed up with a red plastic shopping basket, filled with ten boxes of assorted candy and a bright yellow *Good Times* T-shirt. He held up the shirt and squealed, "J.J.!"

I would have said, "Dy-no-mite!" but that seemed too obvious, so I just said, "J.J.!" too.

Ron paid for his candy and T-shirt, and then handed me a wrinkled dollar bill. It seemed like a very serious transaction, so I shook his hand and said formally, "Thank you, Ron."

I then gave the dollar back to the cashier, and she put my "Convoy" single into a small brown paper bag. And now I had a record. A record that I'd heard on the radio. It was mine.

We dropped off Ron at his house, with his candy and his T-shirt. As he walked up to the entrance I rolled down the window and yelled, "I can't believe you found five dollars!"

When we got home I ran inside and turned on my mom's stereo, put the plastic 45 rpm spindle in the middle of my copy of "Convoy," and hit "Start" on the record player. I'd listened to records on this turntable before, but they'd always been my mom's. This was the first time I had ever played my own record. The tone arm magically knew where to go, lifting over the empty part of the rubber platter and finding the beginning of my record.

There were two seconds of hissing vinyl silence, and then came the military snares that began the record. The verses played, with their

we are all made of stars

dark mix of orchestral arrangements and southern spoken-word, followed by the bright AM-radio choruses. And I was transfixed. It felt like the record was over before it had even started. But I loved my record. I loved it so much I hit "Start" again.

The tone arm lifted, I held my breath during the two seconds of empty-vinyl sound, and then "Convoy" played again. I sat in front of the stereo, still and transfixed. Three minutes and forty-nine seconds later the song ended, so I hit "Start" and listened to it again. I never wanted this to end. And it didn't have to – I could listen to my record as many times as I wanted. I played it for a fourth time, and a fifth, motionless in front of the turntable.

After the twentieth listen I knew I had taken things to an absurd length, but each time I played it I felt like I was in the presence of magic. So I hit "Start" and listened again. And again. After the thirtieth or fortieth listen, my mom yelled, "Dinner's ready, Mobes!" and I finally stopped listening to "Convoy."

"You love your record?" my mom asked, while she spooned spaghetti onto my plate.

"It's so good," I said, still in a trance after spending two hours listening to the same song over and over.

We ate spaghetti, while the cats slept on the kitchen floor. After dinner, as we were doing the dishes, my mom said, "Oh, Kip's coming over later."

I didn't like Kip. My mom had met him at the gas station in Bridgeport where he worked and where she bought cheap gas. He had long black hair and smelled like motor oil, and he always looked at me like I was a stray dog who was in the way. My mom had dated other guys who worked in gas stations and auto-body shops, but they all seemed like they'd made the effort to bathe before coming to our house. Also, if Kip was coming over, it meant that he and my mom would be in the living room and I wouldn't be able to listen to my record.

"Okay, I'll go do homework in my room," I said. I consoled

myself with the knowledge that I'd be able to listen to "Convoy" the next day.

In the morning I came downstairs for breakfast. My mom was sitting at the kitchen table, clutching a cup of coffee and looking pale. She was never happy in the morning, but she seemed particularly upset. I never asked if she was okay; I just tried to be quiet, because I didn't want to make things worse. But this time she asked me, "Mobes, are you okay?"

I stopped spooning sugar onto my Cheerios. "What do you mean?"

"Are you okay? After last night?"

I was confused. "What do you mean?"

She stared at me, growing upset. "After what happened last night?"

Now I was extremely confused. "What happened?"

"You really don't remember?"

I stood by the refrigerator. Time slowed and the light from the old glass ceiling fixture felt soft and distant. I had no idea what she was talking about, but when I tried to remember the night before my brain got foggy. "No, I don't know," I said. "After I did my homework I went to sleep."

She lit a cigarette and looked me in the eye. "After you went to sleep Kip came over. We started fighting, do you remember?"

"No," I said. "I was asleep."

"He was screaming because I told him I didn't want to see him anymore. You know, be his girlfriend anymore." I was relieved because I didn't like Kip, but I was also worried because my mom tended to be at her saddest when she didn't have a boyfriend. "But then he stopped screaming and he grabbed a big knife and said, 'Is it going to be you or me? One of us has to die.'" She took a drag from her cigarette and collected herself. "He came after me with the knife. That was when you appeared."

we are all made of stars

"I what?"

"You appeared. You were standing there. But we didn't hear you come into the kitchen. You just showed up. Kip dropped the knife and ran out the door."

"Was I asleep?"

"No, you were awake. But you didn't talk. When Kip left you went back to your room."

I'd never not remembered something, but I didn't remember this, even though it happened just a few hours earlier. My first thought was, *No, I was still in bed,* but that was impossible. But in that moment I knew that somehow I had been in bed, but I'd also been in the kitchen. Remembering felt like moonlight through Kleenex, but I felt like this had happened before: being in two places, being asleep but being able to see other places. I didn't know how, but I knew. I also knew that to say "I was in both places" would have sounded crazy.

So I just said, "I guess I was sleepwalking?"

My mom's face softened and tears welled in her eyes. "You saved my life, Mobes."

24

SALT LAKE CITY, UTAH (2002)

"You'll be on after Kiss," the production manager said, consulting his clipboard, "and before Bon Jovi."

"Okay," I said. "Well, that's interesting."

"I guess so," he said blandly, and walked away.

I was in Salt Lake City to perform at the closing ceremony of the Winter Olympics. The lineup made no sense to me, but was wonderful in its own absurd way. In addition to Kiss, Bon Jovi, and me, the performers included Willie Nelson, Earth, Wind & Fire, Christina Aguilera, and Donny and Marie Osmond. The closing ceremony was in a stadium that held fifty thousand people, and I had been told that the Olympic organizers were expecting a global TV audience of over a billion people.

These were the first Olympics after 9/11, so when I landed at Salt Lake City airport it looked like a sterile Mormon war zone. Soldiers clad head to toe in black body armor, wielding massive black automatic weapons, were planted between Starbucks and Cinnabon. In Salt Lake City itself the same black RoboCop soldiers were on almost every street corner. The crowning touch to these apocalyptic Olympics: Vice President Dick Cheney was going to be in the audience while I played.

"If you want to meet the vice president, we could maybe arrange it," my liaison told me in the car ride from the airport into town.

"No thanks," I said. I was polite enough not to say that as far as I was concerned, Dick Cheney was an architect of evil, the devil's henchman. He'd run Halliburton, a company that had made billions of dollars from oil and munitions, and as vice president he was the embodiment of everything that was wrong with the Bush administration and the Republican Party.

In a perfect world I'd meet him face to face and be courageous enough to ask him how it felt to profit from war after he had dodged the draft himself. At which point the Secret Service would put a bag over my head and send me to Guantanamo Bay. It was probably best to stay in my dressing room, eat vegan bagels with peanut butter and jelly, and confine my opinions to posts on MySpace and Friendster.

After going over my set with the orchestra conductor and the leader of the fifty-person choir I would be playing with, I walked into the backstage green room to get a cup of tea. Willie Nelson was there in an American-flag bandana and denim jacket, joking with Jon Bon Jovi, who looked like a male model moonlighting as a rock star. Gene Simmons, who was in full makeup, was talking to one of the members of Earth, Wind & Fire, towering over him because of his platform boots. Christina Aguilera, with a giant mane of hair that made her look like the singer from Twisted Sister, was looking for the bathroom. And Donnie and Marie stood around, looking clean and Mormon and smiling at nobody in particular.

The logistics of the show were complicated: some of the performers were actually going to be playing on the ice in the middle of the stadium, while Olympic athletes skated around them. I was glad not to be on the ice: even though I'd grown up in Connecticut, I'd never learned to skate.

The lights in the stadium went down, fifty thousand people cheered, and the orchestra played the celebratory and plaintive Olympics theme music.

The Olympics made me sad because the majority of people competing would end up losing. Whenever I watched the Olympics I tried to be happy for the winners, but I was always aware of the specter of failure. The thought of anyone spending their life preparing for one particular competition and then losing in front of a global audience seemed almost too depressing for words.

Earth, Wind & Fire played on their ice stage, while skaters swarmed around them. They were followed by Willie Nelson, then Kiss. And then it was my turn.

Before my song started I smiled at the one-hundred-and-fifty-person orchestra and the fifty-strong choir, all dressed head to toe in white and all freezing cold. I heard my name announced to Dick Cheney and a billion other people, played "We Are All Made of Stars," and three minutes later my performance was done.

As the announcer boomed out Bon Jovi's name to the vice president and a global television audience, harried security guards rushed me offstage and into a golf cart. They drove me to a second stage, where the rest of my band were waiting: we were going to play three songs once the main televised portion of the ceremony ended.

"It's not as big as the main broadcast, but it'll still go to a few hundred million people," the broadcast coordinator told me contritely. Only a few hundred million people.

My roadie Kevin put a guitar over my shoulder. "That was weird," he said drily. "Were you cold?"

"No," I said, realizing that I should have been, since the temperature was below zero.

Overhead there was a fusillade of fireworks and then a deafening rumble. Directly above us were two giant dinosaur heads, each the size of a school bus. Their giant mechanical mouths started moving and Donnie and Marie's voices filled the stadium. They were doing a comedy routine. As dinosaurs.

Even though we had only thirty seconds before we went live, I motioned Kevin over to me. I asked him, "This isn't real, is it?"

He shrugged and said, "Nope."

The comedy routine ended, Kevin scurried off the stage, and the giant dinosaurs with the voices of Donnie and Marie said, "Here's Moby!"

I'd grown up watching *The Osmonds* cartoon show. I'd also grown up listening to Willie Nelson, Kiss, and Earth, Wind & Fire. Tonight I felt like I was in a reality show written by Proust and Hunter S. Thompson. I played "Bodyrock" and "Natural Blues," and during our last song a few thousand white balloons cascaded down the tiers of the stadium. When we hit the final note the sky erupted with even bigger fireworks. Donny Dinosaur and Marie Dinosaur said, "Let's give it up for Moby!" And then they introduced Christina Aguilera.

I walked offstage, down a long concrete tunnel and directly into a minivan waiting to take me back to my hotel. This was the strangest part of touring: standing onstage in front of huge crowds of screaming people, and then moments later being in a quiet vehicle or dressing room.

To fill the silence I asked the driver to turn on the radio – but some Toby Keith song about 9/11 was playing, so I quickly asked him to turn it off. He left me at the hotel where I was staying, and I went to the lobby bar looking for debauchery.

Soft jazz was playing on the stereo and a few tourists covered with Olympic paraphernalia were drinking state-mandated light beer, but the bar was almost as quiet as the minivan. After playing for a billion people I wanted a full-tilt rock-star night. I wanted to drink and take drugs and end up in a bed full of naked Olympic athletes and beautiful TV presenters. But it seemed like for the duration of the Olympics any degeneracy had been shipped out of the city, possibly to Halliburton-themed detention centers in the desert.

I had to be up the next morning at 5.30 a.m. for a 7 a.m. flight to LA, so I gave up my degenerate dreams and went to my room, where, tediously and responsibly, I went to sleep.

The Olympic organizers had chartered two private planes for the musicians who played at the closing ceremony: one heading to Teterboro airport in New Jersey and one to Van Nuys airport near

Los Angeles. I was going to shoot the music video for "We Are All Made of Stars" in LA, so I got on the westbound plane with Kiss, Willie Nelson, and Earth, Wind & Fire. I shuffled quietly onto the plane, sat down, and fell asleep before the plane took off.

I woke up as we were landing, blinking and rubbing the grit from my eyes. Theoretically this was glamorous, sharing a huge private plane with some of the most iconic musicians on the planet after playing a show for one-fifth of the population of the planet. But the most famous musicians in the world were napping, drinking coffee, or playing Tetris on their phones.

After we taxied to the gate I got my backpack from the overhead compartment and stepped into the aisle with the other musicians. I felt a tap on my shoulder and turned around. Gene Simmons was standing behind me; even without his platform boots he dwarfed me. I'd never met him, but he looked at me as if we knew each other well.

"Moby," he said, staring into my eyes, "you are a powerful and attractive man."

I didn't know what to say, so I said, "Oh, huh, I wouldn't say that."

He just nodded and said, "Hmm," as we walked off the plane under a cloudless LA sky.

we are all made of stars

25

CHESTER, CONNECTICUT (1976)

I was swallowing pebbles.

It was my third day at summer camp, and I hated it and wanted to go home.

On my first day, after my mom dropped me off, I tried politely asking the counselors if they'd let me leave.

On the second day I'd lied, saying that my grandfather was dying (which was true) and that after his multiple strokes I was the only person who could understand him (which wasn't). I even used the term "intracerebral hemorrhage" in an effort to impress the head counselor, but it hadn't worked and he hadn't let me leave.

On the third day I tried throwing myself down a flight of stairs, like the boy in *The Tin Drum*, but only got a small bruise on my shoulder after rolling down a few steps. After this failed attempt at self-harm I went back to my cabin and wrote a letter to my mom, begging her to pick me up and bring me home. Before sending it I sprinkled tap water on the ink so it would blur and she'd think I was crying uncontrollably while writing it.

Now it was the morning of day four, and I was in the woods swallowing pebbles, hoping that would make me sick enough to be sent home. I'd thought that swallowing pebbles was going to be challenging, but they were small and smooth and went down like hard vitamins.

My mom had sent me to camp for two weeks while she moved us out of our house in Stratford and back into my grandparents' house in Darien. My grandfather had suffered a series of strokes (intracerebral hemorrhages) earlier in the year and now he was nonresponsive.

I'd gone to see him in his hospital room before being dropped off at camp. Holding his hand, I said "Grampa" over and over. But his eyes stayed shut while he slowly breathed in and out. After each labored exhalation there was a terrible pause – a silence that, every time, sounded like the end of his life. And then the core of his still-functioning brain stem would tenaciously keep him alive and his chest would slowly rise.

As I grew up in the middle of hippie chaos my grandfather had been my stable hero – everything my mom's boyfriends weren't. He had short hair and a job. He smelled like gin and tonics and barbershop aftershave. He took me to my first (and only) Yankees game. And he let me drive his riding lawnmower, even when I was so small that my feet didn't reach the pedals.

Sometimes I would sit in the back of his closet, just to feel closer to him and the things that smelled like him. Just touching the old wool overcoat he wore to the train station in the winter made me feel safe. And now he was dying. Or, practically speaking, dead. Nonresponsive. All his strength and stability were gone.

I hadn't been involved in the choice of Camp Hazen. One day my mom announced she was sending me to camp; two weeks later she dropped me off.

Camp Hazen was a generic YMCA camp somewhere in eastern Connecticut. The cabins, made out of old wood, smelled like damp cotton sleeping bags and Eisenhower-era dust. The lake was warm and had the same thick tea color as every other lake in New England during the summer. The humid air was filled with gnats and biting black flies. It was a normal, unremarkable New England sleepaway camp. And I loathed it.

After lying to the counselors and sending letters home and throwing myself down stairs and swallowing five pebbles but not

we are all made of stars

getting sick, I accepted that I was stuck at Camp Hazen for two whole weeks. So, like any inmate, I endured. I canoed. I ran. I made a lumpy ceramic ashtray for my grandfather. And I told people that I wasn't a girl.

Camp Hazen was a boys' camp, but a rumor was flying around that they had started letting girls attend – and that I was the first. In between making misshapen ashtrays and trying to hurt myself, I kept explaining to the other campers that I was, despite my shoulder-length hair, a boy. (My mom the hippie hadn't cut my hair in a year.)

After two weeks of bucolic incarceration the bright morning of my liberation arrived. At 8 a.m., after our last breakfast of eggs, bacon, and Hawaiian Punch, I sat on a bench in front of the dining hall, looking for my mom's car with the orange public-radio sticker on the front bumper.

By 10 a.m. most of the parents had come and most of the campers were gone. "Do you want to come inside, Moby?" one of the counselors asked.

I wanted to say, "I'm sure that deep down you and this camp are okay but for some inexplicable reason I hate this place with every fiber of my being and by association I hate you and right now the only meaning I have in my shitty little life is waiting for my mom to drive through the gate in her used car to take me away from this prison."

What I actually said was, "No, thank you." And I waited meekly, sitting next to my secondhand red sleeping bag and an old suitcase my mom had used when she went to college in the early 1960s.

At 11 a.m. she arrived in our rusting car. I leaped up and started waving, even though she was only a dozen yards away. As soon as she pulled up I threw my sleeping bag and suitcase in the back and jumped into the passenger seat. We drove away, and as we passed through the front gate I rolled down the window, stuck my head out, and yelled, "I'm free!"

chester, connecticut (1976)

My mom laughed, but I could tell she was distracted. Before getting on I-95 we stopped at a diner to get lunch. "Mobes," my mom said, as I was eating a tower of pancakes, "Grampa isn't doing well."

"I know," I said, confused as to why my mom was reminding me of this.

"No," she said, tears coming to her eyes, "he's gotten worse."

What could possibly be worse than having multiple cerebral hemorrhages and being nonresponsive in a hospital bed?

We finished breakfast and drove west on I-95. We passed Stratford, which surprised me for a moment – I had forgotten that I didn't live there anymore, and that the whole reason I'd been sent to camp was so that my mom could move us back to my grandparents' house in Darien. I was upset about my grandfather being sick, but I was secretly happy that I was moving back to Darien to live in my grandparents' normal house and to see my old friends.

After another thirty minutes we reached the Darien exit – and drove right past it. "Aren't we going to Grampa's house?" I asked.

"No, we need to go to the hospital."

My heart sank. Hospitals smelled wrong, with a veneer of disinfectant over a fog of dying. And I knew that if we were rushing to the hospital, my grandfather's condition was even worse than my mother had let on.

We pulled into the parking lot, and it started raining. A hot August rain, not cooling the heavy air but thickening it. "Can I just stay in the car?" I asked, hoping to spend an hour playing with the radio, while my mom and our family sat and watched my grandfather die.

"No, Mobes," my mom said, getting out of the car and lighting a cigarette.

We took the elevator to the third floor. When we walked down the hallway we saw my aunts and uncles crying and holding onto each other. My mom stopped short, her sneakers squeaking on the hospital floor. Almost whispering, she said, "No."

My aunt Jane and my aunt Anne ran up to my mom, enfolding

her. I could see my grandmother, stoically talking to an administrator, making arrangements to have my grandfather's body brought to the funeral home. And my uncles were watching their wives grieve with my mother.

I looked through the half-open door to my grandfather's room. He was still there. Lying on the overbleached sheets, he looked like he was sound asleep – but I knew he was dead. I wanted to go in, but I was scared. I'd never seen a dead body before.

I turned and walked away; everyone was absorbed in their own grief, so nobody saw me go. I wandered down the hallway until I found an empty alcove with a few fiberglass chairs and a vending machine making a low hum.

Growing up with a dead father I'd assumed that I had been given enough death for one person, at least until adulthood. But now my grandfather, who had always been there for me, was gone. He was going to miss my birthday on September 11, when I was going to turn eleven, the only time in my life when my age and my birthday would be the same.

Some hospital orderlies walked by me as I sat in my fiberglass chair. I didn't want them to see me, so I put my face in my hands. I'd grieved for cats and dogs that we'd lost, but I'd never grieved for a person before. When my dad died I was only two. And now I didn't know what to do.

With my hands over my face I thought about George, my grandfather's dachshund. My grandfather and grandmother had adopted George the year before. Even though he worked all day, my grandfather made a point of walking him before he went to work at 6 a.m. and when he came home at 6 p.m.

My grandfather was a stoic ex-Marine and ex-college football player, but he softened up around George. When George had been a puppy I had even seen my grandfather playing with him. He didn't know anyone was watching him, and as he played with George he was lighthearted and sweet, almost goofy.

chester, connecticut (1976) 135

I thought of George waiting for my grandfather to come home, looking for him and not finding him, and I started crying. I was hiding my face in my hands, but I still felt too exposed. I turned my chair so it faced the wall, pressed my hands tightly against my face, and sobbed.

26

LOS ANGELES, CALIFORNIA (2002)

It was 2 a.m., and I was wearing a spacesuit in a fast-food restaurant with Gary Coleman and Todd Bridges.

We were shooting the video for "We Are All Made of Stars." The director, Joseph Kahn, thought that it should be a bright, 1980s-inspired look at how Hollywood and fame had damaged people. It was an odd take on a song that had been inspired by quantum mechanics and astrophysics, but I loved the director's other videos, and I trusted him to make something special.

Over the past two days we'd shot O. J. Simpson's pal Kato Kaelin in a dive bar, Verne Troyer in a strip club, Dave Navarro in a crack den, Tommy Lee in a brothel, Sean Bean in a rented DeLorean, Corey Feldman in another crack den, and Angelyne, the patron saint of LA, in her pink Mustang convertible.

The nod toward the astrophysics in the song's title was to have me wearing a decommissioned NASA spacesuit while celebrities lip-synched the lyrics. I'd grown up obsessed with all things involving outer space, and was thrilled on the first day of shooting to put on an actual spacesuit. But after a few minutes of filming I learned that while a spacesuit was perfect for staying alive in a vacuum, it wasn't very comfy in eighty-degree January sunshine on the corner of Hollywood and Highland.

When the camera rolled my job was to stand still while other people lip-synched the words to my song. Sweat rolled down my back in thick beads, feeling like ants on my skin, but I couldn't scratch myself because my hands were locked in thick outer-space gloves. Between takes I'd beg to have my helmet removed and to have a production assistant reach into my suit and scratch me.

I'd thought that having Hollywood legend Bob Evans lip-synching my song poolside at his condo was the weirdest moment we'd shot, but being with Gary Coleman and Todd Bridges in a fast-food restaurant was much stranger. And sadder. Everyone else we'd shot for the video had enthusiastically agreed to be in it either because they liked me or because they liked the song. But I'd heard from one of the casting agents that Gary Coleman had agreed to be in the video simply because we were paying him $500.

I tried to make conversation with Gary and Todd while we sat in the fast-food restaurant, but it was hard. Gary was laconic and morose, and I was wearing a spacesuit. A video had recently surfaced of him in his new job as a parking-lot attendant, wearing a small beige uniform and chasing down a car full of kids who'd refused to pay. It was humiliating and heartbreaking.

I wanted to tell him and Todd that I'd grown up watching *Diff'rent Strokes* and reading interviews with them in borrowed copies of *Bananas* magazine. But the cameras rolled, they sang their lines, and the video shoot for "We Are All Made of Stars" came to an end. I took off my helmet so I could thank them and say goodbye, but as soon as they were done they quietly slipped out the side door.

Diff'rent Strokes, the show that made Gary and Todd famous, seemed cursed: almost everyone involved with the show had ended up dead or damaged. Dana Plato, who played the bright and charming Kimberly, had become a drug-addicted porn star after the show ended. Eventually she died of an overdose in the desert outside LA.

While not everyone in the video had been destroyed by fame, everyone had certainly been damaged by it. Except for me. I loved fame and I knew that it would never hurt me. Before fame I had been a short, insecure, bald guy from Connecticut. Now I was a platinum-album-selling rock star who lived in hotels and tour buses and had famous friends. Fame had saved me and made me whole.

My cell phone rang as I was in my dressing room, changing out of my spacesuit and back into my jeans and black T-shirt. I didn't recognize the number, but I answered anyway. I heard a burst of loud techno and a woman's voice yelling, "It's Jaguar!"

Last night I had gone to the Seventh Veil strip club on La Brea with some friends from the video shoot. Before I left at 2 a.m. I had a long conversation with a stripper named Jaguar. She told me she was a business student from Ohio who was stripping in LA to make money. I had given her my number.

"Moby?" she yelled into her phone.

"Hello?" I yelled back, hoping to be heard over the din of the dance music playing wherever she was.

"Hey! It's Jaguar! From last night! Can I come see you?"

It was 3 a.m. and I'd been shooting in my spacesuit for twenty-one hours, but all I had to do in the morning was wake up and fly to London. I gave Jaguar my hotel information and took a limo back to the Four Seasons, where I was staying. As I entered the lobby I realized that my two-bedroom hotel suite cost more per night than the entire budget for my first video, "Go," which we had filmed for $1,500.

I still wanted to see myself as a punk-rocker at heart, somebody who rejected million-dollar videos, limousines, and $2,000 a night hotel suites. But I had just taken a limo to my $2,000 a night hotel suite after shooting a video that had a budget of $950,000. When I thought of myself as spiritual and temperate I felt good about myself. But thinking of myself as a rock star who stayed in fancy hotel suites and had sex with strippers also made me feel good about myself.

When I considered this paradox I engaged in sophistry, telling myself that I had enlightened neural wiring that enabled me to be in the world, but not of it. The truth was that I clung to anything that made me feel good, and ignored the overwhelming evidence that I was simply a selfish hypocrite.

los angeles, california (2002)   139

I took the elevator to my room, shut the door with an expensive thud, turned on the fireplace with a remote control, and sat on the overstuffed couch in the living room of my suite to wait for Jaguar.

Only a few minutes later the doorbell rang. I opened the door and Jaguar walked in, smelling like her job was smoking cigarettes in a perfume factory. Which, since she was a stripper, in some ways it was. She had long bleached-blonde hair and was wearing a thin gray metallic dress. In her stripper shoes she was slightly taller than I was.

"Hi," I said, by way of a clever intro.

"Do you have anything to drink?" she asked, making a beeline for the minibar. She located a can of Pepsi and a small bottle of Baileys Irish Cream and poured them into a heavy crystal tumbler. She considered the drink, looking worried. Then she rooted around the minibar again and emptied two small bottles of vodka into her Baileys-and-Pepsi.

"Do you have ice?" she asked.

"No, but I can get some."

I was in one of the fanciest hotels in the world, but when I walked down the hall I discovered that the Four Seasons ice-machine room was identical to the ice-machine rooms in Holiday Inns and Motel 6s. For some reason I'd thought that Four Seasons ice would be fancier.

When I got back to the room with a filled ice bucket Jaguar had already finished her drink and lit a cigarette. "Oh," I said. "Do you still want ice?"

She held out the crystal tumbler and I filled it with ice. Then she went back to the minibar and made another cocktail: 7 Up, Southern Comfort, and rum. "It's like a hangover in a glass," I said.

"Not if I don't stop drinking," she said.

I was annoyed that she was smoking in my hotel suite, but I didn't want to complain – even though she was clearly out of her mind, I still wanted to have sex with her. I leaned in to kiss her, but she pulled away.

"Do you want to do some Special K?" she asked. Special K was a powerful animal tranquilizer, ketamine, that had become a club drug in the early rave years. I'd never tried it and suspected this wasn't the right time to experiment, since I had to be at the airport in a few hours.

"No, thanks," I told her.

Jaguar took out a large baggie filled with white powder and started to cut multiple lines on the suite's glass-topped table. "Oh, I'm not having any," I reminded her.

"I know," she said, and kept chopping up the ketamine, dividing it into four lines. She leaned down, snorted the first line, and then asked me, "Are you spiritual?"

"How so?"

"Have you read *The Celestine Prophecy*?" she asked.

"No," I said. I knew of the book, but without actually having read it I'd smugly decided that it was facile, self-serving spirituality for dumb people.

"See, I saw you last night at Seventh Veil and I just knew you were spiritual," she said, leaning down to do the second line of ketamine. "You should read *The Celestine Prophecy*. It's amazing. It tells you everything."

Her phone buzzed and she picked it up.

"I used to teach Bible study," I said, "but now I tend to be more of an undefined agnostic."

She was ignoring me, staring intently at the glowing screen of her phone. She got up from the couch and walked to the window, where she talked quietly and furtively for ten seconds. Then she sat down and did the third line of Special K. "That was N——," she said, naming one of the best-known male models on the planet. She snorted the fourth line, her eyes visibly shimmying in their sockets. "He's at the Hermitage. I'm going to meet him."

Before standing up she looked around my suite, trying to figure out whether staying at the Four Seasons and having sex with a rock star was a better option than driving to the Hermitage to have sex with a famous male model. Aside from the living room where Jaguar had done her Special K, my $2,000 suite had a fireplace, two bedrooms, a dining room, and a patio overlooking palm trees and a pool. She walked to the door, deciding on N—— the model over Moby the musician.

I wanted to be annoyed, but spending twenty-one hours in a spacesuit and then being subjected to her five-minute whirlwind of sugary drinks and perfume and cigarettes and ketamine left me feeling like I'd watched a particularly stressful episode of *Storm Chasers*.

As she walked to the door in her stripper shoes, she stumbled and almost fell. "Are you okay to drive?" I asked.

"What? Ha, what? Oh, sure, I always drive high."

I was going to remonstrate with her, but she walked away.

"Read *The Celestine Prophecy*!" she called as she walked down the hotel hallway. "It's spiritual, like you."

27

NEW YORK CITY (2002)

I was dressed for a trip to McMurdo Station in Antarctica, even though I was only walking two blocks to David Bowie's apartment. A brutal cold front had settled over New York City, and to stave off the sub-zero cold I was wrapped in a long gray scarf, a faux-fur-lined jacket, heavy-duty Patagonia gloves, and a black balaclava.

The week before David had been at my apartment to rehearse for a charity event we had agreed to do together. He got off the elevator on the fifth floor, by my front door, held out a coffee for me, and said, "Delivery boy!" He sat down on my couch and placed the deli coffees on the coffee table. I took my guitar out of its case.

"I have an idea," I said, aware that David Bowie, a demigod, was sitting in my living room and I was talking to him as if we were equals. "What if for the event we played '"Heroes"' on acoustic guitar?"

He smiled kindly and said, "Sure, let's give it a try."

I'd practiced playing the chords to '"Heroes"' the night before, rehearsing by myself on the off-chance that he would agree. I quietly strummed the opening D-major chord. David took a sip of his coffee and started singing.

I was somehow able to focus on playing, even though I was having an out-of-body experience: David Bowie was in my living room, sitting on my couch, singing the most beautiful song ever written. During the second verse his voice rose dramatically and I had to remind my little alcoholic heart to keep beating.

After our thirty-minute rehearsal was over and we'd finished our coffees, David mentioned that he was having dinner at his apartment the following week with Lou Reed and Laurie Anderson. He smiled and said he'd love for me to join them. "Iman and I can even make you something vegan," he added.

The first few times I'd gone to David's building I'd entered under the suspicious squint of the burly doorman at the entrance. But now I'd been to his apartment enough times that the doorman just looked at me and said, "Go on up."

I got in the elevator to go to the eighth floor and started shedding my winter garments. The elevator door opened, I turned right, and I stood in front of David and Iman's front door. I'd been to their apartment fifteen or twenty times, but every time I stood here, about to knock, I froze. I was seconds away from crossing the threshold into David Bowie's apartment, with its long hallways, hypermodern but warm chef's kitchen, dark wood library, and banks of tall windows looking at the hole in the sky where the Twin Towers had been.

What I could never process was that each time I entered, I was visiting David Bowie as a friend. As a peer. Well, "peer" seemed absurd. Bowie was the greatest musician of the twentieth century, while I was a bald degenerate with an accidental hit record. He was a demigod; I was most likely a fluke.

I knocked and heard footsteps. The door opened and there he was: David Bowie. He was wearing gray slacks and a black T-shirt, and he smelled like expensive soap. "Look at all of this!" he said, regarding my jacket and gloves and scarf and balaclava. "Are you walking to Canada later?"

"I hate being cold," I said, stepping inside.

"Here, let me take your things."

I paused for a tenth of a second, marveling at the wrongness of David Bowie "taking my things." You didn't show up in Heaven and hear God say, "Here, let me take your things."

He stowed my winter gear in their hall closet and we walked into the kitchen, where Iman was cooking and talking to Laurie Anderson.

"Moby!" Iman said, and hugged me.

She looked like sculpted royalty: tall and radiant and poised. But even though she looked like a beautiful alien queen, she was always remarkably down-to-earth, kind, and opinionated. We'd spent election night together in 2000, and as we realized that Florida hadn't been called for Al Gore, she got into a testy but funny exchange with Dennis Hopper, who, disappointingly, was a Republican.

"Do you know Laurie?" Iman asked.

"Yes. Hi, Laurie," I said, giving her a polite kiss on the cheek. I saw Laurie often at fundraisers and art openings, and she always looked happy and mischievous underneath her spiky Johnny Rotten hair.

"And you know Lou?" Iman asked.

Lou Reed was wearing a shimmering metallic jacket, holding a drink, and looking at David and Iman's books.

"Hi, Lou," I said. He gave me a long, warm hug. I always expected Lou to hate me, as he seemed to hate most people. But for some reason I couldn't fathom, he seemed to like me.

"Moby," he said in the distinctive voice I'd heard on "Heroin" and "Pale Blue Eyes" and countless other iconic songs. "How are you?"

"I'm good." I paused awkwardly, suddenly aware I was surrounded by alien gods. "Cold."

He looked around. "But it's warm in here."

"Moby walked all the way over from his apartment," David said, joining us.

"But you live across the street," Lou said, confused.

"I know. I'm a big sissy."

"You've been to Moby's apartment?" David asked, almost proprietarily.

"When I was building my studio I went to Moby's studio to look at the carpentry," Lou explained.

My brain had involuntarily compartmentalized itself. One part was having a calm, pleasant conversation with a couple of friends while dinner was being prepared. The other part of it was screaming,

Lou Reed and David Bowie know where I live! They've been to my house! Fuck! The world is upside down!

"Oh, Moby," David said, "have you ever seen a Stylophone?"

"No. What's that?"

"Let me show you." We left Lou and Laurie and Iman and walked down a long, quiet hallway. I'd been here dozens of times, but I always felt like every inch of the apartment was worthy of reverence. We passed his bedroom (where David Bowie slept) and his bathroom (where David Bowie peed and brushed his teeth) and came to his studio (where David Bowie worked).

David's home studio was modest, more of a guest bedroom with some equipment than a sprawling, elaborate place to record music.

"I'm just finishing the next album," he told me, "and today I recorded a Stylophone part on a song about Iggy."

David held up a small pink cardboard box. I opened it and took out the world's smallest synthesizer. "You play it with a pen!" he said, beaming. "It might be the best instrument ever invented."

I turned it on and dragged the metal stylus across the keys. It sounded broken and scratchy, but surprisingly beautiful.

"You can get them on eBay, so I've been buying them up," David said.

"Can I hear the song?" I asked.

"Well, it's not mixed."

"That's okay."

He inserted a disc into his studio's CD player, pressed "Play," and lit a cigarette. The song started slowly and quietly. "It's called 'Slip Away,'" David said, smoking. The song progressed and I recognized some references to *The Uncle Floyd Show*, a strange children's show I had watched in the early 1980s. The song built, and then built some more, beautiful and vulnerable and full of longing. After four or five minutes it ended and we sat there, David smoking and me wondering if I was allowed to gush like an honest fan.

"David, it's beautiful," I said, sincerely.

"Thank you."

"No, really, it is. And I loved the *Uncle Floyd* references."

"Iggy and I used to get high and watch *Uncle Floyd* and fall on the floor laughing. It was our favorite."

"It's a beautiful song. Thank you for playing it for me."

He stubbed out his cigarette. "Should we go see about dinner?"

The song had stunned me. It wasn't ironic or cool. It wasn't dance-influenced. It wasn't even particularly modern. But it was one of the most beautiful and vulnerable David Bowie songs I'd ever heard.

During dinner we kept up a constant stream of chatter – except for Lou, who seemed content to eat and to drink his vodka and soda. We talked about the war in Iraq, about our disdain and contempt for Republicans, about new movies, about the cold, about our new albums, about everything. My vegan food was average, but I didn't care: I was dining with gods and goddesses on Olympus.

After dinner we sat in the library, where David told us about an island called Mustique and the man who had founded it, but who at some point had been banned.

David was happier and more relaxed than I'd ever seen him. He stood up and started pantomiming, imitating this strange, sad man. "You know, I taped a documentary about him and Mustique. Would you like to see it?" David asked.

"Of course!" Laurie and I said. David found the VHS tape and put it on, providing his own narration and fast-forwarding to the most absurd bits, like the founder of Mustique crawling through the jungle trying to get a glimpse of Princess Anne.

Laurie and Iman and I were smiling and laughing, but Lou had fallen asleep on the couch. Laurie reached over and carefully took the drink out of his hand, making sure he didn't spill it on himself.

The movie ended and Lou woke up with a start, confused for a moment, but then remembering where he was. "What time is it?" he asked.

"Eleven," I said. "Time for us to go?"

We all walked down the hall. I mummified myself in my winter gear, while Lou and Laurie donned their jackets, which were not as warm as what I was wearing, but far more stylish.

"Thank you for a wonderful night," I said to Iman, giving her a hug and a kiss.

"Oh, hold on," David said, and ran down the hall. He came back holding a Stylophone. "Here, you can have this," he said, handing me a faded pink box adorned with a cartoon of 1960s hipsters dancing to synthesizer music.

"Are you sure?"

"I bought five of them on eBay!" He pressed the pink cardboard box into my hands. "You're the disco king, you take this one."

I gave him a quick hug. "Thank you, David. And your new song really is beautiful."

He looked a bit uncomfortable but smiled and said, "Thank you, Moby."

Lou and Laurie and I rode down in the elevator together, quiet and companionable. "That was so nice," I said.

Laurie smiled. "It really was."

"What did he give you?" Lou asked.

"A Stylophone – it's a strange old synthesizer." I held it out to him.

He took the box and studied it earnestly as we walked across the lobby. On eBay this was an antiquated trinket, a relic you could buy for less than $50. But in David Bowie's hands it was an instrument capable of heartbreaking beauty.

Lou took it out of its box, and I turned it on for him while Laurie and the doorman watched. The Stylophone made its distinctive, thin sound. Lou looked up at me. Then he looked back at the Stylophone. Dragging the stylus around on the tiny keys, he smiled at the broken music.

28

DARIEN, CONNECTICUT (1978)

On the playground of Middlesex Junior High I heard some of the other seventh-graders talking about how their older brothers were trying to buy pot.

"Oh, I have pot," I said with a nonchalance I didn't feel.

I was weird and small and poor and didn't have a dad. Scott Dekker, Keith Morgan, and Nigel Draycott were three of the coolest seventh-graders in our school. We had the same homeroom, but I'd never registered on their status radar.

"No, you don't," Scott scoffed.

"I do. I'll show you," I said.

"Okay, bring some to school tomorrow."

I knew where my mom kept her pot: in a black lacquered box on top of the upright piano she'd been given by her grandmother. After school I had a couple of hours before my mom got home from work, so I took a small amount of pot from the plastic bag in her black drug box. Also in the box: rolling papers, a small pipe, a few Quaaludes, and some partially smoked roaches. I got a sandwich bag from the kitchen and put the pot in it, adding a little bit of oregano to make it seem more substantial.

The next day Scott and Keith and Nigel pulled me into the boys' bathroom by our homeroom. "Here it is," I said triumphantly, handing over the illicit plastic bag.

There was a hush. None of them had ever come into contact with illegal drugs, especially not at 8.30 a.m. in the boys' bathroom at Middlesex Junior High. "Whoa," Nigel said, examining the bag reverentially.

"Okay, Moby, cool," Keith said, looking at me with something resembling respect. They walked out of the bathroom, while I stood next to the blue toilet stalls, breathing in the smell of disinfectant and powdered soap.

Keith had said I was cool. And all I'd had to do was to give them drugs I'd stolen from my mom.

After I proved myself to Keith by giving him drugs he invited me to have a sleepover at his house – so long as I brought more drugs. His parents were out of town, he told me, so we were going to drink vodka and do the pot and hash I stole from my mom, along with the pills in his own stash.

Keith's other source for drugs was his older sister, who had been institutionalized for schizophrenia. When he visited her at Silver Hills, the local facility for rich people with mental illness and addiction issues, she gave him the antipsychotics she'd been prescribed.

"Your parents are really gone?" I asked. I'd never had a sleepover with someone whose parents weren't there. It made me nervous, but I wanted Keith to keep thinking I was cool.

"They're in North Carolina, so we can get high!" he said cheerfully.

Keith's neighbor, Vicki, was looking after him while his parents were away. She was a cute blonde sophomore at Darien High School. She'd invited a bunch of her older friends to Keith's house and she was bringing a case of beer she'd stolen from her parents' garage.

Vicki, Keith and I watched *The Muppet Show* before the party started. "I'm going to get so high tonight," Keith said, during one of the commercial breaks.

"Me too!" I said. But I was scared.

I wanted to hang out with the cool kids. I craved their approval and longed for invitations to their houses and boats and country clubs, but almost everything about them scared me. They were relaxed and confident, but they weren't actually very nice. And none of them liked the things I liked: science fiction, books, animals, Casey Kasem's *American Top 40*, the Beatles.

The doorbell rang and Vicki's friends started showing up. Someone handed me a joint and I inhaled, making sure not to cough. I'd started smoking pot behind Royle Elementary School at age ten, when I realized that it let me hang out with the older kids. Since then I'd smoked pot enough times to learn how to inhale without coughing.

The truth was that I hated the way pot made me feel: scared and paranoid. But stealing pot from my mom and smoking it with cool, older kids was my only entrée to their world.

"Whoa, you're a pro, little dude," one of Vicki's older friends said to me. He was on the tennis team at Darien Country Club and his dad worked in finance, but with his Molly Hatchet T-shirt and his long black hair he looked like an underage roadie for Lynyrd Skynyrd.

Keith and I made cocktails out of vodka, orange juice, brown sugar, and Dr. Pepper. We used brown sugar instead of white because it seemed more sophisticated. "These are good," I said, surprised that the alcohol wasn't making me gag. Some of the alcohol I'd tried before, like beer and whiskey, made me retch. Whereas sweeter drinks, like champagne and crème de menthe, tasted wonderful.

The night progressed and more older kids in Led Zeppelin and Yes and Rolling Stones T-shirts showed up, contributing pot, beer, and vodka. Keith and I smoked the pot and hash I'd stolen from my mom, drank the vodka he'd stolen from his parents, and took some of the antipsychotics that his sister had given him.

By midnight everything was spinning and I was having a hard time standing. Vicki was making out with one of her high-school friends. A group of football players in the kitchen were drinking beer and listening to a Jimi Hendrix tape. I walked over to them, slurred, "I'm so high," and fell down.

I assumed I'd earned their respect, as I was legitimately fucked up. But through the haze of drugs and alcohol I heard one of them say, almost worried, "If he's like this now, what's he going to be like in five years?"

And I got scared. All of this terrified me. The big kids. The music. The drugs. I realized that I'd intentionally stepped into my mom's world. I wanted to have friends, and I wanted to wallow in the legitimacy granted by the cool kids in black concert T-shirts, but all this darkness scared me.

While I was lying on the floor having my epiphany, the lights turned on and the music stopped. I heard a loud, deep, adult voice say, "What the hell is going on?"

"Oh shit," one of the football players said.

It was Vicki's dad, checking on his daughter's first overnight babysitting job. "What the hell are you people doing?" he yelled.

I stood up on the yellow linoleum floor, slowly and unsteadily, like a baby deer.

Vicki's dad was wearing khakis and docksiders and a faded blue Izod shirt. He was tall and terrifying, like a clean-cut Viking in suburban clothes.

"Dad?" Vicki said, suddenly looking scared and young.

"This is how you repay our trust, young lady?" he bellowed.

She started crying.

"Where's Keith?" he asked. "His parents need to hear about this right now."

Vicki's dad had said the most dreaded word imaginable, even for the coolest kids: "parents." Teenagers in Darien stole whatever they could get their hands on. They drank and smoked and had sex, all the while hoping that their parents would never find out. Even the toughest fifteen-year-old in a faded Blue Öyster Cult T-shirt was terrified at the prospect of his parents catching him sneaking out of the house with a six-pack of stolen beer.

"Where's Keith?" Vicki's dad asked again. The formerly cool kids in the kitchen were now staring at the kitchen floor, abashed. "You kids get out of here," Vicki's dad said, pointing at them. "I'm calling all your parents tomorrow."

I followed him as he walked down the thickly carpeted hall. He found Keith passed out on a bed in the guest room, wet from his own urine and vomit.

"Keith," he said. "Wake up, Keith." He shook him. "Keith!" he yelled, slapping him lightly. Keith didn't respond.

I watched from a few feet away, terrified. I was thirteen years old, high, and drunk. And I was looking at my new friend, who might be dead.

"Vicki, call 911," Vicki's dad yelled. He saw me standing in the doorway. "Who are you?" he said angrily.

"I'm Moby," I said, on the edge of tears, my voice small. He ignored me and went back to Keith.

"Keith, wake up."

He hadn't woken up, but I had. The fear had washed the drugs and alcohol out of my system, leaving me wide-eyed and terrified. The EMTs arrived, briskly intubated Keith, and put him on a gurney. He wasn't dead, but he was nonresponsive and possibly in a coma. One of the EMTs asked me, "What did he take?"

I knew that pot and hash were illegal and I didn't want to get in any more trouble, so I said, "Vodka and some pills from his sister."

After the ambulance took Keith away, Vicki's dad looked at me and said, "I'm taking you home, mister." We walked next door and got into his BMW.

"How old are you, son?" he asked, as we drove down the quiet country streets.

"Thirteen, sir," I said, willing myself not to burst into tears.

"Thirteen," he said, shaking his head. "Thirteen. . ." He started to tell me to get my act together, but then shook his head and stopped, driving me the rest of the way in silence.

We pulled up to my grandparents' house, where my mom and I had been living since my grandfather died. Vicki's dad rang the doorbell and banged on the door. After a minute the lights turned on and my mom came to the door in her beige nightgown and green terrycloth robe.

"Are you this boy's mother?" he asked, tall and stern.

"Yes," my mom said, blinking away sleep. "What happened?"

"He and his friends were drinking and doing drugs. His friend almost died," he said, seething. He got back in his car, conveniently not acknowledging that his daughter had organized the party and provided us with most of the alcohol.

"Mobes, is this true?" my mom asked.

I finally started crying.

"Okay," she said. "Go to bed. We'll talk about it in the morning."

She led me to my bedroom and I cried myself to sleep.

When I woke up in the morning everything seemed clean and quiet and calm. The sun was touching my yellow-and-white striped sheets. I could hear cicadas and a distant lawnmower. I walked into my mom's room, where she was folding laundry.

"Tell me what happened," she said calmly.

I hesitated, not sure what I should say. I didn't want to admit that I'd stolen drugs from her black lacquered drug box, so I said, "Some big kids gave us drugs and beer, and then Keith passed out and went to the hospital."

She lit a cigarette and looked out the window. "And how do you feel?" she asked.

I didn't know how to describe how I felt. I felt like a piece of cloth on a muddy field after a football game. I felt like a dog who had volunteered to be kicked. I felt like a little boy who'd stumbled into a cave filled with demons.

"I feel terrible," I said, and started crying again.

"It's okay," my mom said, patting my hair in the sunlight. "It's okay."

29

NEW YORK CITY (2002)

In the spring of 1987 I dated Melanie: dark, beautiful, French, and living in Connecticut for a year. As we gradually overcame the language barrier we realized that we didn't actually have much in common, but I saved up money for a plane ticket and we flew to France and spent the summer together in Paris anyway.

I was worried the Parisians would know I was American, so at a used clothing store near Notre Dame I bought a striped sweater, an old navy-blue blazer, and secondhand black factory-worker shoes. When I put them on I looked more or less like Marcel Duchamp and the other French surrealists I'd been obsessed with in high school. I wanted so badly to seem Parisian that I tried smoking unfiltered French cigarettes. And I spent hours in a tea salon called L'Ebouillanté – at first to fit in, but then because I loved it. L'Ebouillanté was in a seventeenth-century house in the Marais. I'd sit at a table on the second floor and drink pots of Darjeeling and read Foucault and Rimbaud and send pretentious black-and-white postcards to my friends in Connecticut.

The summer in Paris ended, Melanie and I broke up, and I went back to living in my mom's house by I-95. I was insufferable, peppering my speech with French phrases I'd picked up over the summer and constantly reminding everyone I knew that I'd spent a few months living in Paris. I also told everyone that I'd had a realization: my new life goal, in addition to making records and being a philosophy professor, was to someday own a small tea shop like L'Ebouillanté.

In 1999 I'd been DJing at a small club in Boston, where I met a girl named Kelly. She'd heard *Play* and liked it, and after my set she brazenly walked up to me and said, "You rock."

Kelly was my dream girl: smart, blonde, bookish, and compulsively devoted to old new-wave music. She even wore vintage Joy Division and Cure pins on her tweed jacket. We dated sporadically from 1999 to 2001, and two months after 9/11 decided that we should try actually being boyfriend and girlfriend.

One morning after a long night of vodka and MDMA I told her about my old dream of owning a little tea shop. Her eyes lit up. When Kelly and I met she had just finished working in the Clinton White House, but now she was bartending at a tourist restaurant in midtown New York. "I'd love to run a little tea shop," she said.

We started looking at Lower East Side real estate and soon found a store that had previously been a hair salon. The landlord was desperate to rent to us: after 9/11 all his tenants were either going out of business or fleeing lower Manhattan.

After we signed the rental agreement Kelly and I went on my roof to talk about what we would call our new business. The sun was setting while we brainstormed, so I held my hand up to block the light. Then I choked up and had to stop talking – I realized I could see the sunset only because the Twin Towers were no longer in the way.

"Are you okay?" Kelly asked.

I had broken down crying a few times with Kelly after 9/11, but now some time had passed and I'd gotten better at reining in my emotions. "I'm okay," I told her, and we resumed our discussion about the tea shop's name. I wanted to call it "Platypus" – for some reason I had a weird fascination with platypuses, and thought that was a good name for a small tea shop.

But then Kelly said, "What about 'teany'?"

"'Teenie'?"

"'Teany,'" she repeated, frustrated. She went downstairs to get a piece of paper and a pen and wrote "teany." She handed it over to me. "See? 'Teany' because we're small, we'll sell tea, and we're in New York. 'Teany.'"

I thought for a second, looking for flaws in her creative logic. But no, she was right. It was a great name. "That seems perfect," I said.

There were a few hurdles in opening teany. One was that neither of us had ever opened or run a business. Another was that neither of us had any restaurant experience, other than being customers.

I was finishing my album *18* and getting ready to do a three-month promo tour, followed by what my managers expected to be a two-year concert tour. So we agreed that I would put up the money and Kelly would learn how to do everything else.

We wanted teany to be modern, but not too modern. Clean, but not sterile. Thoughtful, but not pretentious. On my way to the airport to fly to Singapore, the first stop on the *18* promo tour, I summed up the ethos in a text: "just make it cute :-)"

While I was gone, Kelly sent me menu suggestions and music playlist ideas and dessert possibilities and links to teacup purveyors and pictures of tile samples and fabric swatches and updates on all of the myriad things required to open an adorable two-hundred-square-foot tea shop.

After three months of talking about myself and my new album to strangers I returned to New York and a 90 percent finished pristine little tea shop. I also came back to a girlfriend on the edge of collapse. Kelly had been working sixteen hours a day, seven days a week, doing everything. I felt some guilt, like a Victorian father who goes off to war and upon his return is handed a well-mannered child by a beleaguered wife in need of institutionalization.

We decided to open teany in May 2002, a week before I was leaving for the *18* concert tour. I invited everyone I knew to the opening party, from Matt Groening to the Strokes to David Bowie to Norah Jones to Jimmy Fallon to Claire Danes to TV on the Radio.

On opening night I showed up an hour late to the party, happy and already a bit drunk.

Kelly's tireless work had paid off: teany looked amazing. The sconces gleamed softly through the plate-glass window, the stainless-steel countertops shone like in an expensive Dutch bistro, and the new white tile was pristine. Everything was perfect.

Except for Kelly, who was exhausted, pale, and one inch away from a nervous breakdown. She took me into our basement office and started crying.

"What's wrong?" I asked, cluelessly.

For me the world was my vegan oyster. I was a rock star releasing the much-anticipated follow-up to *Play*. I was getting ready to play arenas and headline festivals. And my dream from fifteen years earlier had come true: I was now the proud owner of a jewel box of a tea shop.

"I can't do this," Kelly said, holding herself and shaking.

"What, teany?"

"No, I love teany. I can't be just one of the people you're sleeping with."

Oh.

Kelly and I were boyfriend and girlfriend, but we had an open, non-monogamous relationship. She dated other people, or so I assumed. And I dated other people, as I well knew. In fact, everyone knew that I dated other people. My promiscuity in lower Manhattan had become a thing of legend. A recent magazine article about me had quoted Richard Johnson, a gossip columnist at the *New York Post*, as saying, "Moby gets more ass than the toilet seat in a ladies bathroom." I knew I should feel some shame or remorse about my slutty ways, but I didn't. I told myself I had no reason to feel guilty about sleeping with other people while being Kelly's boyfriend, because she and I were in an explicitly open relationship.

"You want to talk about this now?" I asked, baffled and annoyed that she was interrupting my golden years with legitimate concerns.

"I have to," she said, looking at me with heartbroken eyes.

For years I'd told myself and my friends that what I really wanted was a loving relationship with a wonderful woman. I'd talked endlessly about my fantasy of being married and having children. But now I was at a turning point. Standing in front of me was a wonderful woman who wanted to marry me and have my children. I'd avoided relationships because they gave me panic attacks, but I also realized that I'd been lying to myself: I ultimately wanted fame and debauchery, not domestic bliss.

I was about to travel around the world to play in hockey arenas and football stadiums. I had my own tour bus with a personal bedroom suite. And I'd just hired an assistant, Fabienne, whose primary job was to throw after-show parties for me. I'd met Fabienne in a bar and hired her after we had sex in the backseat of a taxi. I wanted to *carpe* every single *diem* as compulsively and degenerately as I could.

"Okay," I said, trying to sound magnanimous, "out of respect for you, let's just be friends." She clenched her jaw, and in that moment I could see the loathing she'd built up for me.

I knew that for the two years we'd been dating she had been in love with me, waiting for us to get married and make New England babies together. She'd watched while I'd circled the globe, every day trying to outdo myself with drunkenness and dissolution. When we met she'd seen me as a sensitive musician from Connecticut who was having a licentious phase. But now she knew that I didn't want my degeneracy to be a phase. I wanted to kill off the sensitive musician and replace him with a hardened rock star.

In my mind I hadn't done anything wrong, as I'd never lied to Kelly. I'd never cheated on her – we'd been in an open relationship – and I had been profligate within the letter of the law we'd agreed upon.

"Fine," she said, and stood there, seething.

"Hey, you did a great job with teany," I said, trying to mollify her. She looked like she wanted to punch me in the face.

"Kelly?" I asked, not so much contrite as afraid of being punched in the face on the opening night of my restaurant.

"We're done," she said bitterly, and pushed past me.

I walked up the tenement stairs and heard the sound of our party. Teany held only twenty or thirty people, so the hundreds of people who'd shown up were on the sidewalk and street, drinking our champagne and beer and eating the cookies and crostini that Kelly had made.

I leaned against the iron railing in front of teany and drank a beer with Matt Groening and one of the bosses at my record label. "I wanted to tell you," the executive said, "*18* has shipped gold and platinum in twenty different countries."

"Congrats, man," Matt said, shaking my hand with his big bear paw.

Kelly walked by. "Matt," I said happily, "this is Kelly, who single-handedly opened teany."

"Great job, Kelly!" he boomed.

Kelly glared at me and then nodded at Matt. "We just broke up," she told him. "Your friend's a fucking asshole."

30

NEW YORK CITY (2002)

For my first interview on *Charlie Rose* I was still drunk from the night before.

After a day of interviews promoting my new album, *18*, I'd gone out drinking with Andy Dick and his gaggle of degenerates. Andy and I weren't close, and he repeatedly told me he was sober – but he was always up for going out until 5 or 6 a.m. We'd gone to bars and nightclubs until 3.30 a.m., when we were kicked out of a strip club on the West Side Highway for being too loud and unhinged.

We rounded up our expanding posse of strippers and degenerates, took cabs across town, and at 4 a.m. went back to my apartment. Some people I'd never met disappeared into my bathroom to smoke crystal meth, while Andy and some of his friends had an orgy in my tiny bedroom under the stairs.

I was watching this group of strangers ruin my sheets when a tattoo-covered woman with bright-red hair took my hand and led me to the roof. It was a few minutes before dawn; the city was quiet and the dark horizon had an edge of blue. "I have a present for you," she said, pulling down my pants.

As she took my penis in her mouth I looked down through the skylights and saw some other people I'd never met doing what I assumed was coke on my breakfast table. After I came, she stood up, smiled, and introduced herself: "I'm Liz."

By 7 a.m. everyone was gone, leaving my apartment covered in drug residue and littered with empty champagne and vodka bottles. I had to leave at 8.30 a.m. for a long day of promo – an interview with Charlie Rose, a bunch of foreign press interviews, a record signing in Times Square, and my first appearance on *Saturday Night Live* – so I wanted to sleep for an hour. Since my post-orgy sheets looked like they belonged in a badly run Victorian hospital, I lay down on my living-room couch.

I tossed and turned for thirty minutes, and then my alarm went off. I stood in the shower, wondering if I could get through the next eighteen hours without sleep. After putting on a pair of black jeans and a black T-shirt, I walked out of my building and into the limo that was waiting for me. As we sped uptown I smiled at the bright morning sky through the tinted windows and decided that I was simply too happy to be tired.

At the *Charlie Rose* studio a production assistant asked if she could get me anything. "Coffee, please," I said. "I haven't been to sleep and I'm hungover." That sounded like a more palatable confession than admitting I was still drunk.

She smiled. "It's okay. We're all hungover too."

A different production assistant led me to a dark room lined with TV cameras and escorted me to a black chair. Charlie Rose walked in and sat opposite me in his own black chair. He was a venerated interviewer, but with his bloodshot hound-dog eyes, it seemed to me that he might also have been recovering from the night before.

Charlie asked me about the success of *Play*, my relationship to Herman Melville, and 9/11. After fifteen minutes our interview ended and I ceded my chair to Paul Auster. Paul was handsome in ways that I assumed made every other straight male writer in Brooklyn jealous. "I love your work," I said to Paul as I stood up.

"And I love yours," he replied as he sat down.

I wanted Paul to see my interview and be surprised by my erudition and my charming-but-insincere self-deprecation. I wanted him to be impressed enough to invite me to boozy dinner parties at his Brooklyn brownstone, where I'd join his cadre of hard-drinking, *Paris Review*-reading friends.

I left the television studio feeling the patina of legitimacy. As I walked out to my limo a delivery guy on a bicycle passed by me. "Yo, Moby!" he yelled, excited.

"Hey!" I yelled back. And then as I sat in the back of my limo I smiled at myself for being a man of the people, magnanimous even to delivery guys.

The limo took me a few blocks to a hotel just off Times Square, where I was whisked by record-label employees to the penthouse. I spent three hours there talking to journalists about my opinions, my creative process, my idiosyncrasies. I wanted to share everything so that the journalists would tell their friends and bosses and readers that I was bright and kind, the best person they'd ever interviewed.

I was like a prostitute: I spent prearranged chunks of time in hotel rooms being intimate with strangers. The difference, I told myself, was that I was motivated by enthusiasm, not money. Well, enthusiasm and a longing to be the most famous person in the world.

After the interview my limo took me to the Virgin Megastore in Times Square, where a line of fans were waiting to meet me. The line went from the downstairs signing table, up a long flight of stairs, out the front door, and up 7th Avenue.

I'd always been interested in the nature of God and manifestations of divinity. As security guards whisked me from my limo to a folding table stacked with copies of my record, I wondered if I was actually divine or perhaps coming into my divinity. Maybe I was a new god. A benign god. But a complicated god, with a secular dominion over sweetness and filth. Mercurial, but only if someone kept me from my holy sacraments of sex and alcohol and fame. Maybe I was Bacchus or Baal reincarnated? Any type of divinity seemed fine, even if borrowed from a demon.

The autograph session lasted for ninety minutes. I tried to give everyone who'd waited in line what they were looking for. A signature, a smile, a moment in my presence – small tokens of my blossoming divinity. I hugged a few crying women, even though my security guards asked me not to.

After the signing my security guards cleared a path through the horde and placed me back in my limousine. The driver took me to 30 Rock, where the *Saturday Night Live* studios were. I'd grown up watching *SNL*, and now I was walking through the entrance of the towering art deco facade of Rockefeller Plaza, where it was shot.

A new phalanx of security guards brought me to my dressing room. I looked around at the black mini-fridge, the brown sofa, and the white side table, and realized I'd been in this very room before, when I was on *Late Night with Conan O'Brien*. Recognizing a late-night TV show dressing room felt like a confirmation of my fame and legitimacy.

I closed the door to the dressing room – my dressing room – and tried to sleep on the couch. But I couldn't keep my eyes closed. My synapses were alive; the air around me was alive. Every minute of this day was everything I'd ever wanted, and better than I'd ever thought possible. So I poured myself a cup of coffee, resolving to stay more awake than I'd ever been.

Tonight, after I performed on *Saturday Night Live*, I'd be even more stratospherically famous than I already was. I vaguely assumed that at some point I'd have enough fame, but I found it hard to imagine that scenario.

My tour manager, Sandy, had arranged for an acoustic guitar to be left in the dressing room. I strummed and sang "We Are All Made of Stars," which I was going to perform later. Then, sitting alone in my dressing room, I played "Lucky Man," the 1970 song by Emerson, Lake & Palmer. As I played, I thought that maybe I was the lucky man, with his perfect life. He was royalty, longed for and beloved by the world.

Then I reached the last verse, where the lucky man's hubris and foolishness destroys him. Suddenly remembering the lyrics,

I abruptly stopped playing and put down the guitar. *Fame might destroy other people*, I thought, *but not me.* I would be the lucky man who figured out how to avoid the last verse of the song.

31

DARIEN, CONNECTICUT (1978)

I'd started masturbating, even though I was sure it was wrong and that I was making God angry. Some hormonal switch had been thrown in my brain, and now every woman I saw was painfully erotic: my English teacher, Jane Pauley on the *Today* show, every girl in my junior high school. A few weeks earlier it had never crossed my mind to masturbate, but now it was all I could think about.

I was a Protestant Portnoy, masturbating before school, during school, after school, after school again, and before bed. Sometimes for erotic fodder I would think about a woman I'd seen on TV or at school; sometimes I would look at naked women in old copies of *National Lampoon* that my mom's friends had left lying around the house.

I had never talked about sex with my mom or anyone, but I'd always known that it was scary and bad. In third grade I'd seen a copy of *The Joy of Sex* and was frightened by the drawings of furry men doing unspeakable things to slightly less furry women. And whenever I'd seen or heard my mom or her friends having sex it terrified me.

Since I knew that sex was dirty and wrong, I reasoned that pleasuring myself was also dirty and wrong, but I couldn't stop. After a few weeks of furious masturbating I gave myself friction burns on my penis. I didn't know that these burns were just the result of rubbing myself raw; instead I believed that God had punished me and given me a terrible STD.

I had never prayed before, but I got on my knees and made a deal with the Almighty: "God, if you can take away this terrible STD, I will stop masturbating." A few days later my friction burns healed and I gave God the credit. He had healed me, so now I had to keep up my end of the bargain.

The first thing I did to make God happy was to take the old copies of *National Lampoon* into the woods and burn them while I prayed. I thought that the smell of burning cartoon porn would be pleasing unto the Lord. Then I found the Bible I'd been given in sixth grade, covered in thin red vinyl and signed by our golf-playing Presbyterian minister, and started reading it whenever I wanted to jerk off.

It worked – for an entire day. But three and a half billion years of evolution was too much for thirteen-year-old me, and after twenty-four hours of abstinence I started masturbating again. And feeling terrible guilt, and then masturbating some more.

Even though I was back to compulsive masturbation, I tried to pray and spend more time reading the Bible, as a way of keeping God from getting angry and giving me another STD. Genesis was interesting, and even Exodus held my attention. But when I got to Leviticus and the endless chapters on obscure Hebrew law, I got bored and had to go masturbate.

I didn't know what else to do: I'd burned my cartoon pornography; I'd tried reading the Bible; I'd prayed as best as I knew how. But I couldn't stop masturbating five or six times a day.

I knew that some of the kids in my English class were Christians, so one day I went to their lunch table to talk to them. The thirteen- and fourteen-year-old Christians looked like the other preppy kids in Darien, except they didn't wear black concert T-shirts and gave the impression that they took several showers a day, most likely while wearing bathing suits. I asked them if there were any Christian youth groups they could recommend, and their eyes lit up. Apparently this was every Christian's dream: to be approached by a filthy heathen who bathed only once a day and to be asked about Jesus.

I didn't talk about masturbation because nobody ever talked about it. I only knew the word "masturbation" because I'd read about it in a Boy Scout handbook. The chapter on sex clearly stated that only bad people masturbated, and God wanted us to wait until we were married before having sex. This had been my secular junior-high-school Leviticus: codified Boy Scout law stating clearly that I was gross and that God was mad at me.

The smiling Christians at the lunch table told me about a Christian youth group at Noroton Presbyterian Church every Monday night. "I was baptized there!" I exclaimed. "That's my church!" I felt both kismet and the guiding hand of John Calvin.

"So you're already saved?" one of the girls asked me.

I didn't know what she meant, but I wanted to be agreeable, so I smiled and said, "Yes!"

On Monday night I rode my green ten-speed Schwinn to Noroton Presbyterian Church. Even though I wasn't much of a Christian, I'd spent a lot of time at the church because my grandmother helped put out their weekly newsletter. The Youth Shack, located behind the church, had been an old barn until a year before, when the new youth minister enlisted volunteers to fix it up and paint it. When the fixing and painting were finished he hung a small hand-lettered "YOUTH SHACK" sign by the front door.

The youth minister, who looked more like a twenty-two-year-old tennis coach than a saver of souls, welcomed me inside and led me to a table where twenty or so other kids were putting spaghetti and iceberg-lettuce salad onto paper plates. I immediately knew that coming to this Christian youth group had been a good idea: I loved spaghetti and they had full bottles of Italian salad dressing for the lettuce.

I saw some cute girls from school, girls with glowing skin and streaks of sun in their straight blonde hair. I'd never spoken to any of them, even though I'd known some of them since kindergarten. But here in the Youth Shack they smiled and welcomed me.

All these years I'd wanted these beautiful girls to notice me, and it turned out all I had to do was pretend to be a Christian.

We ate our spaghetti, had some ice cream, and played some Christian games. The Christian games were a lot like regular games – freeze tag, duck duck goose – but as they took place on church property they were Christian. After the games we sat down to listen to the youth minister talk about Jesus.

I'd always assumed I was a Christian. I'd been baptized in the church, and everyone I knew – apart from (1) my uncle and his Jewish family, and (2) a black Muslim my mom dated for a month – was Christian. But I'd never read anything about Jesus and I'd never heard anyone talk about Jesus. I was just a Christian because I was white and lived in Connecticut.

Now, as I sat between two cute girls from my school and tried to ignore my growing erection, this youth minister told me that Jesus Christ was my friend and He loved me. I raised my hand and asked, "But what if we do things that Jesus doesn't like?"

He smiled at me. "Then Jesus forgives you."

What? I couldn't understand how being forgiven for doing bad things was part of the same religion I'd been reading about in the Old Testament. The God of the Old Testament seemed more like an angry mayor than a forgiving friend. But if the youth minister, who had clearly been to college, told me that I was forgiven, then who was I to doubt him?

After the talk we held hands and prayed. The youth minister asked us, "Do you accept Jesus as your lord and savior?"

Filled with spaghetti and ice cream, my head spinning from a Monday night spent with cute girls from school, and elated by the knowledge that I was forgiven for masturbating, I happily said, "I do."

I rode home and put my bike next to the old push-mower in the garage. After brushing my teeth I said good night to my mom, who was smoking on the couch while she watched *Maude*.

My guilt was gone and I felt free. I still knew that sex and masturbation were dirty and wrong, but I believed what the youth minister had told me: I had already been forgiven. I got into bed and masturbated, while thinking about the cute Christian girls from the Youth Shack.

32

NEW YORK CITY (2002)

Even though Kelly and I had been making each other miserable on and off for three years, we cautiously tried to date again. A few days before the US tour for *18* began we made plans for a picnic in East River Park.

I went to teany to pick up Kelly and her new dog, Pineapple, a happy little rescue who was possibly a cross between a Chihuahua and a golden retriever. Carrying sandwiches, cake, and a thermos of peach iced tea, we walked to the park with Pineapple. As usual the East River Park was empty, apart from some senior citizens fishing in the river and a group of older Puerto Rican men riding elaborately decorated bicycles.

For the first two years after I met Kelly I'd felt like I could do no wrong in her eyes. But now that she'd been repeatedly subjected to my drunkenness and promiscuity, it was as if I could do nothing right. I wondered if one of the reasons she wanted to keep dating me was so she'd have lots of opportunities to let me know how much she'd come to dislike me.

A friend of mine who was studying to be a therapist asked me why I wanted to be in a relationship with someone who appeared to loathe me. Without hesitation, I said, "Because I can't leave."

"She's not your mom," my friend said, adopting his new professional voice. "Have you considered therapy?"

Kelly and I set up our picnic on a patch of grass near some statues of seals. It was a perfect spring day: a salty breeze wafted in from the East River, while the sun shone through the bright green leaves of trees that somehow had figured a way to stay alive in the traffic exhaust of the FDR Drive. Pineapple was delighted to be with people who cared about her, if not each other. It was such a beautiful day that Kelly even seemed less angry at me than she usually did.

We ate our vegan *pan bagnia* and drank peach iced tea, and while we shared a slice of peanut butter chocolate cake Kelly gently said, "I think you might be an alcoholic, Moby."

I gave her the same lighthearted response I had given for years to worried friends and family members: "I'm not an alcoholic, I'm an alcohol enthusiast."

Kelly's tender facade disappeared and she said, "Okay, then stay sober for a month."

I panicked. A month without alcohol? Why would I, of my own free will, spend a month without alcohol – my best friend, lover, godhead, and muse? Plus I was going on tour. Even though Kelly and I were dating again, we still weren't monogamous. Touring meant vodka and ecstasy and promiscuity. I didn't want to stop drinking. But I also didn't want to admit to Kelly, or myself, how terrified I was at the thought of going a month without alcohol. So I said, combatively, "Fine. I'll stay sober for a month."

The first week of being sober on tour was hard, but it gave me something novel to talk about. "I'm sober!" I would crow smugly to whichever gaggle of drunks I was with that night.

After twelve days of my sobriety experiment I had a night off in Dallas, so I went to see Tommy Lee from Mötley Crüe play a solo show. After the concert I went backstage to say hi to Tommy and a few people in his road crew who used to work for me. Tommy was dripping wet after a long show, but gave me a bear hug, anointing me with his sacramental rock-star sweat.

I was getting ready to leave the venue and head back to my hotel, where I would read a Greg Iles book and get a sober night's sleep, when Vinnie Paul and Dimebag Darrell from Pantera came back-stage with a bunch of their Hells Angels friends.

I'd never met Pantera, but I loved their records. The first time Kelly had visited me, in 1999, I'd put on *The Great Southern Trendkill* while I was making dinner. She liked Belle and Sebastian and Fairport Convention, and was baffled that I would put on a Pantera album while adding organic basil to a vegan spaghetti sauce. When Phil Anselmo screamed the incredibly hostile first line, she looked at me and asked, "You *like* this?"

"I love Pantera!" I said, adding *fusilli* to the boiling water.

She ran to the CD player, ejected the disc, and put on a Smiths album instead.

And now I was meeting Pantera, my speed-metal heroes. Darrell and Vinnie and their friends were all big, all bearded, and all wearing black leather pants and jackets. They looked like the people you'd see behind a bar in Alabama before you got killed for believing in climate change.

"Moby!" Darrell yelled. "We need to get you on our video!"

Someone pointed a video camera at Darrell, Vinnie, Tommy Lee, and me, and we started singing "We Are All Made of Stars." I'd seen the legendary Pantera home movies. They were debased and remarkable. I swelled with pride that I might be included in the next one. A six-foot-eight Hells Angel with a red beard opened a bottle of Crown Royal and pushed it into my hands.

What was I going to say to him? "See, my girlfriend Kelly thinks I have a problem with alcohol, so out of respect to her I'm trying to have a month of abstinence."

Instead I took the bottle and gulped down the whiskey. "I guess I'm not sober anymore," I said as I gave the bottle back to the giant Hells Angel.

He looked surprisingly concerned. "You're sober?" he rumbled.

"For two weeks."

He laughed and passed the bottle back. "Fuck! Drink up, my man!"

After we drained the bottle of Crown Royal, Vince yelled, "Y'all need to come to the Clubhouse!"

I'd heard of the Clubhouse, Pantera's strip club on the outskirts of Dallas, so I immediately accepted his invitation. In the mid-1990s, when I started going to strip clubs with my friend Damian, I'd felt guilt and shame. "Who are these women?" I'd wondered. "And am I a bad person for supporting this?" But my guilt abated when I realized that some of the strippers would actually date me and be nice to me.

We drove to the Clubhouse and entered like demonic royalty. Pantera were Texas gods and this was their strip club. Tommy Lee was perpetually enshrined near the top of the depraved rock-star pantheon. Then there was me, the group's little demon imp. With our coterie of Hells Angels I felt like I was part of a dark army.

We sat at the center of the club and were soon surrounded by strippers and bottles of vodka and whiskey. A thin stripper with short blonde hair sat next to me and looked at me shyly. "Hi, I'm Cassie," she said, shaking my hand. She was wearing a small silver bikini bottom and no top.

"Hi, Cassie, I'm Moby," I said.

"Look, I know you're partyin', but I wanted to say your music helped me get through some really rough times." Her face softened and her eyes misted over.

"Thank you," I said, holding her hand and feeling a fragile connection, even though Ozzy's "Crazy Train" was playing.

The six-foot-eight Hells Angel with the red beard sat down between us and handed me a bottle of Ketel One vodka. "Hey!" he yelled. "Moby's sober!"

I drank straight from the bottle, the way a marathon runner would drink from a bottle of water. "Not anymore!" I yelled, feeling the vodka burning my throat and filling my stomach with soft fire. Everyone cheered.

"Fuckin' Moby!" Darrell yelled. "We should start a band."

"Seriously," Tommy said, balancing one stripper on each knee. "We should. It would blow people's minds."

Starting a band with Darrell and Vince and Tommy Lee sounded like the best idea I or anyone had ever had. Ever. My own fame gave me a veneer of rock stardom, but starting a band with actual depraved rock gods would give me a strong metal carapace. We'd go on tour and stay drunk and be the most feared and immoral rock stars on the planet. "I'm in," I said. "What are we called?"

"The Sober Fucks," Darrell said. We laughed and drank to the Sober Fucks.

Two strippers sat next to me and started making out with each other. I looked around for Cassie, but she had disappeared. One of the strippers turned to me, kissed me with her wide open mouth, and said, "Man, I'm takin' you home tonight."

The other stripper took a long drink from an open bottle of vodka and said, "Well, honey, you need help bangin' him, you just let me know."

33

DARIEN, CONNECTICUT (1979)

The best thing about my junior high school was the library. And the best thing about the library was the subscription to *Rolling Stone*. I couldn't afford my own copy of the magazine, but every two weeks the librarians – who liked me because I liked books and was polite – would hold the new issue of *Rolling Stone* for me to pore over before the older kids stole it.

Rolling Stone was filled with long and fairly tedious articles about establishment rock bands like the Kinks and the Rolling Stones and the Who, but sometimes they deigned to slip in small pieces about new-wave and punk-rock bands. After hearing some Clash and Elvis Costello songs on the radio and seeing Sid Vicious perform "My Way" on *Mr. Mike's Mondo Video*, I'd decided that I liked new wave and punk rock. I had to keep this burgeoning love to myself: the cool kids in school had collectively decided that any new music made by musicians with short hair was "weird" or "gay." If a song by Gary Numan or Talking Heads came on the radio in the lunch-room, the cool kids in their Lynyrd Skynyrd and Led Zeppelin T-shirts would chant "Turn it off!" until the song ended or the station was changed.

In elementary school I'd learned from other kids that David Bowie was especially "weird" and "gay," even though I didn't actually know what "gay" was at the time. When my mom bought *Changesonebowie* as one of her Columbia Record Club twelve-for-a-penny albums, I fell in love with it, but knew I could only ever listen to it in private.

In the last issue of *Rolling Stone* before my summer vacation, Greil Marcus reviewed Bowie's new album, *Lodger*. The review was ambiguous, but the way he described the album made me long to own it. My personal record collection was small: my "Convoy" seven-inch, the first Aerosmith album (a birthday gift from the year before), and the blue-cover Beatles greatest hits album (a Christmas present). I didn't own any new-wave or punk-rock records, but I did have a partial recording of "I Fought the Law" by the Clash, which I'd taped off the radio with my grandfather's old Dictaphone.

I didn't have anything else to do in my summer vacation, so I decided my primary goal for the next three months would be to make enough money to buy *Lodger*.

The day before ninth grade ended I was sitting in biology class next to my lab partner, Matt. He was talking to one of his friends about a boat party he was throwing, when he caught me looking at him expectantly. "Oh, I'm having a party," he said offhandedly. "You can come, if you want."

We were lab partners, but we weren't friends. Matt was cool and I was not. I'd had a moment of being quasi-cool in seventh grade, when I gave stolen drugs to Keith and his stoner friends. But after Keith was hospitalized my quasi-cool status was rescinded. Now that I'd weaseled an invite to Matt's boat party, I had two goals for the summer: earn enough money to buy *Lodger*, and re-ingratiate myself with the cool kids.

For two weeks before Matt's party I planned what I was going to wear and how I was going to act. If I wore the right clothes and stood the right way and kept my burgeoning love for new wave to myself, I would get invited to more cool-kid parties. I hoped that I might even end up with a girlfriend – although I realized that was probably too absurdly aspirational.

I mainly owned secondhand clothes, but my grandmother had given me a new striped Izod rugby shirt for Christmas. I decided it looked like something Matt and his friends would wear on a boat.

The day before the party I put on the rugby shirt and my Wrangler jeans and stood in front of the mirror in my mom's bedroom, practicing how I would stand at the party.

I tried standing with my hands in my pockets. That was okay, but I didn't think it looked cool enough. Then I tried standing with my hands at my sides, which looked fine but felt uncomfortable. Ultimately I decided that I'd stand around all day with my arms folded over my chest. When I folded my arms and pressed my forearms together really hard, it almost looked like I had muscles.

The day of the party I put on my outfit, practiced standing in front of the mirror one last time, and rode my green Schwinn to Matt's family's private dock. It was a shiny new dock, made out of aluminum – but nobody was there.

I walked out to the end of the dock, smelling the brackish salt water and blinking against the sun reflecting off the aluminum. I squinted: in the distance I could see a few boats and some people who looked like Matt and his friends, waterskiing. I almost waved to get their attention, but then I realized it was easier to get on my bike, ride home, and watch TV.

A week later my friend Rob called to tell me that Wee Burn Country Club, the most expensive and exclusive country club in Darien, was hiring caddies. Rob didn't need to work – his dad was a senior vice president at Exxon – but he knew I was looking for a job. (Rob and I had become friends over a shared secret love of science-fiction books like *A Wrinkle in Time* and *Dune*.) Caddying sounded promising, even though I'd never held a golf club and didn't know anything about golf.

I needed a job if I wanted to buy *Lodger*. My mom gave me fifty cents a week to mow the lawn and do chores around the house, but at that rate it would take me almost three months to buy a new album. And I couldn't get a real job because I was only thirteen. Rob told me, however, that you didn't need to be sixteen to be a caddy.

As soon as I hung up the phone on Rob I rode my bike to Wee Burn and parked it by the caddy shack, a crumbling wooden shed next to the staff parking lot and out of sight of the members. I knocked on the door and heard a muffled "What?"

I opened the door. Inside it was as hot as a southern prison. A very round man in a blue golf shirt looked up from behind a battered desk. He was sweating profusely. "Yeah?" he said.

"I'd like to fill out an application for caddying?" I said uncertainly.

He looked me over. "You ever caddy?"

"No," I admitted.

"You know how to golf?"

"No," I said again.

He rolled his eyes. "Okay. Get one of the caddies to show you around and wait. If we need a caddy, I'll get you."

By the side of the shack a group of caddies were seated around a table, playing cards. They were all high-school kids, sixteen and seventeen years old. Working up my courage I interrupted the game as meekly as possible: "The guy asked me to ask someone to show me around?"

A couple of the kids looked at me, then back at their cards.

"Tom," one of the card players said, without even looking up, "your turn."

"Shit," said a blond caddy. He threw down his cards and stood up. He was wearing brand-new Adidas sneakers. "Okay, this way," he said, walking away. I ran to catch up with him.

"You ever caddy?" Tom asked.

"No."

"You play golf? Your dad play golf?"

"No," I said. "My dad's dead."

He stopped and looked at me with something approaching sympathy. "Oh. Sorry. Well, you put your name here," he said, pointing at a piece of paper on a clipboard. "When it's your turn you'll get called."

He walked over to a small putting green and picked up an old bag of golf clubs. "Here, put this on," he said, handing me the bag. I stumbled a little bit under the weight, but hoisted it over my shoulder. "So it's not complicated," Tom said. "You carry the bag and you give the douchebags a club. You're little, so they'll give you the old fuckers. They walk slow, don't have as many clubs, and tip for shit." He paused. "Why are you doing this?"

"I need a job so I can buy records," I said, leaving out that I actually needed only one record, David Bowie's *Lodger*.

"You can't cut lawns?"

"We don't have a mower."

I could see him doing some quick calculations. I didn't have a father and I needed a job to buy records, but my family didn't have a lawnmower. So I was poor.

He finally smiled at me. "Okay, I'll help you figure this out," he said. I almost started crying with gratitude.

I didn't get called to caddy that day, but I showed up the next day, put my name on the sheet, and sat with the other caddies playing Hearts, the only card game they played. All the other caddies went out a few times a day, but I just sat around playing Hearts and drinking lukewarm tap water out of a plastic cup.

I returned for a third day, and around noon the round man in the office came out and read my name off the sheet. "Moby?"

"That's me," I said.

"Okay, you and Phil get these next two."

Phil and I stood up. Phil was the smallest of the caddies, except for me. We walked around the corner and met our golfers, a married couple in their eighties wearing head-to-toe white golf clothes. We picked up their bags and followed them.

"Phil, can you let me know what I should do?" I asked as we approached the first tee.

"Hand them clubs, try not to pass out or kill them," he said under his breath.

I walked behind the wife as she and her husband slowly made their way around the course. By the ninth hole I had sweated through my shirt. Younger, faster golfers passed us by, their caddies smirking at Phil and me as we stood with our geriatrics. When we finally reached the eighteenth hole, after four and a half hours, I was covered in perspiration and mosquito bites. "Thank you, young man," the elderly woman said to me. "Here's something for you." She handed me four quarters.

When I got back to the caddy shack the other caddies started applauding. "You got the Wilsons," Tom said, looking up from a hand of Hearts. "They are the slowest. The cheapest. The worst golfers you'll ever get."

But I had a dollar in my pocket, so I was 20 percent of the way to *Lodger*.

The next day I went out with the Wilsons again, and this time the wife gave me $1.50. "I remember you from yesterday," she said as she counted out six quarters.

"Thank you, ma'am," I said, after carrying her golf bag for almost five hours. Now I was 50 percent of the way toward buying *Lodger*.

The next day was rainy and only a few caddies showed up. By 2 p.m. I was all alone in the caddy shack. The round man emerged from his office. "Moby," he said, "I'm sending you out with Mr. Landon. Don't fuck it up – he's a real golfer."

Mr. Landon looked like all the dads I met in Darien. He was tall and seemed like he'd be more comfortable commanding troops than walking around a golf course in yellow slacks. He handed me his bag of clubs, which weighed about twice as much as Mrs. Wilson's, and we headed out. We walked in the drizzle, our feet squishing in the grass. He asked for clubs, I handed him clubs.

At the eighth hole he asked whether I thought he should play a wood or an iron to get off the fairway and onto the green. "An iron?" I said, not sure which clubs did what.

He nodded and I handed him his club. He hit the ball, sending it onto the green. "Good call," he said, granting me a small smile.

After his round Mr. Landon gave me $5 as a tip. An entire $5 bill. I thanked him, went straight to the caddy shack, got my bike, and rode in the rain to Johnny's Records.

Johnny's had started as a head shop in the early 1970s, selling drug paraphernalia to the bored children of rich parents, but a few years ago Johnny had started selling records alongside the bongs and the rolling papers. I walked in, headed for the "B" rack, and there it was: David Bowie's *Lodger* for $4.99. I looked at the other David Bowie records. *Changesonebowie* for $5.99. A *Ziggy Stardust* picture disc from Japan for $12.99. And a cutout of *"Heroes"* for $2.99. With the money I'd made from caddying, and some of the allowance money I'd saved, I had almost $10. I realized I could buy both *Lodger* and *"Heroes"*. I didn't know what *"Heroes"* was, but it was David Bowie and it was only $2.99, so it had to be good.

I brought my records to the front desk. Johnny and my mom had been friends in high school. He snarled at most of his customers but he was always kind to me, even when I browsed through his records without buying anything. "You know this is a Mexican pressing?" Johnny asked, gesturing at the copy of *"Heroes"*.

"What's that?" I asked.

"The vinyl's really thin," he explained.

I would be playing it on my mom's twenty-year-old record player with one small speaker, so I didn't think thin vinyl was going to matter. And it was $2.99. Plus it was a record. In a cardboard sleeve with a picture of David Bowie on the front. It was precious, even if it was thin.

I had a twenty-five-minute bike ride home in the drizzle. The whole way I cradled my records in my right arm. By the time I got home the brown paper bag was dissolving in the rain, but the records were safely shrink-wrapped.

I unwrapped the plastic and took out my new David Bowie albums. First I listened to *Lodger*. The music made no sense to me, but I loved it anyway. My favorite song on the album was "Look Back in Anger," which felt grand and beautiful.

I was sitting in front of my mom's record player in the living room of our small house by the freeway. We had a sofa from the Salvation Army and a chair covered with a tapestry my mom had found at a garage sale. The rain stopped while I was listening to the album and sunlight leaked tepidly through the windows. My cat, Tucker, was asleep on the floor next to me, and our new puppy Queenie was lying on the couch. But listening to "Look Back in Anger" made me feel like I was flying with huge, sad angels in a faraway place, possibly with mountains.

A musician my mom had dated a few years ago had left a guitar at our house when they broke up. And recently I'd started taking guitar lessons with Chris Risola, a teacher who my mom had met one day when she was at the Stop & Shop. He was teaching me chords and scales and some basic music theory, but I couldn't imagine how I'd ever be able to play a song like "Look Back in Anger," which hurtled along like a Japanese train.

After listening to *Lodger* I put on *"Heroes"*. At first it sounded menacing and illicit, like I was peering into an adult world. Listening to "Joe the Lion," I closed my eyes. Gone was our Connecticut living room with musty furniture and sleeping animals. With the sweet absence of light I was in a dark bar with unspeakably sad people. "Joe the Lion" was subterranean music, made by thin, pale people who lived in subway tunnels.

Then "'Heroes'" came on. I'd heard this once before, late at night on the New York classic-rock radio station WNEW. I didn't even know what instruments made these sounds. Guitars? Synthesizers? Growing up obsessed with science fiction I'd thought that the future was going to be sterile and safe. "'Heroes'" sounded like a different future, full of beauty and regret. It was sad and calm, like an abandoned space station.

I read the lyrics about eking out small, quotidian victories, and it all made sense. The world would always defeat us. Cruelty would always win. But for a brief moment we could find love and a quiet happiness. "'Heroes'" ended and I moved the record needle so I could listen to it again. It ended again and I listened to it again. This was the most beautiful song I'd ever heard. Why was "The Devil Went Down to Georgia" on the radio twenty times a day, but this perfect song was relegated to cheap vinyl?

Eventually I turned the album over to hear side two. Aside from "The Secret Life of Arabia," it was all quiet music, without drums and vocals, like music from a late-night science-fiction film. I didn't understand – I'd never heard of almost an entire side of an album that didn't have words or drums. But David Bowie was my new favorite, and I figured he knew what he was doing. He was an alien-lizard musician from London, England; he'd made multiple albums and had been on the radio and TV. So if I didn't understand this non-song "ambient" music, it was clearly my fault.

My only job was to listen to side two of *"Heroes"* until it made sense.

34

NEW YORK CITY (2002)

"So why does Eminem hate you so much?"

Every interview I did involved some version of this question. Having been raised by progressives and a steady diet of Norman Lear TV shows, I had learned at an early age that bigotry and discrimination were antiquated and wrong. The 1960s and 1970s had their shortcomings, but at least they'd given lip service to tolerance and inclusion.

In the early 1990s Bill Clinton was elected president, alternative rock exploded, and Nirvana and R.E.M. and other modern rock icons reaffirmed what we all knew: racism was wrong; anti-Semitism was wrong; misogyny was wrong; homophobia was wrong.

Then something strange happened. In the late 1990s musicians started unapologetically glorifying misogyny and homophobia in their lyrics and videos. I believed we were trying to leave bigotry in the past, but too many musicians were singing and rapping about abusing women and gay people. Being the product of hippies, Norman Lear, and *Sesame Street*, I spoke up. I assumed all the other musicians who'd been raised by progressive families would also object, but I was wrong. I quickly realized that in speaking up against homophobia and misogyny, I was largely alone.

I criticized some of Eminem's lyrics, even though it was clear that he was talented. I even got the sense that his misogyny and homophobia were, to some extent, poses. But I also understood that his fan base of junior-high-school students didn't understand the nuances in his songs. They just knew that their platinum-album-selling hero was rapping about hurting women and gay people.

In early 2001 I was doing an interview at the MTV studio in Times Square. I sat down in their familiar black cushioned chair, while the familiar sound person clipped a lavalier microphone onto my jacket. For the hundredth or maybe five hundredth time I was asked, "Why does Eminem hate you so much?"

People were increasingly accusing me of being a compromised sellout, which I was, but in the deep recesses of my heart part of me was still a punk-rocker who admired the Situationists. So I said, jokingly and provocatively, "I don't know – maybe Eminem's gay and he has a crush on me."

Which I soon discovered was the equivalent of pouring gasoline on a brush fire. Eminem saw the interview, was incensed, and for his "Without Me" video dressed up like me and had me violently thrashed. Then he shot me in effigy onstage every night of his tour.

At first I thought it was funny. I was even a little flattered that this huge pop star was so obsessed with me. I had been clear in other interviews that Eminem wasn't the only, or worst, misogynist or homophobe. Countless musicians and rappers seemed to be out-doing each other in their expressions of bigotry. I had even heard of homophobia in the dance community, which baffled me, since house music was born and nurtured in gay clubs.

On a tour stop in Detroit I did an interview with a local journalist in an Ethiopian restaurant. We were mopping up our spicy food with spongy Ethiopian bread when he asked the inevitable question: "Why do you have a beef with Eminem and Kid Rock and those guys?"

I swallowed. "Because bigotry is dangerous and bad. How would people feel if, instead of denigrating women and gay people, Eminem and Kid Rock and all the nu-metal guys were espousing violence toward blacks and Jews? How is it that some bigotry is accepted by MTV and the record companies, and other bigotry is hateful? Shouldn't all bigotry be condemned?"

we are all made of stars

He paused and said, "Yeah, but a lot of women are bitches."

I was stunned. This was a journalist, a writer, a supposedly erudite member of the fourth estate. "What?"

"You know, these guys deal with a lot of gold-diggers and bitches."

Now I was horrified. "And that justifies misogyny?"

I wanted the world to be as progressive and inclusive as the world I'd grown up watching on TV. It was clear back then: Archie Bunker was a loathsome old bigot and he represented a world we were leaving behind. And now the Archie Bunkers of the early twenty-first century were programming radio stations and selling millions of records. And bigotry wasn't simply a matter of aesthetics and mores, it was behind the worst atrocities in human history. Genocide is just bigotry on an industrial scale.

The day before the 2002 MTV Video Music Awards I received a phone call from Robert Smigel. He was a troubled writer and comedian, most famous as the voice of Triumph, the Insult Comic Dog. I'd been interviewed by Triumph a few times, and even though he'd been scathing toward me, I admired Robert's comedic genius.

Robert had an idea: in the middle of the show he would have MTV put me in a seat behind Eminem and his posse and then have Triumph come out and insult us both. I happily agreed.

The day of the show I arrived early and spent an hour on the red carpet talking about myself. I loved talking about myself and got very cranky if I didn't have enough time to do every interview with every journalist and TV host on the red carpet. An MTV intern escorted me to my first seat, in between Ludacris and Justin Timberlake. I won an award for the "We Are All Made of Stars" video and was then reseated, behind Eminem and in front of Jack and Meg White.

Eminem turned around to glare at me. As I looked into his eyes I realized this wasn't a joke for him. He truly seemed to hate me. I'd been offended by his lyrics, but deep down I'd assumed that we were two public figures having an overly dramatized show-biz feud. He looked at me and said quietly, "You're dead."

I felt vulnerable: even though we were surrounded by thousands of people in the middle of Radio City Music Hall, he was with his posse of very large, very angry men, while I was alone.

I was also confused. Apart from the misogyny and homophobia, I felt a strange kinship with Eminem. We'd both grown up in grinding suburban poverty. We both had complicated single moms. We'd both found refuge in music. And neither one of us was very tall.

Robert Smigel came over with his dog puppet on his hand, trailed by a mobile camera crew. He interviewed me in the voice of Triumph, gleefully insulting me in front of millions of people. "I wouldn't let you hump *my* leg," he said. I laughed because, well, it was funny.

Then Triumph went to interview Eminem, and Eminem punched the puppet. Smigel looked at him in horror. In all his years of doing Triumph, the Insult Comic Dog, no one had ever punched his puppet before.

They cut to a commercial, and Eminem angrily handed me a picture he'd drawn. I looked at the drawing: it was of him strangling me. I had to concede that it was quite good and wondered when he had found the time to draw it. It was a second draft; on the other side of the pink paper there was a rough version of the same drawing, hastily scribbled over.

The show started up again, and Eminem left his seat to accept an award from Christina Aguilera. As he reached the podium he was clearly agitated. "Yo," he said, "that little Moby girl threw me out of my zone for a minute." The crowd started booing, but I didn't know if they were booing him or me.

Eminem kept lambasting me – "I will hit a man with glasses," he promised – and the crowd booed more. I still wasn't sure who was being booed, me or him. Eminem took his Moonman award and stormed off the stage.

I was shaken. The realization sank in that I'd just been threatened and embarrassed in front of an audience of millions. All along I'd assumed that Eminem hadn't really been that upset with me and that someday we'd meet up and have a friendly conversation in which he'd explain that he wasn't actually a misogynist or homophobe. We'd talk about growing up poor and scared, and maybe even become friends. Instead I was the object of vicious public ire from the biggest and angriest pop star on the planet.

I was also shaken because I was worried people weren't on my side. As hard as it was to admit, a lot of the reviews for *18* had been negative. Not just critical of the music, but of me. Some journalists weren't even bothering to talk about my music anymore; they were just singling me out for ridicule.

I'd seen the ticket counts for some of the upcoming dates on my tour, and they weren't great. I'd hoped that *18* and the subsequent tour were going to cement my position in the pantheons of music and fame. But as terrifying as it was to consider, I knew that the album wasn't doing nearly as well as *Play* had.

I walked out of the awards show, feeling the eyes of five thousand audience members on me. On the sidewalk behind Radio City I met up with Julian Casablancas and some of the other members of the Strokes. They were playing a private after-show party, so I rode with them to the loft in Hell's Kitchen where they were performing. Once there I was escorted backstage, where I drank as much of the Strokes' vodka as I could.

I'd wanted to hate the Strokes: they were good-looking and successful, plus they had grown up rich and privileged. But over the past year we had become friends. And I loved their music, with its unsubtle fan-boy appropriation of the Velvet Underground and Hoboken bands like the Feelies and the Bongos.

They went onstage at midnight. I stood on the side of the stage, drinking from a bottle of champagne and singing along to "Is This It."

I'd first met Julian, the Strokes' singer, a year before, when we had both been getting drunk at a bar in the East Village at 4 a.m. I told him how much I loved "Is This It," and how it reminded me of hot, drunk summer nights on the Lower East Side. I drunkenly told him that "Is This It" reminded me of the moment when everything in New York City seemed to hold you: the warm, soft August air, the bar full of friendly drunks, and the beautiful woman who'd kindly taken you to her fourth-floor walkup in an old tenement building.

Julian smiled and hugged me drunkenly, saying, "You get it."

As the Strokes started playing a new song, I spotted André from Outkast standing backstage with some friends. We'd toured together in 2001, and I wanted to collaborate with him on my next album. I walked over to him and tried to hug him, but he quickly stepped backward.

"What's up, Moby?" he asked.

"I'm working on some music and I was wondering if you wanted to collaborate on some songs?"

He shook his head and gave me a quick, sad smile. "Moby," he said, "you know I like you, but just too many people are hating on you right now."

Section Three:

In My Dreams I'm Dying All the Time

35

BARCELONA, SPAIN (2002)

Through plate-glass windows twenty feet tall I gazed at the Mediterranean Sea, a sparkling blue-gray carpet stretching out to the horizon. I was in Barcelona, on a short break from my European tour for *18*, to perform at the European MTV Awards. The luxury hotel where I was staying was crowned with four opulent apartments; my penthouse neighbors were Madonna, Jon Bon Jovi, and P. Diddy.

To get to our shared penthouse level you had to pass muster with security at the entrance of the hotel, then more security at the first bank of elevators, then armed guards at the private elevator going to the penthouse. After my tour bus dropped me off with my knapsack, I'd ridden up to the penthouse with Madonna's head of security. "So you know Eddie?" he asked me.

Madonna's personal yoga teacher, Eddie, had been one of my best friends in the 1980s. We met while watching John Waters's *Pink Flamingos* at a dive bar in St. Mark's Place. At the time he was a high-school dropout with a ten-inch red Mohawk. Now he was a yoga teacher, teaching Ashtanga to Madonna and Gwyneth, and organizing spirituality workshops with Deepak Chopra.

In addition to the wall of glass twenty feet tall facing the Mediterranean, my hotel penthouse had a chef's kitchen, a dining room for ten people, a formal living room with a grand piano, and three bedrooms on a second level that was reached by a wide glass staircase. The MTV Awards were tomorrow, so tonight I was going to have a party in my suite for my band, my crew, and some people from my record company. I was expecting fifteen or twenty people, so my assistant had ordered three cases of beer, a case of champagne, two liters of vodka, a liter of whiskey, and club soda and limes. The hotel staff had come in before I arrived and set everything up on the sideboard in the living room, along with crystal glasses for cocktails and flutes for the champagne.

I took another elevator to the private rooftop spa, where I received a very quiet $200 massage from an eastern European woman who didn't speak English. I didn't like getting massages – they made me feel syrupy and nauseated – but I felt like it was my duty as a rock star to spend money on things that other public figures seemed to like.

After my massage I had a couple of hours before my guests were supposed to arrive, so I walked down the hall to the other three duplex apartments. I knocked on P. Diddy's door. A security guard answered. "Hi, I'm Moby," I said. "Is Sean here?"

"Hold on," he said, shutting the door. I stood on the thick gray carpeting and inspected the hallway's sconces and walnut panels.

P. Diddy opened his door. "Moby? Come on in."

I walked into his suite, which was the mirror image of mine. "We're neighbors, so I wanted to say hi," I said.

"What's up?"

I had met P. Diddy a few times over the last year at different clubs and awards shows. I didn't know him very well, but every time I saw him he was unfailingly nice to me, so I liked him. "I'm having some people over later, if you want to stop by," I said.

"Thanks, I'm headed out to dinner with Bono and Jay," he said. "But you should come to my party later. I rented a villa outside town. It should start around 1 a.m."

"Okay, thanks, maybe see you later," I said, shaking his hand and heading back to the door. "Oh, and let me know if you need to borrow a cup of sugar."

He looked at me, considering what I had said, and nodded. "Because we're neighbors. That's funny," he said earnestly.

in my dreams i'm dying all the time

I walked further down the hall and knocked on Madonna's door. It was opened by the head of security I'd ridden in the elevator with.

"Hi, is Madonna there?" I asked.

"She's getting her hair done," he said. "Can I help you?"

"Oh, I'm having people over later, if she wants to stop by," I said.

"Okay, I'll tell her. What time?"

"Nine?" I said uncertainly, suddenly nervous that I'd done something wrong by having the temerity to invite Madonna to a party. But I'd known her for years, and two years ago she'd given me my third or fourth MTV Award at a ceremony in Sweden.

"Okay, thanks," he said, and shut the solid wooden door with a soft thunk.

I'd never met Jon Bon Jovi, although we had both performed at the Winter Olympics, so I decided not to knock on his door to introduce myself. Instead I wrote him a note on hotel stationery and slipped it under his door: "hi, didn't want to bother you, but i'm having a little party at 9 pm. your neighbor, moby."

Back in my suite I went into the chef's kitchen and made myself some brown rice, black beans, and steamed broccoli. I took my plate to the living room, along with a Harlan Coben book. Sitting at a burled maple desk, I ate my food and read my book while the sun set over Barcelona.

Scott, my drummer, and Steve, my sound tech, were the first to arrive, at 9 p.m. "Whoa, this place is insane," Steve said, walking up to the walls of glass so he could take in the delicate lights of Barcelona and the inky blackness of the Mediterranean Sea.

After my macrobiotic dinner I'd made myself a couple of very strong vodka and sodas, so I was already kind of drunk. "I used to live in an abandoned factory and pee in a bottle!" I said, gesturing to the wall of windows with my tumbler of vodka.

"This doesn't suck," Scott said respectfully.

The doorbell rang. I opened it to find Madonna, along with her security guard and a few hangers-on. "Moby, hi!" she said warmly.

"Hi! Do you want to come in?" I asked, taken aback that Madonna had actually shown up.

"No, I'm heading out. I just wanted to say hi."

"Hi," I said again, awkwardly. "Will I see you tomorrow?"

"I'm announcing one of your awards again," she said. "Well, hopefully."

"Fingers crossed," I said.

We looked at each other for a second, and then Madonna said, "Have a good night! See you tomorrow." She turned and padded down the soft gray carpeting to the elevators, trailed by her entourage and expensive perfume that smelled like flowers in a yoga studio.

I walked back in and made myself another drink. "That was Madonna," I said.

"Really?" Scott said.

"She and Bon Jovi and P. Diddy are my neighbors," I explained.

The doorbell rang a few more times. By 9.30, there were fifteen people in my suite, all drinking and staring out the windows. The room could have easily held fifty people or more, and with only fifteen of us it felt desolate, no matter how much we drank.

My tour manager Sandy had parked himself on a beige leather sofa, but at 10.15 he stood up. "Well, busy day tomorrow," he said. "I should head back to the poor people's hotel."

"How is it?" I asked.

"Apart from the rats and the holes in the walls, it's great."

"You're kidding."

He smirked. "Yes, I'm kidding. It's fine."

For the *18* tour I'd been staying in hotels by myself. I'd heard that real rock stars stayed in extremely nice hotels, while their band and crew stayed elsewhere, in somewhat less nice hotels. I missed the early days of the *Play* tour, when we all crammed into Holiday Inns and Motel 6s, sometimes sharing rooms. But I was a rock star, so I felt obligated to stay by myself in $3,000 a night hotel suites.

The rest of the guests politely agreed with Sandy, finished their drinks, and headed back to their own accommodations. I'd imagined a room full of rock stars and fans and beautiful women, drinking and partying with me until the sun rose over the Mediterranean. But by 10.45 p.m. I was alone in my glass-walled penthouse with a lot of alcohol and empty glasses.

I made myself another vodka and soda, put Massive Attack's *Protection* on the stereo, and went to my laptop to check my email. I had messages from my aunts, my stepfather Richard, and a few friends in New York. I couldn't focus on any of them; I was too vexed that my sophisticated and sybaritic party hadn't worked out. I drained the vodka – my eighth or ninth – and stumbled to the bar, where I opened a bottle of champagne.

I was a rock star in a three-bedroom suite by the Mediterranean Sea. I'd been given a thousand times more of everything than I'd ever dreamed of. I had made over $10 million the year before and my loft in New York had a hallway lined with gold and platinum records. I told myself that it didn't matter that for one night things hadn't worked out and I was alone – but I didn't believe it. "Fuck this," I said out loud, spilling champagne on the back of the leather couch. "Fuck you," I said to the air, to my dead mom, to the emptiness. It felt good, so I said "Fuck you" even louder.

Finding the happiness I'd enjoyed for the past few years was getting harder. I had to drink more to get drunk. I had to sleep with more people to feel validated. I had to be in more magazines to feel like I had meaning and worth.

I opened another bottle of champagne and walked upstairs. On the glass staircase I tripped and fell. My shins started bleeding; I ignored them.

I sat on the stairs, took a long drink from the bottle, and started crying. This wasn't how it was supposed to be. Growing up I'd known beyond a shadow of a doubt that if the universe gave me success as a musician, I'd be the happiest person who ever lived.

And if you added wealth and fame and awards and sex and alcohol, that had to guarantee I would never again be a sad, scared boy from the suburbs. It was basic math.

But now I was self-pitying and miserable. And scared – because if this wish-fulfillment life wasn't bringing me happiness, then what would?

In high school I'd found cold comfort in listening to Joy Division and fantasizing about killing myself. Suicide had always seemed like the Swiss Army knife of dramatic action. By killing myself, I'd:

– announce to the world that I was miserable;

– end my life and its baffling sadness;

– join the ranks of esteemed people, like Ian Curtis and Albert Camus and Ernest Hemingway, who had taken their own lives.

Distracted by stratospheric success, I hadn't thought much about killing myself over the last few years. But lately the depression had been whispering to me again.

I stood up, still crying, and made my way back down the glass stairs to the sideboard. I poured another drink, switching back to vodka. "I should die. I'm alone and I should die," I said. Once I uttered the words out loud, they made total sense.

I wondered if my mom would have been proud of me. I remembered playing her a recording of some music I'd made in high school. She sat on the brown foam-rubber sofa that seemed to follow us no matter where we lived, and I put a pair of cheap headphones over her ears. I hit "Play"; she closed her eyes and listened to an early piece of electronic music I'd written. When it was done she opened them wide, smiled at me, and said, "Wow."

This was all she'd wanted for me: to spend my life as an artist, making music and seeing the world. Knowing that made me cry harder, because I had everything she'd wanted for me and I'd screwed it up. I had no idea how to be happy. I was a worthless failure.

I went to the windows, barely staying upright. I wanted to throw myself out, fall 450 feet through the warm air, and land on concrete, dying on impact. I could see through the twenty-foot-tall panes of glass, but I couldn't open them.

I went back upstairs, hoping that maybe I could throw myself out of one of the smaller windows in my bedroom. But no, the upstairs windows opened a few inches for air, but not enough for me to squeeze through.

I lay down on the thick carpet in my master bedroom, sobbing and apologizing to God and my dead mom for being such a disappointment.

36

DARIEN, CONNECTICUT (1979)

My mom and I had made a deal. If I worked hard and did my weekly list of chores, she'd raise my allowance to seventy-five cents a week. So, on a Saturday in October, I spent four hours raking leaves and putting them in plastic bags, which I lined up by the side of our garage.

After the death of my grandfather, my grandmother had sold the seven-bedroom house in Darien that they had lived in for decades. With the proceeds she bought a smaller house for herself in nearby Norwalk and a modest house near the Darien train station for my mom and me. We finally had a house of our own, with a proper heating system and a small lawn. Which meant that I had yardwork.

Raking leaves was my favorite outdoor chore, way better than cutting the lawn with the manual push-mower from 1960 that our neighbor Bill gave us after we moved in. Unless you had a gas mower, cutting the lawn was hot and sweaty and involved running away from wasps and hornets. Raking leaves was civilized; the rake hit the brittle leaves like a snare drum on an old jazz record.

After I finished raking and bagging, my mom and I drove to a nearby orchard to buy apples and apple cider. Then we stopped at a convenience store so she could buy cigarettes. On the way home, with a Styx song on the radio, I casually said, "Oh, I'm going to a party tonight with Dave and Jim." It sounded normal, but I'd never been to a nighttime party that wasn't a birthday or a sleepover. I knew that other ninth-graders had parties, but before tonight I'd never been invited to one.

And technically I hadn't been invited to this party – my friends Dave and Jim had overheard someone talking about it in their English class. I'd met Dave and Jim the year before. They both had dads, and they lived in nicer houses than I did, but we were in the same boat socially: we weren't big enough to play sports and we weren't computer-savvy enough to hang out with the diminutive geniuses in our school who were writing computer code. So we hung out together, watching TV and riding our Schwinn ten-speeds to Johnny's Records to ogle records we wanted to buy someday.

My mom and I had meatloaf with egg noodles for dinner, watching *CHiPs* while we ate. After dinner I had a bowl of chocolate ice cream, and then went upstairs to listen to the radio and get dressed for the party. I listened to WNEW exclusively now, as it was the only New York station that sometimes played new wave and punk rock. They still played classic rock, but every third or fourth song they'd play something fast and new, made by people with short hair.

I wanted to look normal for the party, so I had planned my outfit the day before: a dark-blue polo shirt from Goodwill, Lee jeans from the Norwalk Salvation Army, and a Penguin windbreaker that my grandmother had bought for me at the Darien Community Association Thrift Shop. Tucker the cat and Queenie the dog followed me as I went to the bathroom, where I stood on the edge of the bathtub to look at myself in the mirror over the sink. Tucker and Queenie were kind and loved me unconditionally, but the cool kids who would be attending this party were savages. I knew I'd be ridiculed if any of them figured out that my clothes were all bought secondhand. Leaning in front of the mirror I decided that I looked passably normal. I headed downstairs.

"I'm going out, Mom," I said, milking the moment for all it was worth, "to this party."

"Okay, have fun," she said, turning away from the TV to give me a smile.

"Not sure when I'll be back!"

"Don't stay out too late!"

I thought maybe she was kidding. I'd never stayed out late in my life. Sometimes during the summer I'd ride bikes with my friends until it got dark, around 9 p.m. And occasionally I'd watch TV at my friend Rob's house – he had a color TV and a VCR. But apart from a few sleepovers, including the night when I had watched a friend overdose, I had never been out of the house past ten.

I got on my bike and rode to Dave's house, a few blocks away. His house was small by Darien standards, but nicer than mine and further away from I-95. His mom answered the door. "Dave and Jim are upstairs in Dave's room," she informed me cheerfully.

"Thank you, Mrs. Marden," I said.

I went upstairs and heard the sound of Elvis Costello coming through Dave's door. When I opened the door Jim was sitting on the floor, holding the album sleeve of *This Year's Model*, looking at it with reverence.

"You have an Elvis Costello record?" I asked incredulously.

"Yeah," Dave said off-handedly. "I got it in the city."

Jim and I looked at him, stunned. We each owned a couple of records, but we bought them in Darien, or if we were feeling exotic, Stamford, which was ten minutes away. Even though you could buy Elvis Costello records at Johnny's, this copy came from New York City. New York City was only forty-five minutes away, but it was the dark land of everything we loved.

Dave, Jim, and I weren't as embarrassed about listening to new-wave music as we had been six months earlier. The cool kids in school continued to viciously ridicule new wave and punk rock, though, so we still weren't brave enough to publicly admit that we liked Elvis Costello and the Clash.

I'd heard Elvis Costello's "Pump It Up" on WNEW a few times, and loved how it sounded like a basket of energetic bees. And now I was in a suburban bedroom, listening to the same song I'd heard on the radio, but on a record from New York City. I didn't know what Elvis was saying, or what was being pumped up, but the song was fast and absurdly exciting, and made me want to jump up and down and smash everything in Dave's room and scream an endless "Fuck you!" to the quiet suburbs.

But I was repressed, and I wanted to be cool, so instead I casually asked, "Whose party are we going to?"

"Cynthia Corsiglia's," Dave said, mentioning a girl in my biology class whom I dreamed about and lusted after. Cynthia and I were the same age, but I looked like a child and she looked like an Italian movie star. And we were going to her house. My head filled with visions of her taking me to her room, kissing me, and being my beautiful forever girlfriend.

"Oh, I think I heard about her party," I said, lying.

Jim and I left our bikes at Dave's house and walked to the party. I was happy that we were all dressed almost identically, in jeans and sneakers and polo shirts – it confirmed that I had chosen the right outfit. As we were all the same height, the same age, and had the same generic haircut, we could have passed for brothers.

On the way to Cynthia's house we passed the house where my mom and I lived. I saw light coming from the room where my mom was watching TV. The thought of her watching *Hawaii Five-O* or *The Love Boat* by herself made my chest heavy. I wanted to cancel my plans and run inside to make her feel less alone. But I walked away from my house and its one glowing window.

We cut through some backyards and a few minutes later arrived at Cynthia Corsiglia's house. We stood on the sidewalk, looking at the front door and listening to the Grateful Dead's "Casey Jones" playing loudly inside.

"Should we go in?" Jim asked bravely.

"Well," Dave said, "I just heard about this party."

None of us had actually been invited. And we clearly were not the kids who could just casually show up, stroll in, and open a beer.

"Should we see if we can look inside?" I suggested.

We quietly snuck around the side of the house and put a metal bucket under a kitchen window. Jim, being the brave one, climbed up and told Dave and me what he saw. "There's Tom Rand and Chaz Walker, and Muffy Childress and Scooter Borden. They're drinking beers."

"Who else?"

"Jen Icahn and Matt Porretta are making out by the back door."

This was exciting. We were at a party, even if technically we were outside it getting a play-by-play from a friend standing on a bucket. After five minutes we took the bucket to another window. This time Dave climbed up to deliver live commentary.

"Mark Palmer is there, and he's talking to Cynthia. *B.J. and the Bear* is on the TV. Bill O'Neill is on the couch with Erin Bunch and Scott McBride. Oh, and Steve Larkin's there."

My veins froze. Steve Larkin was my nemesis. I'd never been in a real fight, but in seventh grade he had punched me in the stomach on the playground, and I'd been terrified of him ever since. My sweet visions of going inside and kissing Cynthia Corsiglia were replaced with panicky flashes of being mauled on the driveway by Steve Larkin and his football-playing friends. Trying to sound calm, I said, "Okay, so should we go?"

Dave stepped down from the bucket. We snuck through a neighbor's yard and back to the street. My sadness about my mom being alone had been swept away by being outside with my friends on a crisp October night. We felt like brave adventurers as we'd been to a party, even if we hadn't been inside. Cynthia Corsiglia hadn't fallen in love with me, but I'd been outside her house while she'd been inside. And that was enough.

"Want to go listen to the other side of the Elvis Costello record?" Dave asked.

37

NEW YORK CITY (2002)

When it first opened teany was always busy, but we still somehow lost money. Then a friend who owned a restaurant on Ludlow Street gave me some solid small-business advice: "You can't spend more than you take in."

Oh. So that was the solution.

Kelly implemented the new rule of spending less than we took in, and teany started breaking even. This was wonderful – it meant that I didn't have to close it. Shutting down my tea shop would have been heartbreaking, because teany had become my second home. Every hungover morning I went there for bagels with vegan cream cheese. I had meetings and interviews there during the afternoon, and at night I'd meet friends there and we'd play Scrabble before heading out to get drunk. Plus teany was bright and quiet and clean, unlike the dark tour buses I'd been living on for most of the twenty-first century.

It was the day before Halloween, and I was home on a short break from touring. I was going to a Halloween party later, but first I wanted to stop at teany to have a piece of chocolate cake and to show off my costume. I was dressed up as the keyboard player from Journey, or Loverboy, even though I didn't actually know what the keyboard player from Journey, or Loverboy, looked like. I was wearing red pants, white shoes, a red sleeveless T-shirt, a long dark wig, wraparound sunglasses, and a red multi-zippered Michael Jackson jacket I'd bought on the street from a homeless man in 1986.

I had called Kelly earlier and told her about my costume. She told me that she was going to wear normal clothes for Halloween;

her costume was going to be prosthetic makeup that would make her look like a pig-nosed extra on an old *Twilight Zone* episode.

Kelly and I had broken up the day that teany opened, and since then had gotten back together and broken up again at least a dozen times. At present we were ostensibly a couple, even though both of us were polygamously dating other people.

I walked up to the entrance of teany as Kelly walked out the door that led to the tiny basement office where we also made soup. "Is that you?" I asked, amazed by her prosthetic porcine makeup.

"Is that you?" she asked, taking in my red clothes and long dark wig. We both laughed.

"How's teany today?" I asked.

She looked at me and said earnestly, but in a voice slightly muffled by her prosthetic pig nose, "You really need to go inside."

"What's wrong?"

"Nothing's wrong. You'll see."

I stepped down past our little patio and walked into teany. Our tea shop was very small. It seated twenty-two people comfortably, and on some Sunday brunches we squeezed in thirty. Even though nobody complained, thirty people in such a tiny space felt claustrophobic and barbaric.

This afternoon we were half full. But when I looked around I saw what Kelly was talking about. Teany had become a place where some of the public figures in the neighborhood liked to hang out, and somehow today they had all shown up at the same time. Kim Gordon, Thurston Moore, and Lee Ranaldo from Sonic Youth were at one of the tables. David Bowie and Iman and their toddler daughter were at another table. A few feet away Gus Van Sant was having tea with Ben Affleck, Matt Damon, and Joaquin Phoenix. Outside, Jake and Maggie Gyllenhaal were having scones.

Kelly walked up to me. "You see?"

"This is insane," I said quietly.

I made my rounds and said hello to everyone, with my wig making me feel like a maître d' in a Terry Gilliam movie. After I was done checking on our bizarre gaggle of celebrities Kelly pulled me aside and asked, "Can we talk?"

"Okay," I said, suddenly anxious. Hearing "Can we talk?" terrified me, because it usually meant that somebody wanted something from me or that I'd done something bad. Kelly and I walked west on Rivington Street and stopped in front of an old brick building that housed an AIDS clinic.

"I can't do this anymore," Kelly said flatly.

"Do what?"

"Be in a non-monogamous relationship with you."

When we first started dating Kelly and I didn't talk about whether we were seeing other people. It turned out that we both were. After that we tried being open, dating other people but talking about it with each other, but that made us miserable and jealous. Then, through some convoluted logic, Kelly decided that she was fine being monogamous with me, but that didn't mean I had to be monogamous with her. So I was allowed to be promiscuous, so long as I told her about the other people I was sleeping with. It was dysfunctional, but for a few months it almost worked.

For our most recent spate of dating we'd gone back to having an open relationship, but had started going to couples therapy together. When I agreed to therapy I assumed that we'd go to a wood-paneled office on the Upper West Side and our therapist would congratulate me on my self-awareness, and then politely tell Kelly that she was crazy. But that wasn't what happened.

Our first session was a fairly anodyne forty-five minutes of getting to know the therapist. But during our second session I'd been talking about my childhood and how every romantic relationship I had as an adult gave me debilitating panic attacks. The therapist looked at me kindly and said, in his gentle Upper West Side therapist's voice, "You know, Moby, you might want to consider coming to therapy on your own a few times a week."

I was stunned: I thought I was the sane one. For years I'd told myself that my crippling panic attacks in the face of emotional intimacy simply meant that I hadn't been dating the right people. Kelly and I went back to the therapist a few more times, but the sessions became acrimonious, with Kelly yelling and me wanting to run away. Between sessions I was drinking more, taking more ecstasy, and indiscriminately pursuing one-night stands.

And now Kelly had reached her breaking point with us. With me. She stood in front of the AIDS clinic, in her perfect prosthetic *Twilight Zone* pig nose, and seethed at me. We'd been here many times before. Not in front of the AIDS clinic, but in some version of this argument where she told me that she was tired of me and my panic and my promiscuity. "I've put up with this shit for too long," she said. "I'm done."

In my red Michael Jackson jacket and long wig, I pleaded, "But monogamy gives me panic attacks."

"That's bullshit," she snapped.

"It's not, and you know it. I want to be in a relationship, but I panic."

She stared daggers at me over her flawless prosthetic nose, not saying anything. A nurse wheeled a very sick AIDS patient past us and up the handicapped ramp.

"I'm sorry, Kelly," I said. "I wish I was different."

I could tell that after four years of pain, she wanted to scream at me or stab me or put a hand grenade in my pants. But all she said through gritted teeth was "Fuck you," and then she stormed off down Rivington Street.

We'd broken up countless times, but this felt different. I knew that this time we would not be getting back together in a week and having sex in the teany basement, next to the hot plates where we made soup. This was final. I felt sad, but light. I was free to drink more, free to stop visiting a therapist who tried to get me to look into my panic, free to be alone.

The sun had set. I could feel the hum of New York as the street-lights turned on and the dark city came to life. I hated my panic, but it was my protector. As I walked west on Rivington my panic smiled at me, kindly and cruelly, and wrapped me in its wings.

38

NEW YORK CITY (2003)

The first time I went to Don Hill's I broke my ankle. It was a grimy single-story rock club in Soho, a block away from the West Side Highway. I first visited the club in 1995, and at the end of the night got up on its stage while drunkenly dancing to "I Wanna Be Your Dog" by the Stooges, jumping around enthusiastically until I fell off.

A woman from Elektra, my record company at the time, took me home in a cab, with ice wrapped around my grotesquely swollen ankle. I'd returned to Don Hill's a week later on crutches, and had been a drunken regular there ever since.

Tonight I was at Don Hill's to see the band Satanicide. Two of my friends had started the group, a fake 1980s hair-metal band, as a joke. But after playing a few shows they realized that their ironic metal band was actually really good. By midnight I'd had six or seven vodka and sodas and was on my way to getting drunk. Phil and Dale, respectively the guitarist and singer of Satanicide, pulled me out of the crowd during their encore and gave me a guitar so I could play "Whole Lotta Love" with them. "Whole Lotta Love" was the perfect cover song for a dive bar at midnight: it was universally loved and easy to play while drunk, as it had only three notes.

By day Phil was a lawyer who lived in Chelsea with his wife and son, and Dale was a successful fashion photographer. But in Satanicide Phil would be topless, wearing tiny silver shorts and a long blond wig, while Dale, with his black eye makeup and long black wig, looked like a menacing extra from *Lord of the Rings*.

During my solo they sprayed me with glitter, and then held a bottle of Jack Daniel's to my mouth so I could drink and play at the same time.

The set ended and I walked to the bar, strangers patting me on the back. The woman standing next to me at the bar gave me the look that I'd come to love more than air or friendship: the look that said, "I know who you are and I like you."

"Can I buy you a drink?" I asked, clichéd but sincere.

"Sure, I'll have what you're having."

We took our drinks to one of the black vinyl banquettes, where I introduced myself.

"I know who you are," she said coquettishly. Her name was Pam; she was tall and blonde and looked like a Russian flight attendant. After a few minutes of drinking vodka and trying to have a shouted conversation over "Union City Blue" by Blondie, we just started kissing. "Do you want to go back to my house?" she asked. "I live on Sullivan."

"Of course," I said. We left through the back door, while a band started playing a heavy-metal version of "Total Eclipse of the Heart." Her apartment was two blocks away, on the fourth floor of an old tenement on Sullivan Street, and it was the smallest apartment I'd ever been in. There was a diminutive room with a bed and a small chair, a cramped bathroom, and a tiny kitchen that was essentially a closet with a stove.

Pam closed the front door, and with no fanfare we took off our clothes and started having sex on her small bed. Afterward she opened the window by the bed, lit a cigarette, and said, "I'm so glad we did that again."

Again? I thought we had just met.

Then I remembered: in the late 1990s, when my album *Animal Rights* was failing, we had gone on two dates and had drunken sex. I felt ashamed for not remembering, but in my defense she was blonde now and had been a brunette then.

Also, I'd been a blackout drunk then. Which, to be fair, I still was now.

The apartment buzzer squawked loudly, interrupting my reverie of amnesiac shame. A few seconds later it squawked again. Then again. And again, sounding like a loud electronic duck. Pam seemed unconcerned.

"Do you want to get that?" I asked.

"It's my ex-boyfriend," she said quietly, stubbing her cigarette out in an ashtray. "He's insane."

The buzzing went on and on – and then at last, it stopped. But next I heard feet pounding up the tenement stairs and a fist banging on the door. "Pam!" her ex bellowed as he pounded on the metal door. "Open the fucking door!"

We lay there, breathing as quietly as possible and saying nothing. Because her apartment was so small, we were lying in a bed only a few feet away from the door. The banging and yelling continued. "Pam! I swear, open the fucking door!"

"Ssshhh," Pam whispered to me, as if I needed reminding to be quiet.

Eventually the shouting became crying. "Pam," he moaned, "come on, let me in." A few minutes later he gave up. We heard him walk away, his feet on the worn tiles echoing through the stairwell.

"That was your ex?" I asked, still whispering even though he had left.

"Actually," she said, "he's not really my ex. He's still my boy-friend. He's a cop."

Oh. So there was a cop boyfriend, probably waiting outside the building with a gun, furious and ready to kill the person who'd just had drunken sex with his girlfriend.

"I should call him," she said. She turned on the light and I looked at the postcoital bed. There was blood everywhere.

"What happened? Are you okay?" I asked.

She looked at the sheets. "Oh, sometimes when I have sex I get these burst cysts in my vagina. Or I got my period," she said with disconcerting calm.

There was more blood than I'd ever seen in one place. It looked like a cow had just given birth. There was blood on the sheets. On Pam. On me. I was horrified and oddly proud. I used to be a sober Bible-study teacher, and now I was drunk and covered in blood in a small tenement apartment, while a furious cop waited outside so he could shoot me. I felt like the ghost of Charles Bukowski was in the apartment, sitting in the lone chair and telling me, "Well done."

Pam got on the phone with her boyfriend. "Hey, I'm not home," she said. "Okay, baby. I'm coming over . . . no, don't come here." And she hung up.

I wanted to point out that "I'm not home" and "don't come here" were inconsistent things to say, but I didn't think it was my place.

Pam sat in the chair and looked at me placidly.

"I guess I should go," I said, getting out of bed and pulling on my clothes over my wet, bloody body.

"Walk out by yourself," she instructed me. "If you see him outside, just ignore him." She shook my hand like we were saying goodbye after a business lunch meeting over iced tea and chopped salads. "Nice to see you again, Moby."

"Nice to see you too."

I walked down the fluorescent-lit stairs and out onto Sullivan Street. I looked left and then right: there were no angry cops waiting for me.

I'd already had a full night of drinking, Led Zeppelin covers, and bloody sex, but it was Friday and it was only 2.30 a.m. I bought a beer in a bodega and drank it as I walked to Lit on 2nd Avenue.

Lit was one of the last East Village rock clubs. It amazed me that it hadn't been shut down, as it seemed to be more of a cocaine supermarket than a bar. The only person who didn't do or sell cocaine at Lit was the owner. And me. For as much as I loved alcohol and ecstasy, I'd still never done cocaine.

I went to the downstairs bar and ordered two shots of tequila for myself. I quickly drank both of them and listened to the hipster band playing a Pixies cover. I spotted my friend Fancy in one of the booths, so I ordered two more shots of tequila for myself and walked over to him. Fancy and I had been degenerate drinking buddies for the last decade, but I hadn't seen him much since the success of *Play*. I told Fancy and his friends the story of my one-night stand, including the furious cop boyfriend, but leaving out that I was still covered in drying blood.

I ordered more tequila for myself and danced unsteadily as the band played more Pixies covers. After the fourth or fifth Pixies song in a row, I realized through my drunken miasma that they were, in fact, a Pixies cover band, although they did play a few Breeders songs as well.

At 4 a.m. I saw a few people disappearing through a small, almost hidden black door at the back of the basement. Did Lit have a VIP area I didn't know about? Or maybe a super-exclusive degenerate room for super-exclusive degenerates? I thought of myself as both a VIP and a super-exclusive degenerate, so I stumbled through the room full of coke-addled hipsters and opened the small door. I was excited to have found another belly within the belly of the beast.

I stepped inside a tiny, quiet room, with three people hunched over a table. "Hey!" one of them barked at me. "You can't be in here!"

I was swaying on my feet; at this point I'd had around sixteen drinks. With slurred umbrage, I said, "Don't you know who I am?"

And I stopped cold. I'd never said those words before. And I knew, even through my swaying, drunken fog, that I'd crossed a line. "Don't you know who I am?" was the clarion call of diminished narcissists everywhere. I felt real fear, for I knew that the moment someone has to ask "Don't you know who I am?" is the moment when the tide of fame has turned against them.

A few years earlier I'd been leaving a nightclub that was hosting a

in my dreams i'm dying all the time

Darien, Connecticut, 1966

Norwalk, Connecticut, 1968

Danbury, Connecticut, 1969

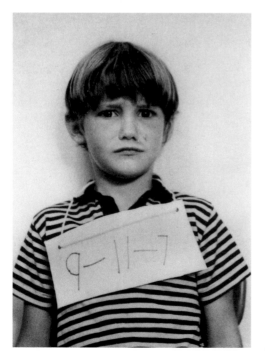

My birthday, Connecticut, 1972

Vatican Commandos (with John Farnsworth), Darien, Connecticut, 1981

AWOL (with Paul Johnson and Andrew DeAraujo), basement, Darien, Connecticut, 1983

Calvin Klein advert, corner of Broadway & Houston, New York City, 1999

Backstage, Texas, 1999

Performing in San Francisco

Self-portrait with some awards, 2002

Performing with The Little Death, New York City, 2006

Disco birthday party, New York City, 2007

El Dorado 'Sky Castle',
2006

The view from one of the five terraces at the El Dorado 'Sky Castle'
apartment, 2006

Acting in the vampire movie
'Suck', Canada, 2008

Working on the album *Wait For Me*, 2008

party for Wyclef Jean, and the singer from a successful 1980s new-wave band was trying to get in. His face was florid with outrage that he was being denied entrance, and he yelled "Don't you know who I am?" at the stoic doorman. I shook my head, sadly, and congratulated myself on the fact that I wasn't a faded celebrity.

But now I had just said those same sad words.

The three people in the quiet room looked up at me nonplussed. "I don't care," one of them said. "This is an office. We're counting credit-card receipts."

39

DARIEN, CONNECTICUT (1979)

I had saved up $70 from doing yardwork for some of our neighbors and bought a used electric guitar and an old Fender amp from the classified ads in the back of the *Stamford Advocate*.

The year before, I'd started taking guitar lessons. Since it was the late 1970s, the apex of the glorious age of guitar gods, my twenty-one-year-old teacher, Chris Risola, wanted me to become the next Steve Howe or Jimi Hendrix. Chris had long black curly hair and taught guitar in his bedroom at his mom's house, next door to the fire station. I took lessons from him because he was a great teacher and I wanted to learn to play guitar, but also because his sister was one of the most beautiful girls I had ever seen and sometimes she would smile at me after my lesson.

I wanted to be a good student, so I practiced every day on my knockoff Les Paul guitar (manufactured in Asia by the Memphis Guitar Company), playing my scales as fast as I could and even trying to learn Van Halen's "Eruption." But I had two dirty secrets that I couldn't share with my teacher. One was that I didn't like the complicated guitar music that he loved so much. I knew that Eddie Van Halen and jazz-fusion solos were technically impressive and very hard to play, but they meant nothing to me emotionally. My second secret was my love for new wave and punk rock. I tried to like the complicated music that Chris loved, but when I heard Gary Numan and the Clash on the radio they excited me in ways that Eddie Van Halen and Larry Carlton simply didn't.

At the end of one of our lessons I'd tested the waters, asking

Chris what he thought of Talking Heads. "Did you see them on *Saturday Night Live?*" he asked, vexed and shaking his curly hair. "That weird dude's 'guitar solo' was just one fucking note!"

So I learned my scales and my transposed versions of jazz standards and Bach cantatas and David Gilmour solos. But all I wanted to do was sit in my room and play new-wave and punk-rock songs.

I had a new friend, Paul, who lived down the street from me. Paul and I were the same age, but he had grown up in England and carried himself like a young Errol Flynn, making him conspicuously out of place in late-1970s suburban Connecticut. One day when I was visiting Paul's house he told me that his older brother Simon had a copy of *Never Mind the Bollocks, Here's the Sex Pistols.* His older brother scared me: he was tall and usually hung out with giant friends who looked like they could effortlessly crush me with their pinkies.

One day I worked up enough courage and asked Paul if he'd ask Simon if I could borrow *Never Mind the Bollocks.* Vinyl was precious, and I'd never heard of anyone loaning anyone else an album, but I was desperate to see what it would be like to have a real punk-rock record in my house. I had my mom's records to listen to – everything from Dvořák to Babatunde Olatunji to CSNY – and my own tiny collection, featuring two David Bowie records, but the only punk music I had was a few songs I'd taped off the radio with my grandfather's old Dictaphone.

Paul went into Simon's room and came back thirty seconds later with *Never Mind the Bollocks.* "Here you go." He handed it to me casually, as if loaning someone a bright-pink-and-green-and-yellow punk-rock LP was the most normal thing in the world.

"Thanks," I said, holding the album like a glowing totem.

I took it home, put it on my mom's turntable, and dropped the needle on "Holidays in the Sun." It was so angry and confident. And fast. I couldn't believe I was playing it on the same stereo my mom used to listen to Dave Brubeck and Taj Mahal. I felt like I was looking at pornography in church. And I loved it.

I listened to the whole Sex Pistols album from start to finish, and then listened to it again. I plugged my $30 guitar into my $40 amp and over the next hour learned to play "God Save the Queen" as best I could. I'd never thought about what I was going to do with the guitar skills I was acquiring. But now I knew: I wanted to start a band.

I wasn't the only one who wanted to be in a band. My mom had met some Connecticut musicians in a band called Shakedown Street, and they'd invited her to play piano with them. She said yes, and told them they could rehearse in our living room. The three musicians – Ron, Ted, and Shaun – showed up late on a Wednesday afternoon with a drum kit, a bass guitar, and a bass amp. "Oh," my mom said to me, "Shaun doesn't have a guitar and an amp. Can he borrow yours?"

I looked at Shaun in his dirty corduroys and faded Jerry Garcia Band T-shirt, and wanting to borrow my amp and my guitar to play old country-rock songs with my mom and two other hippies. I didn't know if he was my mom's friend or if they were dating, but I wanted to say, "No." Just straight-up "No," as in: *No, you cannot take my amp and my guitar, my two most prized possessions in the entire world, and sully them with your greasy pot-smoking hippie fingers*. I wanted to say "No" as loudly and as many times as I could.

But I was a musician, and weren't musicians supposed to be cool and relaxed, even generous? There was no part of me that was actually cool, relaxed, or generous, but I said "Okay" to Shaun and my mom. And then, as a meek codicil, "Just take care of them, okay?"

I had a math test in the morning, so I went to my room to study. I sat down at my plywood desk, opened my textbook to study, and my mom's band practice started. They were playing in the living room, which was right below my bedroom. And even though they were playing Grateful Dead-inspired country rock, they were extremely loud.

My mom had been playing piano since she was five or six years old. She played delicately; I loved listening to her play Bach and Leonard Cohen at the old upright piano her grandmother had given her. But now her unamplified piano was drowned out by Ron the drummer, Ted the bassist, and Shaun the dirty hippie playing my beautiful guitar through my beautiful amp.

I wanted to be cool, but I started panicking. I needed to study for my test. I wasn't a great student, but I did okay and I always did my homework. After the first song I went downstairs. Somehow, in the space of one song the living room had filled with cigarette and marijuana smoke.

"Mom?" I asked, panicking but trying to appear calm. "How long is your band practice going to be?"

"All night, dude," Shaun said, peeling out a subpar Jimi Hendrix guitar lick like he was onstage at Monterey Pop and not standing by some aloe plants in a small suburban living room.

My mom gave Shaun a dirty look and said, "Not too late, Mobes."

I went back upstairs and sat down as they started their second song, which was louder than the first. Shaun's guitar was too loud. No, *my* guitar was too loud. I couldn't study because a smelly hippie was befouling the two loves of my life – my guitar and my amp – with old hippie music that I now hated. Up until that moment I'd thought that Talking Heads and the Sex Pistols could coexist with classic rock, but now I wanted to shave my head and tattoo "I'M A PUNK-ROCKER, FUCK YOU, SHAUN!" on my forehead.

This band of wannabe Jerry Garcias in my living room were the stand-ins for every shitty hippie my mom had ever dated, every entitled stoner who worked in a music store and wouldn't acknowledge me, every motorcycle gang member who'd ever scared me, and every long-haired kid in school who made me feel smaller than I already was. They were the past, and I wanted to destroy them.

Mercifully the song ended abruptly. Once it did, I could hear loud, aggressive banging on our front door. I ran to the top of the stairs and looked down.

One of our neighbors, Bill Sanford, was on our doorstep, livid, drunk, and holding a gun. He started screaming, "You fucking hippies, what are you doing in my neighborhood? It's a Wednesday night, for God's sake!" My panic and rage had apparently all been channeled by our elderly, peaceful neighbor. Bill Sanford, usually found in his backyard wearing old madras shorts and drinking a gin and tonic, had turned into the Monster from the Id in *Forbidden Planet*.

"I'm sorry, Bill," my mom said, trying to placate him.

"I should call the police!" he said, drunkenly waving his gun around.

Shaun stepped forward. "Dude, just relax, okay?"

Bill Sanford, normally sad and quiet, retired after forty years of being an accountant for local florists and hardware stores, was so drunk and full of rage that he made a noise somewhere between an eagle and a dachshund. Unable to make real words, he bark-squawked at Shaun and my mom, slammed the door, and stormed off.

I went back to my room and opened my math book. I wasn't happy that our drunk neighbor had shown up waving a gun. But at least now it was quiet.

40

UPSTATE NEW YORK (2005)

I was upstate at my gated country estate, trying to meditate. It was a cold Friday afternoon in January, and I was expecting twenty or thirty friends to come up for the weekend. After they arrived we'd make dinner, play some games, start drinking, take drugs, dance in the disco, end up in the spa around 3 a.m., and then hopefully I'd wind up in bed with someone I'd never met before.

I'd bought the estate in 2002, after seeing it advertised in the back of the *New York Times Magazine*. The ad was simple but compelling: "12,000 sq. ft. house w/ 2 guest houses, 60 acres, 70 minutes from Manhattan. $1,250,000." The house was in terrible shape when I bought it, but after eighteen months and over a million dollars in renovations I had a private, gated, sixty-acre compound, tailor-made for huge, decadent parties.

The main house was a five-level chalet with ten bedrooms. It had a disco, a spa with an eight-person jacuzzi, an elevator, and as it was completely surrounded by hundreds of acres of protected woods and forest, no neighbors. Not having neighbors was important, as I'd installed a huge sound system in the disco, and it was very loud. But I also wanted as much privacy as possible, because a lot of what happened at the parties involved celebrities and illegal drugs. To that end I installed a metal security gate at the bottom of the half-mile-long driveway to prevent surprise visits from the police.

The property was serving its purpose as a debauched party compound, but I hadn't bought it just to be a degenerate. I believed that I had depth and spirituality, and I thought that the estate's sylvan isolation would help foster those qualities. Meditation seemed like it should be part of a spiritual person's life, and I'd been reading more and more articles in the Sunday *Times* about the benefits of meditation. My mom had tried to teach me to meditate when I was six years old, even though I had always quit after a few minutes so I could go play with my Hot Wheels. But today I was going to start my meditation practice, as I was pretty sure I knew the fundamentals: you said "Om" to yourself, and then after a few minutes found enlightenment as the divine secrets of the universe revealed themselves.

I sat in a vintage Eames chair in my bedroom, positioned next to a long, snow-covered balcony. My house was at the highest point in Putnam County: looking out the wall of windows I could see for fifty miles, all of it white and pristine and beautiful. If ever there was a perfect place to meditate, this was it. I closed my eyes and started saying "Om."

After thirty seconds of meditation I started to worry that my assistant hadn't ordered enough alcohol for the weekend. Fabienne's usual job was to organize after-show parties on tour, but now that I was taking a short break from touring, her main responsibilities were arranging limos to take me to parties in New York and making sure that my houses were stocked with alcohol. I said "Om" a few more times and then worried: Did we have enough vodka? Would anyone bring ecstasy?

I decided that I would meditate better if first I made sure we had enough liquor. I walked downstairs and stepped into the liquor pantry. The original owner had built it as a walk-in pantry for food, but I thought it made more sense to stock it with alcohol, so I moved my organic spaghetti, oatmeal, and raisins to cupboards under the sink. I had eight cases of Stolichnaya vodka, ten cases of red wine, ten cases of white wine, ten cases of Veuve Clicquot champagne, sixteen cases of beer, eight cases of club soda, and two cases of tonic water. It was enough alcohol to kill an army, so we were good. I went back upstairs and sat down in the Eames chair. Now that I knew we had enough alcohol, I could calmly meditate.

I said "Om."

Was the hot tub hot enough? I walked downstairs and checked on the spa, lined with white tiles and cedar panels. I'd set the hot tub to 104 degrees, and the LED readout said "104." People came to my country estate expecting to be naked in the jacuzzi, so now I was sure it was working and that they wouldn't be disappointed.

I wanted to start meditating again, but I realized that first I needed to check my email to make sure all my guests were coming. I opened my laptop on the dining table I had bought from a failed dot-com. It was twenty-two feet long and made from a single piece of rosewood. Even though the dot-com had spent $75,000 on this massive table, I was able to buy it for my new house for only $10,000.

I had lots of emails from people saying they were coming up from the city, bringing vodka and drugs and food and friends. Okay, now that everything was set for the weekend – alcohol, drugs, friends, hot-tub temperature – I could meditate.

I closed my laptop and returned to my master bedroom, once again taking in the fireplace, the skylights, and the wraparound balcony. My 1,500-square-foot bedroom suite was bigger than the house my mom and I had lived in when I was in high school. And this sixty-acre compound was bigger than my entire neighborhood when I was growing up. A few weeks ago some friends and I had been walking around the woods outside the house and I'd said, with no ironic intent, "I've never seen this part of my property before."

I had money, status, and huge swaths of pristine land. But the increasingly noisy and demanding truth was that unless I was drunk or having sex with a stranger, I wasn't happy. And although I had decided that I was a spiritual person, I never actually did anything spiritual. I never helped anyone else or put other people's needs before my own. But I knew I was spiritual. I had to be. Otherwise I was just another entitled, narcissistic public figure.

I closed my eyes once more. If I could meditate, that would prove I was a spiritual person. And maybe I'd find the happiness that was eluding me. I said, "Om."

I wanted a sandwich. And I was restless. Maybe I'd go for a pre-enlightenment walk around my property and have a sandwich. And then, finally, I'd be ready to meditate.

I put on my boots and my gloves and my heavy coat and my hat and my scarf and stepped outside. Upstate New York in the winter is quiet (especially when you have no neighbors) and profoundly cold. Tonight my friends and I would fill the quiet and cold with alcohol and drugs and Guns N' Roses and sex. At some point, when we were perfectly drunk and high, we would stand on the balcony at the top of my five-level manor house and stare up at the dark sky. We'd see our breath in the night air and the thousands of stars far above our heads. And we'd yell at the emptiness. The wind would blow and the cold would slap our faces and we'd hurry back inside, shivering and congratulating ourselves on being brave enough to drunkenly yell at the void.

I stepped off the front porch and headed to the northeastern part of my property. My contractor had told me I had streams there, and I'd never seen them. After twenty minutes of crunching through the thick frozen snow, I came upon a dead animal. It was big, so I assumed it was a deer, but its body was so mangled I couldn't be sure. Its head was gone and most of its skin was flayed, revealing viscera and muscles that were frozen and waxy. Something had destroyed this animal, but what? A hunter? A mountain lion?

I looked around, panicking and hearing only my fast breathing. I wanted to leave this dead, skinless creature and these barren woods and go back to my house – which was now so far away that I couldn't see it. The emptiness of the woods had looked safe and pastoral through my bedroom windows, but now it felt desolate and filled with death.

in my dreams i'm dying all the time

I hurried back up the hillside, crushing the hard snow under my feet. Had the dead thing in the woods tried to run away from whatever had killed it? What had it thought as it died? What assumptions about its life had been torn from it as it took its last breath? I ran faster, and after ten minutes I got back to the driveway. In the cold shadow of my hulking house I felt calmer.

For most of my life I'd assumed that the universe was empty or supportive. But maybe it was neither. I thought of the Nietzsche quote: "If you gaze too long into the abyss, the abyss will gaze into you." Maybe the emptiness wasn't placid. Maybe the universe had no interest in supporting me.

I went upstairs to the master bathroom, took off my winter clothes, and turned on both of the ceiling-mounted Swiss rain-shower heads in my giant glass shower stall. I felt the torrents of hot water on my skin, while I looked outside through the ceiling-to-floor windows. This felt right. The malevolent cold was outside, and I was conquering the elements by being inside. An inch away was an environment that ripped the skin from animals and cared nothing for what I loved. But I was warm and naked and smug.

Tonight I would fill myself with vodka and spaghetti. I would laugh and yell at the empty sky and find someone to have sex with, while the void waited as it always had, patiently.

41

NORWALK, CONNECTICUT (1980)

The week before high school started I hit the motherlode at the Norwalk Salvation Army. I was shopping for clothes with my mom and I found an almost-new Fred Perry shirt. I fingered the small embroidered laurel-wreath logo, making sure it was real.

I owned two other polo shirts: my grandparents had given me one with a little trophy over the left breast, and I had found one at Goodwill with a little J. C. Penney fox on it. Even though I was a fledgling punk-rocker, it was still one of my dreams to own a new Izod shirt, with the proud little alligator taking up residence over my heart. I also dreamed of having a new pair of Levi's and an actual pair of Adidas sneakers. They didn't have to be new, so long as I could go to school and not be ashamed of my clothes.

"Mom, can I get this?" I asked, holding up the Fred Perry shirt. She was looking through the rack of used sweaters and had found two that she liked, which were draped over her left arm. One was brown with gold threads and the other was dark green.

"How much is it?"

I looked at the tag. "$1.50."

She frowned. "That's kind of a lot for a shirt. But you really like it?"

"I do," I said, nervous and hopeful. I really wanted this shirt.

"Okay, let's get it."

At the end of the summer I took the train to New York City with my friends Jim and Dave to see Talking Heads in Central Park. I was fourteen and had never been in the city without my mom

226   in my dreams i'm dying all the time

or my grandfather. We walked from Grand Central Station to the skating rink in Central Park and stood in line with over a thousand new-wavers and punk-rockers, staring at the beautiful women with pink hair and the stratospherically cool men with leopard-print pants.

We had expected to see the four members of Talking Heads onstage, but they brought an extra bass player, some percussionists, and African American backing singers. Somewhere around the moment the band played "Life During Wartime," I realized that we had been converted: we were jumping up and down and sweating, part of the ecstatic, surging crowd of new-wavers.

The night before high school started Jim called me up and told me he was going to cut his hair and wear the $5 Talking Heads shirt he'd bought after the show. I assumed he was trying to sound tough, but after first period I saw him walking in the hallway, his hair clipped short, proudly wearing a black shirt emblazoned with electric blue letters that spelled "TALKING HEADS." I was in awe, and chastened: I had come to school trying to fit in with my Fred Perry polo shirt and longish late-1970s suburban hair. I was a coward.

By lunchtime Jim had been called "freak" and "homo," and had been pushed into the lockers by the preppy jocks. I wondered when and if I'd be courageous enough to cut my hair and wear a black T-shirt to school.

Ever since I'd played along to "God Save the Queen" in my living room I'd wanted to start a punk-rock band so I could play covers of the Clash, the Sex Pistols, and Richard Hell and the Voidoids. If Jim could cut his hair, I reasoned, I could start a band. I asked Jim to be the singer. Excited, he agreed immediately.

I knew only one other musician: a drummer named Chip, whose family lived on a cul-de-sac by Long Island Sound. He and his family were Darien middle class, meaning they belonged to one of the less expensive country clubs. I sat next to Chip in my third-period history class, and on the second day of school I asked him if he had a drum set. He said yes, he did.

Then I asked the bigger question, trying to be as relaxed and conversational as possible: "Do you like new wave?"

"Like Talking Heads?" he said. "Yeah, it's alright."

That was better than I'd hoped for. "Alright" was more encouraging than what the other kids in high school had to say about new-wave and punk-rock bands. So I went in for the kill: "Do you want to start a band?"

"Sure," he said, as casually as if I'd asked to borrow a pencil.

I met Jim in the cafeteria for lunch and excitedly told him we had a drummer. He had news too: "Some guy in my English class had 'The Clash' written on his notebook," he said breathlessly. It seemed like too much to ask for, that Darien High School might contain one more person who liked new wave and punk rock.

The next day Jim talked to the kid with "The Clash" scrawled on his notebook and found out five things, four of which were remarkable:

1. His name was John.

2. He liked the Clash and Gary Numan and was, in fact, a new-waver.

3. He'd lived in London with his parents and owned records that he'd bought in England.

4. He was sixteen and had a driver's license.

5. He not only knew how to play guitar, he owned a guitar and amp.

Jim invited John, Chip, and me over to his house after school so we could all meet. John was a year older than the rest of us, but with his brown hair and small frame he looked like he could be my cousin. We ate cookies and watched TV and talked about bands.

"Do you like the B-52's?" I asked John.

"Do you like Devo?" Jim asked John.

"Have you heard the Sex Pistols?" Chip asked John.

in my dreams i'm dying all the time

He answered "Yes" to all our questions, then stumped us with a question of his own: "Have you listened to WNYU?"

We hadn't. "What's that?" I asked.

"It's 89.1 and they have the *New Afternoon Show*, every day from three to six, and all they play is new wave. They even have a punk-rock show called *Noise the Show* on Tuesday nights."

I wanted to run home, lock myself in my room, and glue my face to my radio. The next day after school I went straight home and sat in front of the radio from 3 p.m. to 6 p.m., taping everything onto some Radio Shack cassettes I'd stolen from the Darien High School language lab. In those three hours my world expanded like an unfolding gas-station map: for the first time I heard the Damned, Joy Division, Bauhaus, Bad Brains, the Misfits, and Depeche Mode.

A week later it was my birthday. At my request, my family (my mom, my grandmother, my aunts and uncles) got me the first B-52's album, the first Gang of Four album, and the first Madness album. So when I woke up on the morning of September 11, 1980, I had a fledgling new-wave record collection: three new albums, two David Bowie albums, and a growing pile of stolen thirty-minute cassettes full of music that I'd taped off WNYU.

A few days after that Jim, Chip, and I asked John if he wanted to be in a band with us. He agreed almost before we could finish asking.

Jim's TV room had become our de facto clubhouse, so over cookies and orange juice we compiled a list of possible band names, while an episode of *Gilligan's Island* played in the background:

– The Banned

– UXB

– Dicky Hell and the Redbeats

– SS and the Daryans (we had a particular nemesis at school named Steve Smith: he was tall and blond and looked like a Nazi, so we thought it would be funny to name our band after him)

– The Darien Defamation League

We settled on UXB. We'd learned from PBS that it meant "un-exploded bomb," and it sounded cool and British. I'd started writing punk-rock songs for us to play, and one of them was called "Danger! There's a UXB," with the refrain:

Danger! There's a UXB!
It's underground where no one can see

I was cautiously proud of my first attempt at punk-rock songwriting.

Jim's parents said we could rehearse in their basement, so after school on September 23, 1980, we had our first band practice. We didn't have much equipment: Chip's drum kit, my guitar and amp, John's guitar and amp, and an Audio-Visual Club microphone that Jim had stolen and plugged into his stereo. Once all our equipment was turned on and quietly humming, we looked at each other like bashful new-wave Vestal Virgins, as none of us had played music with other people before.

"Should we play a Sex Pistols song?" Chip asked. The Sex Pistols were now his favorite band. He clicked his drumsticks together four times and we played "God Save the Queen."

The drums were louder than the guitars. We could barely hear the vocals. But it was perfect. Terrible. Perfect. We finished, bursting with shy excitement, unable to meet each other's eyes. "Let's play it again?" Jim asked. So we did. And again.

We learned four songs that day: "God Save the Queen," "I'm So Bored with the USA," "Anarchy in the U.K.," and a Voidoids song, "Love Comes in Spurts." I wanted us to play some of my original songs, but I wasn't brave enough to let anyone else hear what I had written.

None of us played sports or had girlfriends, so we practiced at Jim's house as often as his mom would let us. After a month we had an official band meeting in Jim's kitchen: over Nutter Butter cookies and chocolate milk we decided it was time for our first show.

in my dreams i'm dying all the time

John lived in an eight-bedroom colonial house by the New Canaan border, and next to it was a one-acre field where horses sometimes grazed in the summer. In October we figured that there wouldn't be any horses around, so we agreed that our first show would be in the field on Sunday.

At noon on Sunday we packed up our equipment in the back of John's mom's station wagon. We hit the road, driving five miles from Jim's house near the beach to John's house in northern Darien. I looked out the window as we passed Post Corner Pizza, pretending I was an old, jaded musician who'd toured so much that driving two amps, a stereo, and a stolen microphone in the back of a paneled station wagon was a wistful, gentle reverie.

At John's house we stretched an extension cord from his garage to the middle of the empty field, and arranged our drums and amps in the hay. Once our gear was set up I showed the other band members the shirt I'd made for our first show. After two weeks as UXB we'd changed our name to Vatican Commandos because we thought it was funny. So the night before our first show I'd taken my Fred Perry shirt and written "VATICAN COMMANDOS" on the back with a red Magic Marker. Jim, Chip, and John weren't impressed, until I told them the marker I used was permanent.

We wanted an audience for our first show, so we'd invited ten of the computer and art nerds we knew at Darien High School. By 3 p.m. no one had shown up, so we played frisbee. By 4 p.m. no one had shown up and the sun was starting to go down, so I asked, "Well, should we just play?"

We started with "God Save the Queen," and the hair on the back of my neck stood up. I was playing my first live show and it didn't sound terrible. We ran through our handful of songs, while Sparky, John's little terrier, sat in the field where the audience was supposed to be. When we played "Love Comes in Spurts," I even tried jumping around while playing the guitar, until I felt self-conscious and stopped.

norwalk, connecticut (1980)   231

After playing our cover songs we ended with "Space Jam," which was just us banging on our equipment and making as much noise as possible, while Jim yelled into the microphone. It was too much for Sparky, who left and walked back to the house.

As we were loading the equipment back into the station wagon, Chip said, "Our first show, to an audience of a dog."

"A dog who left during the last song," Jim pointed out.

But we were in a band. And we'd played a concert, even if it was in a horse field with a human audience of no one.

42

LONDON, ENGLAND (2005)

"Every day I want to kill myself."

I was peeing next to one of the heads of EMI. His company had just bought Mute, my European record label since 1992, but this was the first time I'd heard him speak. I looked at him to see if he had anything to add to what he'd just said.

He had silver hair, he was wearing an expensive lavender suit with sweat stains in the armpits, and he was drunk. I was wearing jeans, a T-shirt, and a hoodie, and I was just as drunk. He shook his head sadly, zipped up his fly, and said, "Okay, back to the party."

EMI were throwing me a release party for my album *Hotel* at a private club in London. The club, paneled in dark wood, felt like a place where prime ministers met British movie stars and aristocrats for cheese and cocktails. EMI were very happy with me and my new album, as *Hotel* had a huge single, "Lift Me Up," and the album was the number-one seller in Europe.

But not in America. In the US the album had failed before it was even released. The *New York Times* write-up, which had sat stubbornly on their home page for the last six days, was the worst review I'd ever received. Whoever the journalist was hated the album, and me, so much that he'd called the album "the end of music." I tried to focus on the fact that *Hotel* and "Lift Me Up" were doing well in Europe, but I couldn't stop masochistically visiting the *New York Times* website and clicking on the scathing review. It would have been one thing to be viciously attacked in a small music magazine, but knowing that this review was in the *Times* made me want to find the journalist and either beg him to love me or throw him off the roof of a building.

Before working on *Hotel* I'd recorded and mixed all my albums in my tiny bedroom studio. But I was now a successful adult musician, so I'd decided it was time to join the ranks of the real rock stars who made professional albums with professional engineers in big studios. To that end I'd spent tens of thousands of dollars in various top-of-the-line New York City studios, recording, rerecording, and mixing the album.

After it was mixed I realized that the album did have an expensive sheen of professionalism. The only problem was that it didn't resonate with me emotionally, whereas all my previous records did. I had worked hard on crafting and recording all the songs on *Hotel*, but I really loved only one of them: "Slipping Away," a sad, vulnerable song tucked away near the end of the album.

I had a year-long tour planned, starting in Europe and going to North America, Asia, South America, and then back to Europe. The first leg of European arenas was already sold out, but the US tour was going to be a struggle. I was scheduled to play much smaller venues than I had on the previous tour, and even these scaled-down shows weren't selling very well. All evidence suggested that in the States my fame wasn't just waning, it was plummeting. And I was terrified.

I needed my fame to stay exactly as it had been at its height in 2000. When I walked out of my front door on Mott Street I wanted to hear people talking about me. When I entered a party I wanted everyone to look at me.

Once I had loved visiting the magazine store at the corner of Prince and Sullivan to look for mentions of me on glossy full-color pages, but now when I did my daily Google search of my name I was furious. The journalists and the radio programmers and the hipsters who maligned or ignored me didn't know what was at stake. They didn't realize that the consequence of their disdain was that I was

in my dreams i'm dying all the time

becoming less famous. It would take such a small effort on their part to write good articles about me, to play me on their radio stations, to invite me to their parties. All I needed in order to be happy was for them to love and support me, forever.

I left the bathroom in the private club's basement and walked back upstairs to rejoin the party. David Munns, one of the EMI label bosses, came over and clapped me on the shoulder. David scared me a bit: he seemed like a handsome pirate who could become someone's worst enemy in an instant. But for now I was making money for EMI, and he was being nice to me.

"Good first week!" he boomed.

"Yeah, not in America," I shrugged.

"Eh, fuck 'em," he said, and walked away.

I wanted to stay at the party, drink some more, and find someone to go home with. But I was panicking. Was the *New York Times* review accurate? Had I released a bad record? I needed to listen to *Hotel* again and figure out if the bad reviews were right. I snuck out one of the side doors and got in the limo that was waiting for me. It took me back to the Landmark hotel, where I was staying in the presidential suite.

I'd first stayed in the Landmark in 1992, with my former best friend Paul. At the time I'd never stayed in a nicer hotel. It was huge and elegant, with soft carpeting and gray-veined marble bathrooms. Paul and I had jumped in the pool and run down the hallways and watched *Star Trek* reruns and eaten vegan pasties we bought in Covent Garden. I sent my mom a postcard with a picture of the hotel, writing, "This place is amazing!"

And now my mom was dead and Paul and I hadn't spoken since 1999.

A few months ago I'd had a falling-out with Damian, my other best friend. He'd accused me of being a selfish, narcissistic alcoholic; in turn, I'd accused him of being a misanthropic shut-in. We were both right, but the argument had been fierce enough and vitriolic enough that he and I were now ex-friends.

"You better be nice to me," my old friend Lee said, after I told him about my falling-out with Damian. "I'm the only friend you have left." I wanted to disagree with him, but he was right. I had a constant gaggle of people to get drunk with, but no real friends.

Back in my suite at the Landmark I put on my headphones and went for a walk up and down the carpeted hallways of the hotel, listening to my new album. In terms of recording, mixing, and engineering, *Hotel* was impeccable. But during the third song, "Beautiful," I knew that a lot of the bad reviews were right: it was missing something. I'd traded my battered little bedroom studio for expensive rooms filled with the best equipment on the planet, and the result was a compromised album. It had a few moments of beauty, but I didn't love it.

I kept listening, and my panic skyrocketed. I realized I'd made a mistake in releasing *Hotel*. A mistake that had now been shipped around the world for millions of people to experience firsthand. I wanted to buy all of the millions of CDs that had been shipped, bury them in Nevada, and rerecord all the songs on the cheap equipment in my little studio on Mott Street.

Suddenly I needed to drink more and be around people, to be reassured that I still mattered and that things weren't actually falling apart. I got back in my limo and returned to the private club. The party was still going strong, with nobody aware that the guest of honor had left to spend quality time with his shortcomings. The DJ was playing a Robbie Williams remix, and the record executives and minor British celebrities were having loud, cocaine-fueled conversations. I went to the bar and ordered a vodka and soda.

The executive who'd told me "Every day I want to kill myself" in the toilets was holding himself up by the vintage beer taps. His eyes were even more unfocused; he'd had more time to drink himself into near-oblivion. "You see all this?" he barked at me. "You see all this?" he repeated, gesturing at the room full of loud drunks. "This is all shit!" He tried to spit, but his saliva didn't get far – it just dribbled onto the front of his Armani shirt.

He leaned in close to me and poked me in the chest. "But what you do is important. You make art. That is what is precious. Not this." We looked at each other for a long moment. "Fuck this," he said, stumbling off, leaving me holding my drink. He was right, but I didn't want him to be. I wanted uncompromised art, but also unvarnished fame.

I finished my drink and walked into the scrum of the party, looking for a record-company executive to tell me once again how well *Hotel* was selling.

43

STAMFORD, CONNECTICUT (1982)

I finally owned a drum machine and a synthesizer. My mom had saved up and bought me a $75 Mattel Synsonics drum machine for Christmas. I was mildly troubled that it was a drum machine made by the same company responsible for Barbie dolls and Hot Wheels cars, but it was still a drum machine. And apart from a used Nikon F camera my uncle Joseph had given me the year before, it was the nicest present I'd ever been given.

Our Christmases had a structure. My family, including my various aunts and uncles, would spend Christmas Eve at my grandmother's house. On Christmas morning we woke up early and opened the small presents in our stockings. Then we had breakfast at my grandmother's dining-room table. Afterward, still in pajamas and nightgowns, we rushed back to the living room to open the big presents.

Normally Christmas morning was a noisy free-for-all, but when my mom handed me a surprisingly small and lightweight box wrapped in green and red paper, my aunts and uncles and grandmother all quieted down and watched me, smiling. I carefully peeled back the Christmas wrapping paper, trying not to tear it; my grandmother remembered the Great Depression and insisted on saving and reusing wrapping paper. When I saw the words "drum machine" on the box inside, my eyes lit up and I hugged my mom, who had a wide smile and a lit cigarette.

When I'd asked for a drum machine for Christmas my family had been confused – none of them knew what a drum machine was.

in my dreams i'm dying all the time

But I'd noticed that a lot of my musical heroes who'd started off as punk-rockers, like New Order and Killing Joke, were now using synthesizers and drum machines, and I wanted to join them.

I wanted to start recording with my new drum machine right away, but we didn't get home from my grandmother's until 10.30 p.m. on Christmas night. So I woke up early on December 26, went to the basement, and set everything up. In addition to the brand-new Synsonics drum machine, I had my guitar, a delay pedal, a pair of headphones, a Korg M500 Micro-Preset synthesizer I'd bought at a tag sale for $20, and a microphone I'd kind of taken from the language lab at Darien High School. I'd also borrowed a new four-track cassette recorder and some audio cables from the AV department at Darien High School. I'd considered stealing the four-track recorder, but stealing was unethical. Also, the four-track recorder was one of the nicest things in the AV department, and they might actually miss it if it was gone.

I put a cassette in the four-track recorder and started reading the instruction manual. I'd never recorded my own music before, but it looked pretty straightforward. I plugged the drum machine into input 1. I plugged the Korg synthesizer into input 2. I plugged my guitar into input 3. And into input 4 I plugged the stolen, or possibly borrowed, microphone. I turned on the synth and the drum machine and took a step back to survey my achievement: I had turned our moldy basement into a tiny electronic music studio.

I'd started watching *Star Trek* with my grandparents when I was four years old, in the TV room at their colonial house. At first I didn't know it was science fiction, as we'd watched the moon landing on the same TV. I thought *Star Trek* was as real as the moon landing, or at the very least a fiction based on modern reality. NASA showed us what the outside of spaceships looked like, and I assumed *Star Trek* showed us what the inside looked like.

I enjoyed the aliens and the space battles on *Star Trek*, but my favorite thing about it was Mr. Spock and his bank of scientific equipment: light-emitting diodes, oscillators, and plastic buttons that did important space things. A few years later, when I was in elementary school, adults sometimes asked me what I wanted to be when I grew up. I would answer, without hesitation, "A scientist." Because in my mind scientists were like Mr. Spock, working with important buttons in clean environments in outer space.

Our basement wasn't in outer space, or even clean. There was mold and water in the corners, along with a lopsided pile of damp brown boxes filled with old magazines. But in front of me was technology, with glowing red lights and diodes. Even if I hadn't been allowed to touch my drum machine and the four-track recorder, I would still have been happy: they were clean and beautiful.

I took a breath and pressed one of the gray rubber buttons on the drum machine. It made a sound that resembled a cereal box being hit by a spatula. But it was a sound, and it was electronic.

I'd been playing guitar for years, but I was growing increasingly frustrated that I could never get a guitar to not sound like a guitar. Guitars were great, but they weren't drums. They weren't synthesizers. They weren't drum machines. I wanted instruments that would let me make sounds that didn't exist in the real world.

I programmed a simple drum pattern on the Mattel drum machine and hit "Record" on the Tascam four-track. After two minutes I rewound the tape and played it back. It had worked – I'd really recorded a drum machine. My scalp tingled as I realized that I was actually making electronic music. Up until this moment I'd only been able to listen to Kraftwerk, New Order, Depeche Mode, and Heaven 17, and dream cluelessly about how they made electronic music. And now, in our dank basement, with my Mattel drum machine, I'd joined their ranks.

My analog Korg keyboard played only one note at a time, which was why it had been so cheap. I hit "Record" on the four-track and played a simple synth bassline over the simple drum-machine pattern I'd already recorded. And like magic, it worked.

I plugged my guitar into my pedal, an analog delay pedal I'd bought used with $25 my grandparents had given me for my birthday last September, and recorded New Order-style guitar parts over the Mattel drums and the Korg synth bass. I was one person, but in just a few minutes I had recorded a song by myself.

Now it was time to sing something. The microphone was plugged into the four-track, but for some reason no sound was coming through. I panicked briefly, but then I looked at the manual and figured it out: to record a microphone I had to set the input to "Mic." I was a bit chastened, as I probably should have been able to figure that out on my own. But it was my first time recording music and now I knew.

I hit "Record" and did my best to sound like Ian Curtis or Ian McCulloch as I sang over the track I'd just recorded. I hadn't written any lyrics down beforehand, so I just imitated my heroes and sang sad words about losing love and being alone.

I played back all four tracks of audio and saw that there were three rubber knobs that changed the sound. I knew what "Bass" and "Treble" were, but I didn't know what "Pan" did. I turned the "Pan" knob and the sound went toward my left ear. I turned it in the other direction and it went toward my right ear. I grinned – now I knew what "Pan" was. Maybe it was short for "Panorama" or something technical and obscure that I couldn't figure out.

I played around with the bass and treble and listened back to what I'd recorded. It was boxy and flat and thin, but remarkable – because I'd been able to record it all myself. I loved being in a band and playing with other musicians, but other musicians weren't always there. And no matter how good they were, other musicians always sounded like other musicians, not perfect synth robots. I realized that as long as I had a little studio like this, I could work on music by myself at any time. And as long as I had synthesizers and drum machines, I could make sounds that were more than just guitars, basses, and drums.

stamford, connecticut (1982)   241

The two-minute track ended. I rewound the tape. On the other side of the wooden stairs the 1940s boiler was humming. Our cat Tucker was sitting and watching me quizzically. I heard water run through the pipes, meaning my mom was upstairs in the bathroom, or maybe filling up her percolator to make coffee.

Almost everything in the basement – the moldy cardboard boxes, the wooden shelves, the old cans of paint – was old and smelled like mildew. But the clean equipment had the aroma of new plastic and warm electronics and science fiction. I looked at Tucker and hit "Play."

44

ST. PETERSBURG, RUSSIA (2005)

At midnight in St. Petersburg I pulled the thick curtains of my hotel room closed, blotting out the late-night sun, and was about to get a restorative night's sleep when my phone rang.

"Moby! It's Johnny Knoxville!"

A voice in the background: "And Steve-O!"

"We're in the lobby!"

Steve-O was from Darien (along with Gus Van Sant, Robert Downey Jr., Chloë Sevigny, Anne Coulter, Topher Grace, and Kate Bosworth) and also a vegan. I knew him a bit from animal-rights events, where we'd reminisce about teachers we'd both had at Darien High School.

I had wanted a quiet night in, but I put on my clothes and went down to the hotel lobby, where Johnny and Steve-O and the entire *Jackass* crew were waiting for me. *Jackass* had become a hugely successful American franchise, based around kids from the underground skateboarding world doing their best to hurt and degrade themselves on camera. I had no idea why they were in Russia, or why they'd called me, but I loved being around the chaos that followed them wherever they went.

We started drinking in the ornate lobby, next to framed photos of George W. Bush and other heads of state who'd stayed in the hotel, then went to a few techno clubs. I blacked out around 5 a.m., after fifteen or twenty vodka shots, but not before seeing Steve-O force himself into a dance contest where he was the only person onstage not wearing pants.

After thirty or forty minutes of post-*Jackass* sleep in my hotel room I went to the airport and flew to Moscow to play a show for fifteen thousand people in a hockey arena. The show was good, even though I needed three shots of espresso to make it onto the stage.

Backstage after the show I met a group of five people: very tall, very stylish, possibly involved in organized crime, and very Russian. They wanted to take me to the best club in Moscow; as I'd had only an hour or so of sleep in the last thirty-six hours, I was in favor of that idea. I'd battled insomnia for decades, and I found sometimes the best way to handle sleeplessness was to drink vodka and coffee until alcohol, caffeine, and exhaustion created a Hunter S. Thompson level of psychosis.

We glided through the city in a brand-new black bulletproof Mercedes limo. When we arrived the club promoter met me at the car, gave me a glass of vodka, and walked me inside, guiding me by the elbow to have an audience with a woman he told me was Vladimir Putin's daughter.

The club wasn't huge, but every surface was as new and shiny as an arms dealer's Miami penthouse. The promoter led me to a black leather couch, where I sat down and shook hands with a lovely and shy young woman who looked like a blonde grad student at Princeton. I knew that her father, Vladimir Putin, the president of Russia, was ex-KGB, and since I didn't want to end up dead or in prison, I resolved to be on my best behavior.

"Moby," she said loudly, in almost unaccented English, "it's a pleasure to meet you." She told me that she liked my music, asked how I liked Russia, and then listened politely as I drunkenly told her that I loved nineteenth-century Russian literature and considered Leo Tolstoy to be one of the patron saints of veganism. She kept smiling and nodding, but I didn't know if she could hear me over the blaring Top 40 techno.

In my loudest voice I tried to tell her my half-baked theories

in my dreams i'm dying all the time

about Russia: that it was neither Western nor Eastern but simply Russian, and that even after reading Dostoyevsky and Pushkin no Westerner could ever fully understand Mother Russia. As we were talking – or, rather, as I was yelling – a tall blonde woman came and stood in front of me.

"You are Moby?" she yelled.

"Yes," I said.

"I want you sign my pussy," she shouted, and undid her gold jumpsuit, suddenly standing naked in front of me, with her jumpsuit bunched around her ankles.

"Excuse me," Putin's daughter said, hurriedly getting up and leaving with her security detail.

"Do you have a pen?" I asked the naked lady standing in front of me.

She smiled and presented me with a Sharpie.

"They have Sharpies in Russia?" I asked.

"*Da!*" she said, her eyes gleaming like a cat about to kill a garden mole.

"I've never signed a pussy before," I said, unsure of how this was going to work. I'd signed arms, legs, stomachs, breasts, necks, foreheads, hands, feet, drum machines, Bibles, shoes, jackets, cars, and copies of *Moby-Dick*, but never the area around someone's genitals. I hoped that she hadn't been perspiring too much: Sharpies didn't work well on sweaty skin.

"I told your security that I was prostitute," she yelled over a Tiësto remix of "We Are All Made of Stars." "But," she said as if addressing a dim student, "I'm not prostitute!"

I drew a cartoon character just to the right of her labia and then signed my name. "There," I said, happy that the Sharpie had worked so well on her skin.

She pulled up her jumpsuit, sat next to me, and poured us both big glasses of vodka. I said, "*Do svidaniya.*"

She laughed. "*Do svidaniya!* Is like you're Russian!"

st. petersburg, russia (2005)   245

Do svidaniya and *spasibo* were the only Russian words I knew, so when I was in Russia I used them a lot.

"Look!" She gestured broadly at the club. "Everyone is watching!"

She was right. I had assumed they'd been surreptitiously looking at Putin's daughter, but now almost everyone in the club was openly staring at us.

"I like it," she said, pouring us more vodka. "*Do svidaniya!*" she said, and we drank.

She leaned over so she could speak directly into my ear. "This autogram on my pussy will make my boyfriend so much jealous," she said.

"Really?"

"But you know what will make him such more jealous?"

"What?"

She looked at me seriously. "When you fuck me."

I'd been propositioned before, but never so blatantly – with the exception of one night in Finland, when a tattooed and pierced goth woman had walked up to me and asked, "Do you like Nine Inch Nails? 'Cause I want to fuck you like an animal." I thought of myself as a libertine, but being in the presence of true degenerates sometimes made me feel like a nervous eight-year-old.

"You have hotel?" she asked casually, pouring herself another drink.

"*Da,*" I said, smiling awkwardly.

She finished her drink in one swallow, took my hand, and barked some Russian orders at the security guards standing around us. They pushed people out of the way and walked us through the club to the exit. A few people yelled "Moby!" but the guards ignored them. There was no civility in the way the phalanx of security pushed through the club, but even though this was an exclusive club, the well-dressed crowd seemed untroubled by this show of force.

Thirty seconds later we were in the back of another bulletproof Mercedes limousine – mine, I assumed. "Which is yours hotel?" she

246   in my dreams i'm dying all the time

asked loudly, even though we were now in a soundproofed German limo. I told her, and she issued some Russian commands to the driver and security guard sitting in the front. As we headed out, the car behind us turned on flashing lights and a siren.

"Police?" I asked.

"You are VIP," she said casually, pronouncing it "vipp," as if it were a monosyllabic noun and not an acronym. She snapped another order to the driver and the limo filled with music: Billie Holiday.

"Oh, what's your name?" I asked.

She considered the question, listening to the music. "I'm Billie," she decided. "Do you want cocaine?"

"No, thank you," I said, looking through the tinted windows as we sped past Russian pharmacies and supermarkets, closed because it was 5 a.m., but glowing in the light from the unsetting sun. I'd still never done cocaine, and I didn't think that snorting white powder that had traveled eight thousand miles from South America to Moscow was the best way to be introduced to the drug.

She cut lines on the screen of her flip phone, to a soundtrack of "Summertime" by Billie Holiday. She sang while snorting her coke.

"Summingtime." *Snort.*

"And the life goes out easy." *Snort.*

"Fish have something." *Snort.*

"And gotten of high." *Snort.*

Her broken lyrics sounded perfect, and made as little sense to me as being in the back of a bulletproof limo while speeding across Moscow with a police escort at 5 a.m.

We got back to my hotel and walked into my suite. "Wow-a," she said, taking in the living room and the formal dining room, "you really vipp!" She opened the French windows overlooking Red Square. The sky was robin's-egg blue and rays of sun were peeking over the Kremlin.

She turned away from the window and once again undid her gold jumpsuit. "Now you fuck me," she said, stepping out of the jumpsuit.

I took off my clothes. She stood naked in front of me, put her hands on her hips, and said haughtily, "Music."

I handed her my iPod and a pair of headphones.

"Play me 'Lift Me Up' song," she said, and started singing it to me, as if I needed a reminder of which song she was talking about. I spun the dial on my iPod and found it. She put the headphones on and turned the iPod up as loud as it could go. Then she lay back on the bed and pushed my head between her legs, where my cartoon drawing looked balefully at me.

I'd started drawing my "little idiot" cartoons in the mid-1980s, when I'd been living at my mom's house and working at Johnny's Records in Darien. Johnny's policy was that every bag that left the store had to be drawn on. So my primary responsibility, aside from restocking bongs and Grateful Dead bootlegs, was drawing my "little idiot" alien cartoon on paper bags. Since then my cartoon had appeared on T-shirts and mugs, and music videos like "Why Does My Heart Feel So Bad?": a quasi-self-portrait of a slightly sad, nervous little alien.

I remembered a scene toward the end of the David Lynch movie *Twin Peaks: Fire Walk with Me*, when Laura Palmer looks at a small framed painting of an angel. By this point in the movie she's gone down a tragic rabbit hole of addiction and rape. As she looks at the angel it disappears – leaving her alone with her demon, who kills her. I looked at my smudged alien, an inch away from my face, and expected him to disappear like Laura's angel.

The song ended. "Billie" started it again, brusquely positioned me on top of her, and then pulled me inside her. Her eyes were closed and she was singing loudly to music I couldn't hear.

After sex I tried to be affectionate, to find some warmth or connection, but she pushed me away. "No," she said sternly, like she was chastising a bad dog. "For that my boyfriend only."

She got up, put on her jumpsuit, and walked to the door. "Thank you for fucking me. My boyfriend fuck me so good when he jealous," she said, and then pulled the door closed behind her and left.

I wanted to go to sleep, but I had to leave for the airport in an hour so I could fly to the Ukraine. Also, I was full of vodka and coffee, and I'd just had sex with a tall she-wolf aristocrat who'd disappeared like a pale vampire before the sun touched her. I felt like an anonymous, dissipated spy.

I went over to the open French windows and looked at the Kremlin. The sky was pink and blue, like a child's nursery. Red Square, just across the street from me, looked like a fairytale prison.

45

DARIEN, CONNECTICUT (1982)

I assumed I'd never lose my virginity. I'd briefly had a girlfriend at the beginning of the summer between my junior and senior years of high school, but we broke up before ever actually having sex. I didn't just want to be liberated from my virginity, though – I wanted to give it to someone I loved.

For a short-story assignment in English class I'd even written an elaborate fantasy about how I wanted to lose my virginity. The story started with my perfect new-wave girlfriend. She was Canadian, and she was at Darien High School because her father worked in finance and had been transferred from Toronto to New York. She loved Joy Division and Rimbaud and *Star Trek*, and in the story we fell perfectly, sweetly in love, amazed that the universe was kind enough to give each of us a soulmate.

Her fictional parents had a cool downtown apartment in Manhattan, and one Saturday in October she and I took the train to New York to buy records and see Echo & the Bunnymen at Danceteria. After the show we walked back to her parents' cool apartment in the West Village, lost our virginity to each other, and fell asleep in each other's arms while a New Order cassette played in the background.

My teacher gave me a B–.

For a year I'd had an all-consuming crush on Laura Smythe-Stafford. She was blonde and quirky – a self-proclaimed Taoist – and lived with her old-money family in a gated estate by Long Island Sound.

We met on a camping trip to Block Island sponsored by Darien High School's Outdoors Club. I'd pined for her ever since, but she was two years older than me, headed to Cornell in the autumn, and completely uninterested in dating a high-school student. After giving her a poem in which the first letter of each line spelled out her name, I called upon hitherto unknown reserves of bravery and asked her if she liked me. "Well," she said, stepping on my little new-wave heart, "I think you're a nice friend." I wanted us to fall in love and spend the rest of our lives together, but it was clear the feeling wasn't mutual and she wouldn't be helping me to get rid of my virginity.

It was the middle of August, two weeks before I headed back to Darien High School for my senior year. I'd spent the summer writing songs and poems, rehearsing with Vatican Commandos, and making money cutting lawns with a borrowed gas-powered lawnmower.

My mom had left town for the weekend, and for the first time ever I had the house to myself. While she was gone I planned on pretending that I was an adult, doing grown-up things like listening to loud records and getting drunk at a keg party.

At dusk on Saturday, after a day of playing guitar and listening to Joy Division and writing poetry, I rode my bike to my friend Duncan's house. Duncan was a year older than me – he was heading off to Bowdoin College in a few weeks – and was a tall, lacrosse-playing athlete who lived next to a country club. Our friendship was based on the fact that he had recently discovered the English Beat and XTC, and my friends and I were the only people he knew who admitted to liking new wave.

When I arrived Duncan was filling a pitcher with vodka, ice, and Tom Collins mix – his parents were out of town too. We hung out in the living room with his older brother, listening to new-wave records and drinking. Whenever I spent time with Duncan I expected him to realize that he didn't actually want to be my friend. Duncan was tall and handsome and good at sports, whereas my punk-rock friends and I were none of these things. When Duncan hung out with us he seemed like a different species, a human among hobbits. He towered over us, carrying himself with patrician grace and *noblesse oblige*, while the rest of us squabbled over whether the Dead Kennedys were better than Black Flag.

Duncan had a real girlfriend, and he was going to her house later. So after a couple of new-wave albums and five drinks, I left his parents' gated estate and rode my bike to my mom's house, literally on the other side of the train tracks. In an empty house with a stomach full of vodka and sugary Tom Collins mix, I felt like a grown-up. And grown-ups made cocktails.

I put a Birthday Party album on my mom's stereo and poured myself a vodka and orange juice. Sitting on the Salvation Army couch while listening to Nick Cave bleating about releasing bats, I drank my screwdriver and thought about air-conditioning. All my friends had AC, but we'd never been able to afford it. Usually the heat was a scourge, but right now with the alcohol coursing through my blood it felt like a cloying badge of honor.

I made another drink, adding more vodka this time, and pretended I was in Los Angeles. I'd never been to LA, but I assumed it was hot there. In my fantasy I was still finishing my drink and listening to Nick Cave, but I was getting ready to go to a punk-rock club with John Doe and Exene Cervenka from X. I'd seen pictures of them in their house in east LA, surrounded by weird statues and Mexican candles, and they seemed happy.

I finished my drink and realized I'd never been happier in this house. I was alone, I was drunk, I had my growing collection of fifteen new-wave and punk-rock records to listen to, and I was going to a party. A real party where I'd be allowed inside, rather than skulking around the yard and standing on a box to surreptitiously look through the windows.

in my dreams i'm dying all the time

After two more screwdrivers I rode my bike to the party and stumbled through the house. In the backyard a band had set up by the pool and was playing a cover of the Doors' "Break on Through," while people stood around, drinking Schaefer beer out of clear plastic cups.

I spotted my punk-rock friends – Jim, Dave, John, and Chip – gathered in a corner of the yard, unsure of how to comport themselves at a party full of normal people. We knew how to walk around Lower Manhattan and find obscure punk-rock clubs. We knew how to stage-dive at Black Flag shows and not end up with fractured skulls and broken limbs. But we were clueless when it came to talking to girls and civilians.

I walked over to my friends and grabbed Chip's beer. I yelled, "I'm drunk!" and downed the beer in one long gulp, like a skinny new-wave version of John Belushi in *Animal House*. My friend Paul walked over, accompanied by four girls I'd never seen before. I had known Paul since eighth grade, but my friends and I treated him like semi-royalty: he had lived in London and still had faint traces of a British accent. Also, he was taller than us, had baffling self-confidence, and had lost his virginity when he was fifteen.

Three of the girls with Paul were cute and preppy, but one was very tall, very pale, and had bleached hair that was shaved on the sides. Looking at her stopped me in my drunken tracks – I hadn't expected to find an actual new-wave girl at a backyard party in Darien. I was instantly smitten. "Hi, I'm Moby," I said, bravely introducing myself to this tall, translucent goddess.

She smiled coyly. "I'm Victoria."

"Can I get you a drink?" I asked. I'd heard men ask that question on TV.

"No thanks," she said, still smiling coyly, like a bleached Mona Lisa.

I went back to the keg and got two more cups of beer for myself. The band segued into Led Zeppelin's "Black Dog." Some drunk jocks were high-fiving each other and doing chest bumps. I didn't want them to notice me: I was a scared monkey at their watering hole and I recognized these chest-bumping giants as a mortal threat. I scurried back to my corner of the party and tried to sound confident and adult.

"Where are you from?" I asked Victoria.

"Fairfield," she said.

"Do you go to high school there?"

"I graduated in June."

So she was older than I was and taller than I was. And she had perfect new-wave clothes and perfect new-wave hair. I asked her if she'd been to Pogo's, which was the only hardcore punk-rock club in Connecticut.

"No," she said. She was laconic and I was running out of questions. "So where do you like to go?" I asked.

"New Haven."

I was impressed. New Haven had two actual new-wave clubs, but the drinking age was twenty-one, and they carded. Since my friends and I were years away from being twenty-one, we had never even tried to get into these places. One time Echo & the Bunnymen had been playing at one of the new-wave clubs in New Haven, so we parked nearby and hung out on the sidewalk, just so we could eat pizza around people with cool haircuts and black jeans.

Pogo's, on the other hand, was our little punk-rock paradise. It was a dive bar in a decimated neighborhood in Bridgeport, and they had never once asked us for ID. Since Pogo's was halfway between New York and Boston, it had become a stopping point for small and medium-sized punk-rock bands. We'd seen Black Flag, Bad Brains, Mission of Burma, and the Misfits there, stage-diving until 10 p.m. and then driving a half-hour home to sleep in our safe beds.

"I'm going to get another beer," I said, drunkenly stumbling over my words. "D'you want one?" I was pretty sure I was flirting. I'd never felt this confident before, talking to a tall, beautiful, new-wave girl who was clearly out of my league.

At 1 a.m. the party was winding down. After six beers, on top of the five drinks I'd had at Duncan's and the four I'd had at home, I was very drunk. In a surge of drunken courage, I asked the bravest question I'd ever asked: "Do you and your friends need a place to stay? My mom's out of town."

"I'll ask."

Victoria huddled with her friends. I swayed, finishing another plastic cup of Schaefer.

"Okay," she told me.

She was tall and gorgeous and almost invisibly pale. And so quiet. Suddenly I was scared. Why was she coming back to my house? Was she a ghost? Maybe she was going to come to my empty house and steal my soul. I told myself she wasn't a ghost.

We piled into her friend's station wagon. I was going to ask if I could put my bike in the back, but I wanted to seem cool and mature. And cool and mature men didn't ride around town on lime-green Schwinn ten-speeds they'd had since sixth grade.

Back at my house I made myself another vodka and orange juice. Somehow it was hotter than it had been during the day, even though it was after midnight. The windows were open, but the inside of my house was stifling. I tried to turn on lights strategically so these older girls from Fairfield wouldn't see just how threadbare our secondhand furniture was.

"You guys can stay on the couches?" I asked her friends. And then I looked at Victoria. "And do you want to stay in my room?"

She looked at her friends, nodded, and said quietly, "Okay." She was so calm, and I was so drunk and scared. I'd never had girls in my house, but now a tall new-wave ghost was holding my hand and walking up our orange-carpeted stairs.

In my bedroom I put on a cassette of music I'd taped off the radio, finished my drink, and tried to look urbane and sophisticated. Four years had passed since we'd moved into our house by the train station, and my room hadn't changed much – except now my walls were covered in new-wave and punk-rock posters I'd scrounged from the dumpsters behind the local record stores. I still had the same floral-sheeted twin mattress I'd had since third grade, resting on the floor next to a plastic Sears fan. Victoria sat on my thin mattress and took off her shoes as a Cure song came on the cassette. "Oh, the Cure," she said.

"Do you like the Cure?" I asked, trying to find a way to connect with her.

"They're okay," she said, retreating back into her shell.

"Should we go to bed?" I asked, not sure what else to ask, or say, or do.

"Okay."

We got into bed wearing all our clothes, even though it was over ninety degrees. "Should we take off our clothes?" I asked, more out of practicality in the face of oppressive heat than seductive confidence.

Victoria said nothing, but she slid out of her dress and then wriggled out of her underwear. I reached over and touched her skin. My hand moved down and I touched her hip. There was a girl in my bed. There was a *naked girl* in my bed. I was drunk and on the verge of blacking out, but the presence of this tall naked ghost in my bed woke me up.

I took off my clothes as quickly as I could and leaned over to kiss her. The humid air pressed down on us. Through my open window I could hear the trucks trundling down I-95. A Tears for Fears song came on the cassette and I entered her. She exhaled the quietest and softest "Oh."

I'd never been with a naked girl. Apart from some passed-out hippies at communes, I'd never seen a naked girl. And now I was inside a naked girl. I was having sex. And then it was over.

I rolled over, sweating from heat, not exertion. We lay next to each other on the mattress as the cassette ended. It had been a thirty-minute cassette I'd stolen from the language lab at Darien

High School, with only fifteen minutes on each side. So the whole thing – stepping into my room, putting on a cassette, finishing my drink, and having sex for the first time – had lasted just shy of fifteen minutes.

I noticed everything. The feel of the unwashed sheet on my skin. The late-night suburban pink noise of cicadas and truck traffic. The presence of this tall, thin ghost next to me in bed. We didn't speak – and then I was awake and the thick sun was coming through my window. Victoria was standing up, looking at me and wearing her dress.

"I fell asleep," I said.

She stared at me, and then said, "We have to go."

I got dressed under the sheet, as I was embarrassed for her to see me naked. We walked downstairs to find her friends were awake, sitting on the brown foam-rubber sofa in the TV room.

"Hi," I said, uncertain of the protocol for this situation. "Did you sleep well?" This was an absurd question: we had no air-conditioning, it was sweltering, and they'd slept on Salvation Army couches that smelled like our rescue animals.

"It was okay," one of them said, politely lying.

As her friends left, Victoria turned to me and said, "Goodbye, Moby."

I didn't know what I was supposed to do. I was hungover, or maybe still drunk, and I'd just given my virginity to this tall ghost goddess. Was I supposed to hug her or kiss her? I just held the aluminum screen door and said, "Drive safely." She turned away and got into the station wagon with her friends.

I went inside and collapsed onto the foam-rubber couch. I'd finally lost my virginity, but all I felt was hungover. And hot. It was so hot. It was only 7 a.m., but the sun was pushing into our house like angry syrup. And I had to throw up.

I ran to our downstairs bathroom and threw up into the toilet, realizing that whoever had used the toilet before me hadn't flushed. I expelled beer and vodka and stomach acid, which mixed in the toilet bowl with toilet paper and someone else's pee. I lay on the bathroom floor and pressed my face against the cool base of the toilet bowl, feeling like an adult.

46

NEW YORK CITY (2006)

I pointed to the top five levels of the El Dorado, a venerated art deco apartment building towering over Central Park, and said, "That's my house."

My date, Lizzie, was confused. "There?" She pointed at the two-towered castle. "Which apartment?"

"The whole top of the south tower."

She looked at me with disbelief, which was understandable – the towers looked like Batman's Gotham lair.

We crossed Central Park West and I nervously led Lizzie through the El Dorado lobby. I had spent $7 million in cash to buy and renovate my new apartment, but I still irrationally assumed that the security guards in the lobby would look at me and make me use the service entrance. The lobby was vast and had the quiet echo that came with old money and older marble floors. The walls were paneled in dark oak, with a few burnished frescoes from the 1920s showing the early history of New York City. This was one of the crown jewels of Manhattan architecture: two soaring spires, each one looking like a cross between a castle and a limestone rocket ship.

I'd bought the apartment over a year ago. And tonight, after months and months of renovations, was going to be the first night that I slept there.

We entered the elevator as Adam Clayton from U2 was getting out.

"Adam?" I said, surprised.

"Moby?" he replied, equally surprised.

"You live here?" I asked. I knew that Bono and Alec Baldwin and Ron Howard lived in the El Dorado, but I didn't know that Adam did.

"I do!" he said brightly.

"I just moved in," I said. "Or am moving in."

"Well, I hope I see you around!" he said, and strolled off into the night.

We took the elevator to the twenty-ninth floor, and then walked up a flight of stairs to my front door. "I can't believe I live here," I said as I unlocked the ornate metal door. I opened it and flipped a light switch. Lights glowed softly on the first flight of stairs, which were covered in a carpet with a subtle navy-blue fleur-de-lis pattern. We walked up to the living room, which had leaded windows and a marble fireplace. "Do you want a drink?" I asked Lizzie.

"No, I'm sober," she said. I was surprised, because we'd met the week before in a bar at 3 a.m., and I assumed everyone in a bar at 3 a.m. was as drunk as I was.

Lizzie was from Albany. She had short bleached hair and looked like a beautiful elf. We'd kissed at the bar at 4 a.m., just as the place was closing, and I'd asked her to come home with me. She'd smiled and said no, she wouldn't go home with me after just meeting me, but she would happily go on a date if I called her and asked her out.

I called her the next day, and we talked for thirty minutes about music and politics and growing up in the suburbs. She was beautiful, smart, and charming; making plans to meet up with her was both what I wanted to do and what my new therapist had told me to do.

My anxiety around dating and intimacy was getting worse. Sometimes it was so bad that I would panic and have to end things with a woman before we even went on a first date.

Two months ago I'd called a psychiatrist to ask about anti-anxiety medications. Over the phone he asked, "Have you ever done cognitive behavioral therapy?"

in my dreams i'm dying all the time

"No," I said, annoyed; I just wanted drugs that would fix my broken brain.

"I'll give you the drugs, but first try CBT, okay?" He gave me the name of a therapist, Dr. Barry Lubetkin.

I'd had bouts of therapy in the past, but this was the first time I'd committed to showing up for appointments consistently. Every time I sat down in Dr. Lubetkin's office it made me feel like Woody Allen, only balder and more neurotic. After I explained my problem to Dr. Lubetkin – that dating and emotional intimacy gave me debilitating anxiety – he told me that there was only one solution: exposure therapy. Or, more simply: go on dates, get close to people, and don't run away.

"Eventually the anxiety will go away," he said cheerfully.

"But you have no idea how much it hurts," I said, pleading.

He looked me in the eye and smiled, kindly. "*Bubbeleh*, I've been a therapist for almost fifty years. Trust me, I know how painful it is."

I'd started panicking before my date with Lizzie, and wanted to cancel, but I forced myself to be a good CBT patient and met her at a vegan macrobiotic restaurant on Amsterdam Avenue. My anxiety waned during dinner, just as Dr. Lubetkin had said it would. Afterward we walked circuitously through Central Park so I could show her my new home.

"Here, let me show you something," I said once we were inside, taking her hand and walking her onto the balcony off my living room.

"Oh my God," she said, putting her hands over her mouth. From my apartment's balcony, on the thirty-third floor, you could see all of Central Park, 5th Avenue, and the Metropolitan Museum of Art – and even the planes in the distance, taking off from LaGuardia and Kennedy airports. It was the lowest of the apartment's five balconies.

I took her hand to lead her back inside, but she pulled away. "Wait, let me just stay here for a second." She walked to the edge and looked four hundred feet straight down to Central Park West. "It's just, I don't know, like . . ." she said quietly, almost to herself.

"Like a movie?" I offered.

"Like a movie. But that seems too obvious."

We walked back inside and up another flight of carpeted stairs to the third level. "This is balcony number two," I said. This one faced the Hudson River. We could see the last blush of the sunset, fifty miles to the west.

"Unreal."

"There's more," I said, smiling like a proud and arrogant real-estate broker. I led her up an iron spiral staircase to the oak-paneled library, and then out to the wraparound balcony on the fourth level. "Balcony number three," I said.

"Fuck," she said. "This shouldn't exist. Do you need a nanny?"

"Probably," I said. I walked her up to balcony number four, and then to balcony number five at the very top of the tower – careful not to disturb the falcon who had nested there. "Amazing, right?" I said, tritely.

A soft wind was blowing off the Hudson River. Manhattan, normally loud and vicious, sounded distant and calm. "Can I pitch a tent up here?" Lizzie joked.

During dinner she had told me she was a musician, so I asked, "Will you play me some of your music?"

"Sure. Do you have a piano?"

"Yes, back on the second floor."

"Floors in an apartment . . ." She shook her head. "Moby, you know you're the man."

"Ha, thanks," I said.

"No, not like that. You're a rich WASP from Connecticut and you live in a five-level penthouse. You're 'the man,' as in 'Stick it to the man.' As in the person they guillotine in the revolution."

I didn't know if she was insulting me, but I decided to take it as a compliment.

We walked back down three flights of stairs to the living room. "I still can't believe anyone lives here," she said, looking around the living room, with its nineteenth-century Turkish rug, marble fireplace, and walls of bookshelves. "It's so . . . adult."

"I grew up on welfare," I said, wanting to clothe myself in both ostentatious wealth and the street cred that came from growing up poor. "And the first place I lived after leaving home was an abandoned factory in a crack neighborhood."

"And now this."

"And now this," I said with habitual but false modesty.

Lizzie sat down at the piano. I hadn't known what to expect, but her song was haunting. And her voice was dark but strong.

"You're really good," I told her when she finished.

"Thanks," she said, smiling sweetly.

"Do you have a record deal?"

"I'm working with a manager, but you know how it is. Or maybe you don't," she said, gesturing at the penthouse.

"So you'd make music under your name? Lizzie Grant?"

"I don't know. When you say it like that it sounds kind of plain."

"I think it's a nice name." I sat next to her on the piano bench and started kissing her. She kissed me back – but then stopped. "What's wrong?" I asked.

"I like you. But I hear you do this with a lot of people."

I wanted to lie, to tell her that I didn't, that I was chaste, sane, and ethical. But I said nothing.

"I'd like to see you again," she said.

"Me too."

I walked her downstairs to the twenty-ninth floor and kissed her good night at the bank of elevators.

This wasn't how I imagined the night ending. I'd assumed that we would end up christening my new apartment with vodka and sex. But to my surprise, this was almost nicer. I wasn't drunk, and I wasn't panicking. Nobody had been compromised, and I felt almost normal. "Good night, Lizzie," I said, as she stepped onto the elevator. "Thank you for coming to my weird sky castle."

"Ha. Good night, Moby."

Back in my apartment I walked up and down the staircases, looking at the way the soft incandescent light glowed on the old marble and the expensive striated fabric on the couches. I stood on the top balcony and looked at Manhattan spread before me. And I waited to feel complete.

My new apartment was perfect. Beyond perfect. I could stand here and look at all of New York City, or go down a few floors to have tea with Bono or Alec Baldwin. Or I could walk across the street and stroll through Central Park. This was all I'd ever wanted growing up: an elegant, luxurious, respectable home. So why did I still feel incomplete?

I walked down and down and down the multiple staircases to the living-room level and sat at the $20,000 Swiss piano that Lizzie had been playing. I took off my shoes, put my bare feet on the Turkish rug, and played a *Gymnopédie* by Erik Satie. Before moving in I'd told friends and family members that I would grow old in this apartment, and that I'd happily die sitting at this piano. I abruptly stopped playing and walked out to the balcony.

There was all of New York City, twinkling and grand and as beautiful as anything human beings had ever made. And I panicked. I had everything, a million times more than everything, but I wasn't happy. Spending millions of dollars to buy and renovate this unimpeachably elegant apartment hadn't fixed anything.

I went into the kitchen and looked for a glass, but they hadn't been unpacked yet. I poured vodka into a teacup and drank it like water. I poured another cupful and downed it. When I started drinking alcohol in junior high school it made me gag unless I mixed it with soda or juice. But now room-temperature vodka went down as smoothly as a seal on a wet slide. The liquor calmed my panic, just a bit.

　　　　　　　　　　　in my dreams i'm dying all the time

The phone rang. My first phone call on the landline in my new apartment.

"Mo! It's Fancy! We're going out to Sway, come join us!"

When Lizzie left I'd imagined having a sane, quiet night in my new apartment. Maybe I'd read John Cheever's journals by the marble fireplace, while drinking chamomile tea and listening to Handel. Instead I had a stomach full of lukewarm vodka and my apartment felt as small and disappointing as I was.

"Okay, Fancy," I said. "I'm leaving now. See you soon."

47

DARIEN, CONNECTICUT (1982)

The band I started had kicked me out for being a dick.

We'd started off playing Clash and Sex Pistols and Voidoids covers, but over the last year we'd begun writing our own hardcore punk songs: "Hit Squad for God," "Housewives on Valium," and my favorite, "Wonder Bread," a song about white bread killing off entire neighborhoods and then being used as a building material.

Over the last few months I'd canceled Vatican Commandos rehearsals, complained about the music we were playing, and generally been obnoxious to my best friends. I understood why they'd kicked me out. But I didn't know why I was being an insufferable dick to my friends.

The straw that broke the punk-rock camel's back was the Battle of the Bands in the Darien High School cafeteria. Darien was one of the wealthiest towns in the world, but the cafeteria looked like it belonged in a developing-world prison. It was a long room with concrete walls, fluorescent lights, and low ceilings. I'd never been in the DHS cafeteria after dark, and something about bands performing in the space where I normally drank chocolate milk and ate my lunchtime peanut-butter sandwich felt grown-up and thrilling.

I showed up late to the Battle of the Bands, wearing the least punk-rock clothes I could find: bright-blue pants, a yellow sweater vest over a pink T-shirt, and fuzzy slippers. I intentionally played badly, even doing a slow jazz solo during "Hit Squad for God," one of our fastest songs. And after the show I left my equipment behind, so the other Vatican Commandos had to be my ad hoc roadies and pack up my guitar and amp.

I was doing everything I could to antagonize the other band members. Unsurprisingly, Jim called me the next day and told me that I'd been voted out of the band. He also told me that I needed to come and pick up my equipment or he was going to leave it on the street.

I'd started two other groups in the past year: AWOL, which was my best effort at sounding like Joy Division; and Image, a pop group that I started just so I could spend time with Sarah, a beautiful singer I had a crush on. I liked these other projects, but the band I'd been in the longest was the Vatican Commandos.

I'd known Jim and Chip since eighth grade, and John since tenth grade. We'd discovered punk rock together. We'd gone to New York together to buy records and see Talking Heads and Black Flag shows. For the last two years we'd spent almost all our time together, playing music, talking about music, or talking about playing music. These were my best friends, the only other punk-rock/new-wave kids I knew. And I was pushing them away. And I didn't know why.

I took my mom's Chevette and drove to Jim's house to get my amp. He was watching TV on the couch with his brothers. "Your amp's in the driveway," Jim said, not looking up from *The Price Is Right*.

I wheeled my amp over to the back of my mom's hatchback and levered it up into the car. I wanted to be mature, so I went back inside. "Jim," I said, standing in the doorway to the TV room, "I just wanted to say I'm sorry I didn't take my amp last night."

"Okay, Moby," he said dismissively, staring at Bob Barker and not looking at me. I hesitated. I'd hoped he would accept my apology and shake my hand. Or ask me why I was being such a bad friend and terrible band member. Or do something to make me feel like I hadn't just lost my oldest friend.

"You still here, Devo?" his older brother, Mike, said. Mike and his pot-smoking friends listened to the Grateful Dead and ridiculed us constantly for being short-haired punk-rockers. For a while they'd called us "gay" and "weirdos," but after the success of "Whip It" they'd taken to calling us all "Devo," as shorthand for losers with short hair who didn't have girlfriends.

"Okay, see you later, Jim," I said quietly, and left.

I went home, unloaded my amp, and called John. He was older and wiser than the rest of us, and I thought maybe he would be willing to talk to me.

"John?"

"Oh, hey, Moby."

"I guess Jim's mad at me."

"Well, you were a dick last night."

"I know."

"What's going on?"

I paused, because I didn't know. "I don't know."

He didn't say anything.

"Okay, I should go. I hope we can still be friends."

He laughed and hung up.

The weekend before I'd been in traffic on I-95 and I'd seen a bunch of AA bumper stickers on the car in front of me. They all seemed like clichéd nonsense – "Easy Does It," "One Day at a Time" – but the last one stuck with me. It read: "Hurt People Hurt People." At first I couldn't figure it out, but then I parsed it: "People who have been hurt tend to hurt other people."

I was hurting my friends before they could hurt me. They were my friends, but they were people, and I'd learned over and over again in my seventeen years that people weren't to be trusted. My friends had done nothing wrong, but deep down I knew that they would. And I had to push them away before they hurt me.

I didn't want to stay home, so I put a cassette of *Heaven Up Here* by Echo & the Bunnymen in the car stereo and drove to Long Island

in my dreams i'm dying all the time

Sound to look at the nice houses by the water. Before I got my driver's license I'd ridden my bike around Darien, listening to sad British music on my Walkman and looking at the gated estates and the Gatsby-esque mansions. Now in my mom's car I could expand my range, even checking out the gated estates in New Canaan and Greenwich.

I'd grown up visiting school friends in their big, beautiful homes. Whenever I entered their houses I marveled at the carpets, the golden retrievers, the pools, the tennis courts, the space. But what impressed me the most, no matter the time of year, was the perfectly curated light. In the summer these homes had light that was cheerful and inviting, and in the winter the light was soft and quiet. The houses and apartments I'd lived in with my mom had all been dark. Sometimes that was because we had heavy tapestries hanging over the windows, and sometimes because the windows were small and faced a wall.

I parked by my favorite mansion on Long Neck Point, a nineteenth-century brick home that looked like Thomas Jefferson's Monticello. Listening to the last songs on *Heaven Up Here*, I wondered: What would it have been like to have grown up there? To feel unashamed? To feel safe? The ivy-covered brick walls and leaded windows were perfect barriers, I decided. They kept safety in and shame out.

The Echo & the Bunnymen album ended. I pushed the clunky "Eject" button in the car stereo to spit out the tape, turned it over to side A, and pushed it back in. My mom's friend Calvin had given us this tape deck, as we couldn't afford one ourselves. He'd installed it for us, though he'd never installed a car stereo before. He'd needed some duct tape and folded matchbooks to make it sit right in the purple vinyl dashboard. The dashboard had been red at one point, I assumed, but had faded purple in the sun – which was one of the reasons the Chevette had been so inexpensive when my mom bought it secondhand at a gas station in Norwalk.

I cranked up "Show of Strength," the first song on *Heaven Up Here*, but the speaker in the door started rattling, so I turned it back down. I watched tall clouds gliding through the blue sky over this suburban Monticello and imagined what the world looked like from inside.

in my dreams i'm dying all the time

48

NEW YORK CITY (2006)

I would have gone almost anywhere in the world to see Donna Summer perform, but I didn't have to: she was playing a fundraiser at a ballroom in Times Square.

I invited my friend Fancy to come with me to the charity event where she was performing, for he loved Donna Summer almost as much as I did. As we walked into the gold-and-beige hotel lobby, I realized I'd been in this building before. In the late 1980s my former friend Paul and I had snuck onto the roof to make short, surreal films in which we jumped around naked and waved our flaccid penises at New York City. At the time this had been one of the newest, tallest buildings in Times Square. Now, twenty years later, it seemed like a gaudy relic from the era of *Ghostbusters* and Eddie Murphy.

As they seated us at our table in the ballroom I saw that even though the hotel was faded and dumpy, the event was filled with New York royalty: the Bloombergs, the LeFraks, the Trumps, the Kleins, the Sulzbergers. All the New York billionaires had turned out in their best suits to get their pictures taken by Patrick McMullan and to give money to a charity started by Bette Midler to protect New York City's streams and wetlands.

"New York has streams?" Fancy asked, looking at the program.

I loved the idea of protecting wetlands, but I was here to see Donna Summer. I'd grown up with disco in the 1970s, when I just knew it as exciting pop music on AM radio. In the 1980s it died off, but still inspired everyone from New Order to Duran Duran to

Kraftwerk. And then in the late 1980s the ghost of disco came back with a fury, giving birth to house music, techno, rave culture, and even a lot of hip-hop. Disco was the crucible in which most modern music had been born, and within the disco pantheon no one had ever reigned higher or more supreme than Donna Summer.

I'd read a story about Brian Eno discovering Donna Summer's single "I Feel Love" and bringing it to the studio in Berlin where he and David Bowie were working on *Low*. He made everyone sit down and listen to the track from start to finish, and presciently announced, "I have heard the sound of the future." I still played "I Feel Love" during my DJ sets, and thirty years later it still sounded like the future.

Fancy and I drank vodka. I made small talk with *Vogue* editor André Leon Talley, while Fancy tried to flirt with Anna Wintour. "Anna," he said, "you're a good-looking woman. Are you single?" She smiled politely and introduced Fancy to her boyfriend, Shelby. The harried waiters brought me a sad vegan meal of steamed vegetables and white rice. I ignored it, drinking more vodka instead.

Bette Midler welcomed everyone, the auction began, and a room full of billionaires competed with each other to see who had the biggest and most turgid financial penis. After 9/11 New Yorkers had been afraid that the global economy had collapsed, or that Wall Street's pre-eminence had lapsed. But the market came roaring back, and now New York's billionaires were throwing money around like it was dirty confetti.

"Dinner for four at Rao's going once," the auctioneer said. "Going twice, sold for $100,000." The audience clapped politely.

Fancy turned to me. "Someone bought spaghetti for $100,000? Who are these people?"

"New Yorkers," I said, trying to get the waiter's attention so I could order another vodka.

The auction ended, Bette Midler respectfully introduced Donna Summer, and the queen of disco walked onto the stage. She was wearing an understated black suit, and underneath the purple and yellow stage lights she looked like the president of the world.

I went to as many elegant Manhattan fundraisers and events as I could, as I was a Faustian running dog who wanted the New York cognoscenti to love and respect me. I wanted to be invited to their gilded apartments and their sprawling estates. When I told them stories about growing up on food stamps they unconsciously leaned back, afraid that my hereditary poverty might infect them.

I'd spent enough time with the New York billionaires to know that they were miserable. If they were happy, they wouldn't be drinking themselves to death and spending tens of thousands of dollars a week on pills and mistresses and therapy. I also knew that their wealth was hollow, based on getting rich off the fruits of other people's labor. But this was their world, and I could see they never doubted their place in it.

I understood that the men were surrogates for the rich dads I'd grown up intimidated by, and the women were surrogates for the girls in high school who wouldn't date me, but I still craved their approval. But as Donna Summer took the stage my sycophantic longing to be accepted by Manhattan's plutocrats disappeared. The billionaires and their bloated friends were ordering drinks and talking loudly, ignoring the disco goddess who was taking the stage a few feet away. I said, "Fuck it," and ran to the front.

This was Donna Summer. I wasn't going to let my desire to be accepted by New York's anemic monied classes keep me from being as close to the queen of disco as I could. A few more people joined me at the front of the stage, looking around nervously as if to say, "Is this allowed?" But then Donna Summer started singing and we lost our minds.

I was usually too nervous to dance in public, but I couldn't help myself. I was hearing "Our Love" and "Bad Girls" and "MacArthur Park" being played live, just a few feet away from me. Some of the less sclerotic gentry joined us, and soon there was a respectable and sweaty disco quorum at the front of the stage. She ended her set with "I Feel Love," and I forgot that I was in a hotel ballroom. I felt like I was dancing in liquid oxygen at a disco on a space station. She finished singing, said, "Thank you," and those of us at the front cheered as loudly as we could. We'd just seen Donna Summer perform, and she'd been sublime.

I walked back to my seat, happy, drunk, and sweaty. One of the event organizers came to the table. "Moby, would you like to meet Donna?" he asked.

"Yes!" I said, and stood up again. "Fancy, let's go meet Donna Summer."

"Do we look okay?" he asked.

Fancy was wearing a secondhand black suit with wide lapels and a burgundy tie. I was wearing a strangely cut gray silk Versace suit that Donatella Versace had inexplicably given me a few years before. "We look great," I said, even though we looked like struggling eastern European pornographers.

The organizer brought us to a small office next to the ballroom, and Donna Summer came out with her husband. Usually when I met my heroes I tried to stay cool and keep my fandom to myself. But this was Donna Summer, so I gushed, telling her how great her voice sounded and how wonderful the show had been, and how she'd invented techno.

I'd met other divas, and usually they were imperious and haughty, but Donna was personable and humble. She smiled politely, we chatted, her husband said some nice things about my records, and they left to go upstairs to their hotel room.

"Fancy, we need to go out," I said, drunk on vodka and Donna Summer.

"Where?"

"Have you ever been to a strip club in Times Square?"

"No."

"Neither have I."

We turned our backs on the billionaires and left the once-glamorous hotel to look for a strip club in Times Square. It was a cold, rainy Tuesday night, and the streets were empty, apart from damp rats looking for pizza crusts in the piles of wet garbage. Times Square was a thousand times cleaner than it had been in the 1970s and 1980s, but it was still a shithole.

We spotted the blinking marquee for Crazy Girls, paid our $10, and walked in. I'd assumed that a strip club in Times Square would be bigger or stranger or filthier than other strip clubs in New York. But inside I saw that Crazy Girls was identical to every other strip club in Manhattan, with mirrored walls, stages painted black, grimy upholstered banquettes, and sticky cocktail tables.

We sat down and ordered vodka. Some of the strippers came over, excited to have customers other than criminals and syphilitic truck drivers on a wet Tuesday night. Fancy put down his drink and checked his phone. "Shit, it's Penny," he said. "I have to go." He stood up and abruptly left.

I didn't feel alone – I was already drunk, and there was a room full of strippers and a bar full of alcohol. I was talking to one of the strippers while the DJ played a Ja Rule song, and she surreptitiously handed me a small baggie filled with white powder. "Here," she said.

This was cocaine. Or I assumed it was cocaine. My sleazy suit was still damp, and I was by myself in a strip club in Times Square. *When*, I thought, *would there be a better time to try cocaine?*

I'd tried acid and ecstasy and angel dust and opiates, but so far I'd avoided cocaine. It had always scared me: I'd seen so many lives not just ruined by it, but sadly compromised. Heroin addicts died quietly, but cocaine addicts lost their money, talked about themselves endlessly, and made terrible records. But if I'd learned anything from cognitive behavioral therapy, it was that I needed to face my fears, so to conquer my fear of cocaine I took the little bag of drugs to the Crazy Girls men's room.

The walls and toilet stalls were painted black, there was a dented condom-and-lube dispenser next to the urinal, and the mirrors were covered in graffiti. I opened the door to the toilet stall and poured some of the powder on my hand between my thumb and my index finger, the way I'd seen other people do it. The only light in the men's room was a coiled fluorescent bulb in the ceiling. The cold light made the cocaine look synthetic, off-white, and beautifully wrong.

I snorted. It wasn't so bad. So I did it again. And again. Until the bag was empty.

I hadn't known what to expect, but I didn't feel that different – just numb and marginally more awake.

I walked back to my seat, and the stripper said, "Where's the rest of my coke?"

"What do you mean?"

"The rest of the bag?"

I looked at her, suddenly realizing that I wasn't supposed to have done her entire bag of cocaine. Most of the drugs I'd consumed in my life weren't shared. You didn't do part of an ecstasy pill. You didn't drink part of a vodka and soda. I hadn't known that a bag of cocaine was communal.

"You did it all?" she said, astonished and furious.

"I didn't know," I said, scared. "I'll pay you for it."

"Where am I going to get more?!" she screamed, and lunged at me. Some security guards ran over and pulled her off me, while she yelled "Motherfucker!" and rained threats on me.

After she was dragged off, the manager came over with a vodka and soda and said, "I'm very sorry for that, Moby. Here's a drink on the house."

"Oh, no problem, thank you," I said politely. Then I realized I needed to go to the bathroom. I started walking toward it until I realized I *really* needed to go, at which point I jogged across the club. I went back to the stall where I'd done the bag of cocaine,

in my dreams i'm dying all the time

pulled down my shiny Versace trousers, and immediately evacuated everything I'd eaten in the last year.

As I sat on the filthy toilet the cocaine fully hit me. My eyes rolled, my jaw clenched, and my skin felt like it was covered in dirty electricity. I leaned my head against the graffiti-covered wall, tapping my teeth together and grinding my jaw. And I started laughing. "I used to teach Bible study," I said out loud to no one, tapping my sweaty bald head against the wall.

I was by myself in a strip club in Times Square on a Tuesday night, drunk, wearing a hideous shiny suit, and voiding my bowels after doing a bag of street drugs given to me by a furious stripper. I laughed harder. "I used to teach Bible study!" I shouted. Finally, after years of trying, I'd lost my soul. And it was funny.

Someone knocked brusquely on the door of my toilet stall. "Security. You alright in there?"

I giggled. "I'm good."

My eyes were vibrating in my head, but as I sat on the toilet I looked down and noticed the floor. It was old, with black and white tiles that had probably been put down in the 1930s or 1940s. Maybe at one point the floor had been beautiful, but now it was covered in so many layers of accumulated filth it was impossible to tell what it had looked like originally.

I closed my eyes and laughed harder. For most of my life I'd always felt terrible, inadequate, inferior. But now I knew – I *was* terrible, inadequate, inferior. My philosophical preening and my spirituality were just a pretense. This shallow, diarrhea-splattered horror was my actual life.

I was worthless, this was my truth, and the truth had set me free.

Section Four:

Then It Fell Apart

49

FAIRFIELD, IOWA (2006)

"HI, MOBY!" David Lynch said in his high, booming voice, making me feel like a junior FBI agent in *Twin Peaks*. I had loved him ever since seeing *Eraserhead* in 1981, and now I was meeting him for the first time.

I was in London to DJ, when Heather Graham invited me to hear David be interviewed onstage at BAFTA, the British Academy of Film and Television. Heather was a huge movie star, but what impressed me most about her long career was her brief stint as Dale Cooper's girlfriend in the second season of *Twin Peaks*. The first time I met her I blurted out, like a fan with no impulse control, "You were Annie on *Twin Peaks!*"

Heather picked me up at my hotel, with her hair pulled back, wearing a simple floral dress. Every time I saw her I was reminded that my friend was one of the most beautiful women on the planet. We got to the theater, posed for some pictures for the British paparazzi, and found our seats.

The stage lights came up, and David Lynch walked onstage in his trademark black suit and buttoned-up white shirt, smoking a cigarette and smiling at the audience. He was being interviewed by an erudite, Cambridge-educated journalist, but as the interview went further and further down the rabbit hole of insouciant journalistic cleverness, David started shutting down and getting quieter. At one point the journalist asked a long, involved question about David's creative process, assuming that he'd get an equally long and involved response. When the question was finished David just shook his head, fluttered his hands in the air, and said, "See, creativity is beautiful."

His words hit me like lightning on a clear day. When I started making music I wasn't striving for fame; I was responding to the simple magic of music and its ability to make me cry and dance and sing. Growing up, music had given me a comfort and connection that was deeper than anything else I'd ever experienced.

While the journalist kept plying David with clever questions, I thought about what David had said: "Creativity is beautiful." I was excited that I'd seen the truth, and I was chastened and ashamed that for the last few years I'd been so willing to sacrifice creativity in the pursuit of fame.

After the show Heather and I went backstage to meet David. "HI, HEATHER! HI, MOBY!" he boomed, holding a glass of red wine and smiling like a jolly lawnmower repairman in an undertaker's suit. I'd never met David, and I was in awe of his work, but he was so genial and unassuming that my nerves disappeared.

"When you said, 'Creativity is beautiful,'" I said, groping for words, "it just . . . hit me."

David smiled broadly and said in his foghorn voice, "THAT'S BECAUSE CREATIVITY IS BEAUTIFUL, MOBY!"

David and I traded email addresses, and a week later he invited me to the "David Lynch Weekend" at the Maharishi University of Management in Fairfield, Iowa. I had no idea what the Maharishi University of Management was, but I immediately canceled whatever plans I had for that weekend and wrote back, telling him that I'd love to come. I held David in such reverence that if he had asked me to walk to Argentina to make him a cup of coffee, I would have said, "Yes, sir!" and laced up my shoes.

I flew to Iowa on a Friday night and was met at the Cedar Rapids airport by a woman from the Maharishi University of Management. The sky was cold and full of stars, and I was as excited as I'd ever been – I was going to spend the weekend with

David Lynch. In his last email he had promised that I'd learn how to meditate.

"Do you meditate?" I eagerly asked the woman who'd picked me up at the airport.

She laughed. "That's pretty much all we do here."

She dropped me off at a small hotel on a hill next to a cornfield in Fairfield, Iowa. The woman at the reception desk told me that the buildings in Fairfield were all constructed according to Ayurvedic principles.

"What are Ayurvedic principles?" I asked.

"Well, it's complicated," she said. "But basically they all face east."

I was in my room unpacking my bag when I heard a knock on the door. "Who is it?" I called.

"MOBY! IT'S DAVID!"

I opened the door. David Lynch was standing there, in his black suit and white shirt, holding a tray of food. "I brought soup!" he boomed. I was tongue-tied – I had no idea what to say in an Ayurvedic hotel room to David Lynch. He came in like the world's happiest bellboy and put my soup on the small table in my room. Then he shook my hand vigorously. "THANKS FOR COMING, MOBY!" he said, his voice comically loud in my small and quiet hotel room.

"So when do I learn to meditate?" I asked.

David laughed. "BOBBY WILL SORT YOU OUT! OKAY! HAVE A GOOD NIGHT, AND DON'T FORGET: ENJOY YOUR SOUP! P.S. MOBY, IT'S VEGAN!"

He retired to his own room across the hall. I took out my BlackBerry and emailed a few friends in New York who loved David Lynch as much as I did: "i'm in iowa. david lynch just brought me soup. the owls are not what they seem."

David had organized concerts on Saturday night and Sunday night, where Donovan, Chrysta Bell, and I would be performing. I was doing acoustic sets, so my friends Laura and Daron had flown in to play with me. Laura was a political activist who sang like Big Mama Thornton; Daron was her husband, a handsome magazine editor who played guitar and harmonica. After I woke up on Saturday morning I called Laura and Daron's room, and we met in the lobby for a tour of Fairfield.

The woman who'd picked me up at the airport was our tour guide. She drove us around town and told us that Fairfield was the world center for transcendental meditation, but it was also a farming town smack-dab in the middle of nowhere. Laura was originally from Iowa, and she couldn't believe there was a town in her home state full of farmers and Ayurvedic meditators.

"What do the farmers think of the meditators?" I asked our smiling tour guide.

"At first, in the 1970s, there were some issues," she said. "But now everyone gets along. Even the mayor's a meditator now!"

We drove down the main street. A John Deere tractor dealership was next door to an Ayurvedic crystal and incense shop. "It's so . . ." I tried to think of the right word.

"Clean?" said Laura, who had come from Bushwick the day before.

"Weird?" said Daron, because it was.

"And calm," I said. "It's so calm."

Our guide told us that there were centers surrounding the town where people meditated twenty-four hours a day. "They meditate for world peace, but you can feel it in town, can't you?" I wanted to say she was crazy, but she was right. Something was going on here. The molecules in the air seemed to be moving in a less hurried way than they did on the rest of the planet.

We met for lunch with David and Donovan in a white nineteenth-century farmhouse off the town square. I didn't know if it was the town full of meditators, the clean Iowa air, or the presence of David Lynch, but I felt wonderful. I wanted to be an obsessive fan during lunch and pepper David with *Twin Peaks* questions: "Who are Bob and Mike?" "Where is the Black Lodge?" "What is garmonbozia?" "What happened to David Bowie and Chet Desmond?" But I stayed calm and asked about the history of Fairfield instead.

"See, the Maharishi needed a place to go in the 1970s, so he bought this old college and moved here with ten thousand of his followers," David said, in a slightly less booming voice. "And now it's a magical place that's going to save the world!"

I had grown up with the seductive darkness of David Lynch, and I was having trouble reconciling *Twin Peaks* and *Lost Highway* with this smiling advocate of world peace and Ayurvedic teahouses. But as David had said in an interview I'd read, "You don't need to be dark to make dark art!"

I decided to stay sober for the weekend, as Fairfield was a spiritual place and I had come to learn how to meditate and to spend time with David. When David stepped up to the microphone to introduce the acoustic concert on Saturday night, a member of the audience shouted out, "Give me an idea!"

Without pausing, David said, "A BOWLING BALL FILLED WITH RED ANTS FLOATING IN OUTER SPACE!" Creativity *was* beautiful.

After performing our acoustic set I was leaving the venue and heading back to my hotel, when a beautiful woman with short, bleached hair approached me. "Hi, I'm Sophie," she said. "Do you want to get a drink?"

This was my sober, spiritual weekend. But what harm could there be in going out for a drink with a beautiful woman and seeing how people really lived in Fairfield? Plus I wondered if the calm I felt from being in a town full of meditators meant that I'd be able to drink like a normal person. Back in New York I was having fifteen or twenty drinks a night, but I told myself that drinking excessively was my personal choice. I could choose to drink like a normal person, if I wanted to; normal people routinely went out, had one or two beers, and then went back to their hotel rooms.

Sophie took me to one of the only bars in Fairfield, and I ordered each of us a beer. The bar was as clean and normal as the town, and I felt like I could be in any small, progressive college town in the country. I sat down next to Sophie on a vinyl banquette, and people started coming up to me to say that they'd liked my show and to ask what I thought of Fairfield. I was fascinated by these meditators and children of meditators, who were drinking beer and listening to Green Day.

I had a second beer, as that's what normal people in normal bars did. Then I thought it couldn't hurt to have a third beer, as it was Saturday night and I wanted to celebrate being in Iowa with David Lynch. Then I had a fourth beer, since there wasn't really much difference between three beers and four beers. And then someone bought me a shot of tequila. And then another shot of tequila. And then a teenager in a Tool T-shirt asked me, "Do you want to go to a rave?"

I was taken aback. There was a rave? In Fairfield, Iowa? "Yes," I said, starting to slur my words just a bit. "Yes, I do."

I got into a car with Sophie and the nineteen-year-old in the Tool shirt and his nineteen-year-old friends. They passed around a joint laced with angel dust, which I politely smoked with them. After thirty minutes of driving through barren fields we reached an abandoned grain warehouse on the outskirts of town. In the warehouse the air was thick with fog and a few hundred kids in oversized shirts were drinking and dancing. As the bass vibrated my ribcage I felt like I had stepped into a time machine and gone back to 1991. I pulled Sophie to me and said, "We're at a rave! In Iowa!"

A white guy with long dreadlocks came up to me. "Are you Moby?" he asked.

"Yup."

He hugged me. Then he reached into his pocket and handed me a pill. "Here. It's E." Someone else handed me a beer, and I swallowed the pill.

"Can I buy some for my friend?" I asked. I gave him $100 and he handed me three pills. Sophie swallowed her two pills and I washed my second down with a bottle of water.

"You like G?" the young pixie raver who handed me the bottle of water asked me.

"G?"

"GHB – it's in the water."

"I don't know what GHB is," I said, feeling out of touch.

"You'll love it!" she said, and danced away into the crowd.

Sophie and I wandered around the warehouse, hugging ravers, and sat down on beanbag chairs in the chillout room as the ecstasy kicked in on top of the beer and tequila and pot and angel dust and GHB I'd taken. The chillout DJ played "Porcelain" as Sophie leaned over and kissed me.

The room felt like warm birds, breathing on us and sustaining us. Amber and yellow lights moved slowly across the wall. I told Sophie I'd had an epiphany: we were both warm-fusion stars and all of us were creating new stars with our emotions.

"We are all made of stars," she said, smiling at me while wreathed in friendly yellow flames. I'd come to Iowa for sobriety and spirituality and meditation, but I'd found enlightenment while sitting next to a beautiful woman in a beanbag chair at a rave. And all I'd needed for transcendence was alcohol, angel dust, ecstasy, pot, and a water bottle filled with animal tranquilizer.

Sophie went off to get us more drinks, and some ravers came over to talk to me. "Whoa, you're Moby," one of them said. "It's so cool that you're here."

I smiled at them. Like Sophie they were moving like slow trees and were softly wreathed in flame.

"Do you want to get high?" he asked.

I didn't know what he meant, as I was already high. But I smiled and said, "Yes."

He and his friends led me outside, around the back of the warehouse. I could hear the drum-and-bass coming from inside, but above me the sky was black and filled with stars, while the fields next to the warehouse extended forever into darkness.

"Do you smoke?" one of the ravers asked me.

"Smoke what?"

"Speed," he said.

I had to think for a second, as my thoughts were slow and enlightened. I remembered that "speed" meant "meth." I said, "No, I've never smoked speed." He handed me a glass pipe and lit the bowl. I inhaled and promptly felt as though my head had fractured like a calving iceberg.

"It's laced," he said.

I exhaled, feeling like my nasal passages were at the center of a slow explosion made out of cold glass. "Laced?" I somehow managed to ask.

"Dusted," he said.

Oh. I'd just smoked crystal meth that was dusted with PCP. But I felt strong and bright. I'd come to Fairfield for enlightenment, and I'd transcended material existence by smoking meth and angel dust with ravers in a cornfield. I did a few more hits, hugged the ravers, and stumbled back inside.

Sophie came up to me and handed me a beer. "Where were you?" she asked.

At first I couldn't remember. Where had I been? Outside? I was sure it had been a long time ago. "Looking for you," I said, not feeling my skin.

We sat down in the beanbags and held hands and kissed and looked at the lights for an hour. Or four. The music stopped. "Oh no," I said, cold and despairing, "it's over."

Sophie smiled.

"Can you come to my hotel?" I asked, suddenly shaking and filled with dread.

"Moby, I live with my fiancé," she said, sweetly and sadly. I plummeted into darkness.

"But you kissed me?" I said.

"You look so sad," she said, touching my face.

"Can you break up with him?" I asked desperately. "Right now? You can use my phone. Please don't leave me."

"No. I have to go." She gave me a bittersweet smile and walked away.

The remaining ravers were milling around, looking as lost as I felt. I stumbled outside and saw that somehow it had become daytime. I found my way to the field serving as a parking lot and stopped some kids getting into a minivan. "I'm Moby," I said, shaking and struggling to make words come out of my mouth. "Can you give me a ride?"

On the road back to town, one of them offered me a joint and said, "Do you want to smoke?" I still hated pot; whenever I smoked it, I felt like I was filling my veins with dirt. But I needed something, so I inhaled.

I'd already had crystal meth, angel dust, GHB, two hits of ecstasy, and well over a dozen drinks, so the pot didn't make me any more or less high. My neural system was already saturated, so I sat in the back of the minivan, shivering with cold and despair and holding myself.

They dropped me off at my hotel as some of the meditators were sitting down to breakfast. "Moby!" one said brightly, assuming I was coming in from a morning walk. "Join us!"

I felt like a demon with broken teeth, so I smiled and waved, tried to look normal, and went to my room. I lay down on my bed and couldn't think: my mind was a nest of whirling insects. I turned on my computer, trying to do something to make the time pass, but I couldn't focus or even make words. I got in the shower and tried to cleanse myself of the alcohol and drugs, but I just stood there, shaking in the water, saying, "What am I doing?" over and over.

I'd brought Xanax and Vicodin to help me sleep, so I took four Xanaxes and four Vicodins, hoping to pry the chemical vice from my head. I lay down in my bed, whimpering quietly, and put on a pair of headphones so I could listen to *Bryter Layter* by Nick Drake. I felt like my body and brain were both irreparably bruised, but Nick Drake's voice helped calm me. By the third song, I was asleep.

I heard knocking on my door. Where was I? Oh, Iowa.

I was still wearing my clothes from the night before, and I was confused: when I'd gone to sleep it had been light, and now everything was dark. Was I dead? I wasn't sure, but I didn't think so. Every pore ached and my brain felt like it was floating in a pool of ammonia, but I was alive.

"Who is it?" I asked, the words sounding far away, even though I was saying them.

"Moby, it's Daron! Are you okay?"

I opened the door. "What time is it?"

"It's seven," he said. "We're on at eight." He looked at me more closely. "Are you high?"

"I don't know," I said, shaking my head and immediately regretting it. Trying to make normal conversation, I asked, "How was your day?"

Daron told me that they'd gotten Ayurvedic massages, had meditated with a group of people, and had gone for a walk and looked at a herb garden. "What did you do?" he asked.

"I'm just getting up. It was a long night. I went to a rave."

"They have raves in Iowa?"

"They do."

We drove to the venue in a minivan. Once we were backstage I sat on a white plastic lawn chair and tried to restart my damaged brain with coffee. Staring at the floor, I suddenly remembered the dream I'd had before I woke up. It had been about Bob, from *Twin*

Peaks. In many ways, Bob was the central character in the show. He was a demon from another dimension called the Black Lodge, although what he was or where he came from were never explained specifically. But in my dream I'd finally figured it out, who and why Bob was, and I needed to tell David.

The theater was full, with a thousand or so people in the audience. We played a couple of songs, and after "Natural Blues" I took the microphone and addressed David, who was in the front row. "Okay, first off, someone needs to teach me to meditate," I said. The audience laughed, even though I wasn't kidding. "Also, David, this is important: last night, or today actually, I figured out Bob."

David and the audience were quiet, staring at me.

"I was passed out on Xanax and Vicodin, sleeping off my hangover, and I dreamed about Bob. Here's what I learned: he doesn't want to be bad."

I looked at David again, searching his reaction for some sign of confirmation. He was smiling, kindly but concerned, as I was babbling about a demon from a TV show he'd made almost twenty years ago. But I'd had what I thought was a huge epiphany and I needed to share it.

"David," I said, with the zeal of the newly enlightened, "I figured him out. Bob's bad, archetypally bad. But he doesn't want to be. That's who he is, but it hurts him. Being bad hurts him."

50

DARIEN, CONNECTICUT (1983)

After I apologized to the Vatican Commandos and promised that my petulant days were behind me, they relented and let me back in the band. Over Christmas break we'd recorded six songs for a seven-inch single, and now we were embarking on our first-ever tour: a pizza parlor in Ohio, a prep school in upstate Connecticut, and then the Anthrax, a small punk-rock club in Stamford, Connecticut.

We were leaving on Thursday night to drive to Akron, so that day in school I informed anyone willing to listen that I was going on tour. Friday was going to be the first time since kindergarten that I'd skipped a day, or even a period, of school. But I'd already been accepted to Kenyon, Tufts, Fordham, and the University of Connecticut, so I could be a super-tough little punk-rocker and miss a day of school without worrying about compromising my permanent academic record.

The Vatican Commandos lineup had changed a bit. Chip was still on drums, but Jim had switched from vocals to bass. We had a new singer, Chuck, who had a blue Mohawk and was going to be a pre-med at Boston University in the fall. John had left the band to spend more time with his amazing new girlfriend, Lindsay. We still couldn't believe that one of us had an actual girlfriend, especially one from Los Angeles who was tall and beautiful and had been friends with former Germs singer Darby Crash.

On Thursday night the singer for Reflex from Pain – one of the bands we were touring with – picked us up in his dad's van. The van had no windows or seats, so the four Vatican Commandos, the four guys in another band called CIA, the three other guys in Reflex from Pain, and two of our Connecticut punk-rock friends all sat on the metal floor for the twelve hours it took to drive to Ohio.

Our friend Sean had written an article about the Vatican Commandos for *Neirad*, the Darien High School newspaper. As we pulled onto I-95 and headed out of Connecticut, Jim handed me a copy of the paper. There was a picture of us playing at Pogo's, opening up for Agnostic Front, and a complimentary two-hundred-word article. It was our first press, and we took turns reading the article over and over again. I couldn't get past the thrill of seeing a picture of myself in print, even if it was blurry and was only going to be seen by a couple of hundred people at Darien High School.

At 4 a.m. we got to a punk-rock squat in Akron and fell asleep on the living-room floor, a pile of teenage punk-rockers curled up with their leather jackets. I was exhausted after twelve hours in the van, but I went to sleep happy: I was on tour.

Three hours later I was woken by a mangy dog adorned with a Crass bandana who was sniffing my face. A smiling punk-rock kid with a bright-green Mohawk happily announced, "We made lentils and brown rice!"

We had woken up in a vegan squat. I'd heard of vegetarianism; my mom sometimes flirted with tofu. But veganism? Until the green-haired punk-rocker explained it I had no idea what "vegan" was. My diet consisted of Frosted Flakes, pizza, hot dogs, and Burger King, so there was no way I was going to eat anything remotely healthful for breakfast. Especially not lentils and brown rice.

"We need to get real food," I said sotto voce to my friend Jeff, who published the *Connecticut Underground Dispatch* with Jim. The *CUD* was the first punk-rock fanzine in Connecticut, and Jim and Jeff printed each six-page issue on Jeff's dad's Xerox machine. They'd sent copies to Tim Yohannan, the king of punk-rock fanzines and the publisher of *Maximum Rock 'n' Roll*. Tim had sent back a note saying, "Thanks!" – high praise and a high-water mark in Connecticut punk-rock fanzine history.

Jeff and I put on our leather jackets and walked through Akron until we found a fast-food restaurant. I couldn't believe we were in Akron, the home of Devo and Pere Ubu, and I secretly hoped Mark Mothersbaugh or David Thomas might come to the pizza parlor tonight.

"I had the weirdest dream," Jeff said, as we stood in line to order our food. "You were playing at a stadium in front of a hundred thousand people, and you were on top of a tank."

"That's bizarre," I said. "With Vatican Commandos?"

"No, you were playing on your own. You had your shirt off and you were standing on top of this tank, and everyone was screaming."

"Like Freddie Mercury?"

He laughed. We ordered hamburgers and chocolate shakes for breakfast. "You know," he said, "technically they can't call them milkshakes because they don't have any dairy in them."

A handful of people – seven, to be exact – bought $5 tickets to our show in the pizza parlor, but the bulk of the audience was the people from the squat and the other bands. There wasn't a stage, so we cleared away some tables and chairs and set up our equipment between the front door and the jukebox.

We started our set with "Hit Squad for God," and the twenty people in the pizza parlor immediately started moshing. Twenty-five minutes later, after we had played all twelve of our songs, our set was done.

The other bands ran through their equally short sets, and by 10 p.m. the show was over. We packed up the van, ate some pizza, and politely set up the restaurant tables and chairs as best we could.

"We only made $35 at the door," the punk-rock anarchist vegan with the green Mohawk told us apologetically, "but you can take it all."

We stopped at McDonald's to get food for the road and started the long drive back to Connecticut. "You guys," I said, after eating another Quarter Pounder, "I think I need to use the bathroom."

"Okay," the Reflex from Pain singer said from behind the wheel, "I'll find a gas station."

A few minutes passed and I started panicking. "I need to go now," I announced.

"Yo, we're in the middle of nowhere."

"I don't care – I need to go now."

He pulled over and I jumped out of the van, pulling down my pants and making it a few feet before everything came out. "Fuck! Gross!" Jim shouted. Everyone else got out of the van and pelted with me empty beer cans and garbage while I had diarrhea.

"Stop it!" I yelled, trying to run away with my pants around my ankles.

"Hurry up, Moby!" a member of CIA yelled, as he pegged me with an empty beer can. "We're leaving!"

"Guys, leave him alone," Jeff said, earning my undying gratitude.

After five minutes I had emptied my bowels and I got back in the van. The other musicians tried to give me space in the tightly packed vehicle – not out of consideration, but because I smelled like a dumpster.

We stopped a few more times so I could throw up and shit by the side of the road, and got back to Connecticut at noon. I was feverish and shaking, but I reminded myself that things were great, as I was on tour. "I'll pick you up in two hours to go to Choate," Jim said, as I got out of the van.

I slept for ninety minutes and woke up to Jim honking his horn in the driveway. I'd gone to sleep sick, but being seventeen years old and on tour had healed me, so now I felt fine. Jim was leaning on his horn, so I brushed my teeth and ran out the front door.

We headed to Choate Rosemary Hall, one of the prettiest and preppiest boarding schools in Connecticut. A senior at Choate had become a punk-rocker, and on a visit to the Anthrax saw us and Violent Children and Reflex from Pain. He wanted to bring punk rock to Choate, so he offered the three of us $100 to play as part of their spring concert series.

The only issue was that all the bands had to change their names, which were too harsh for the refined sensibilities of Choate. So Vatican Commandos became Velvet Calm, Reflex from Pain became Reflections from Poetry, and Violent Children became Violet Children.

We played in a wood-paneled common room as the sun set behind the ivy-covered brick buildings. A few preppy Choate students stood around and watched, while the seventeen-year-old promoter, who gave himself a Mohawk before the show, tried to start a mosh pit.

While we were playing "Point Me to the End" – one of our darker, faster songs, closer to speed metal than punk rock – I looked at my fellow Vatican Commandos and thought, "We're actually good." Chip had become a fast and solid drummer. Jim was manic and passionate on bass. And Chuck was a little screaming demon, hurling himself into audiences and yelling at the top of his lungs. I was glad I had apologized to the band and they'd let me rejoin.

I was still being punished for my sins, though, so after the show Jim, Chip, and Chuck got drunk on light beer in the parking lot and made me the designated driver. During the car ride home they kept drinking while we listened to the *Flex Your Head* compilation from DC, and they threw empty beer cans at my head.

"Don't shit in my mom's car, Moby!" Jim yelled at me.

I laughed. "I can't make any promises."

51

NEW YORK CITY (2007)

I needed a hit.

My fame was waning: whereas a few years ago I had been billed first or second at music festivals, now I was usually fourth or fifth. At some festivals I'd even been relegated to performing during the daytime. And a daytime slot at a festival was fine if you were up and coming, but playing to a festival crowd of fifty thousand people while the sun was still up was a kiss of slow death if your career was in decline.

My dwindling fame terrified me. A few years earlier I'd been invited to parties every day of the week. Rock-star parties. Movie-star parties. Head-of-state parties. But now the invitations were getting fewer and further between, and the parties were less prestigious than they'd been in the aftermath of *Play*. I hoped tonight would be different – when I was done working in my studio I was going to a birthday party for a billionaire.

Over the last decade fame had given me worth and made me attractive. And I feared that if I wasn't famous, I would never find the right person to finally love me.

If you asked me why I was holing up in my studio, I would say it was because I wanted to make beautiful music. But what I really wanted was to make a hit that would recapture the fame and validation I'd had after *Play*. The song I was currently working on had a pleasant disco chorus, a loop of a woman singing "I love to move in here." I'd added disco drums, percussion, and some old-school house piano, but in its current state I knew the track wasn't going to be the hit that I craved. Grandmaster Caz was on his way to my studio, and I hoped that he would make the song come together, helping to keep me from the curse of sunlight when I played festivals.

Grandmaster Caz was a hip-hop legend. He'd written and rapped on some of the most iconic tracks of the late 1970s and early 1980s; he was widely seen as one of the inventors of hip-hop. I'd reached out to him through my manager's assistant, asking if Caz would consider doing some verses on my new record. To my amazement, he had agreed.

For some reason I didn't understand, the New York hip-hop community still seemed to like me. I'd worked with or remixed some of my rapper heroes, like Public Enemy, MC Lyte, Busta Rhymes, and Nas, and most New York-based MCs and producers were usually incredibly kind to me. More often than not they'd pull me aside and say something along the lines of, "Fuck Eminem, Moby, we got your back." Which was gracious, but cold comfort. Eminem was the most successful musician on the planet, and every year that went by he sold more records and I sold fewer.

Grandmaster Caz came over, I set up a microphone, and he flawlessly recorded his vocals in a matter of minutes. It was always unsettling having someone else in my studio, as the room was small and I usually worked alone. Also, Caz was taller and bigger than Lou Reed and David Bowie and the other musicians who had visited over the years, so after we were done recording his vocals we relocated to my living room. I made us each a cup of tea and we hung out, reminiscing about New York in the 1980s, talking about old clubs like Mars and the Tunnel and some of the hip-hop records that were big back then.

After Caz left I put the song together, adding more percussion and keyboards. By 7 p.m. it was done. I played it back and judged the results: it was slow and sinewy and special in places. But it wasn't a hit.

I was angry, anxious, and ashamed. Angry at myself because I couldn't write a hit. Anxious that my career was spiraling downwards. And ashamed that I'd become a sad joke among the hipsters: a faded star who was still out every night, getting drunk and going home with anybody who'd say yes. But deep down I was angry because I knew that I had perverted my own music.

I almost couldn't admit this to myself, but my primary method for judging the music I was working on had become the contemptible criterion "Will this help my career?" I'd hoped that my epiphany at hearing David Lynch say "Creativity is beautiful" would fix me, and then, freed of my lickspittle desire for fame, I could go back to making music without worrying about its commercial potential. But here I was, judging a perfectly nice little song because it wasn't a hit. I felt like a disgrace.

I turned off my studio, repulsed by what I'd become, and put on my nicest suit. I'd been invited to the birthday party of billionaire real-estate developer Richard LeFrak by one of his assistants, who apparently thought I was still young and cool. I wanted to bring a guest, but I'd alienated most of my friends, and the few I hadn't lost were now in their forties, happily married, and living in the suburbs. I thought about staying home instead of going alone to a stranger's birthday, but LeFrak had rented the Hammerstein Ballroom and hired Earth, Wind & Fire, and I'd never seen Earth, Wind & Fire play live.

I took a cab to the Hammerstein Ballroom, one of the most beautiful old theaters in New York, and gazed up at the marquee. I'd played here in 2000. Originally I'd been booked for one night, but it sold out so quickly we added a second, and then a third. My skin ached with desire for the halcyon days when everything came so easily.

The Hammerstein held up to three thousand five hundred people, but tonight's party was for a hundred. They'd set up tables and chairs in front of the stage, and although everything was exclusive and elegant, it still felt like having a tea party in an airplane hangar. I was seated between one of the Hearst daughters and an heir to the Sackler pharmaceutical fortune. I surveyed the room. Donald Trump was there. Michael Bloomberg was there. Some of the new hedge-fund billionaires were there. "We should take them all hostage and start a new country with their money," I said to the Hearst heir sitting next to me.

She paled, and I was flooded with regret, remembering that her mother had been kidnapped and taken hostage in the 1970s. "I'm sorry, I'm an idiot," I said, sincerely contrite.

"It's okay," she said, but turned away to talk to the hedge-fund manager seated on her right.

I ordered vodka and more vodka and drank quietly, while waiters brought course after course of food I couldn't eat. After dinner a cadre of staff pushed the tables to the side of the dance floor, the lights dimmed, and Earth, Wind & Fire took the stage. A few people clapped, the sound evaporating in the cavernous room, but most of the billionaires chatted with their friends or, like Trump, scowled while checking their phones.

It wasn't a glamorous gig, but Earth, Wind & Fire had been paid to play, so they played. I'd had six or seven vodkas, so I got up and danced by myself. When the band played "September," a few of the billionaires even stood up to dance joylessly with their Botoxed mistresses.

"September" was one of those songs that seemed light and jolly on the surface, but was deeply melancholy at the core. I looked at the cavernous theater and heard the surprisingly mournful, elegiac words bouncing back from all the empty seats. Only seven years ago I had filled all those empty seats with happy people.

The singer for Earth, Wind & Fire seemed exhausted. When he reached the last verse, his words filled the theater like a lamentation.

A few songs later they played "Shining Star," and almost all the people at the party finally got up to dance. A few of the younger guests had smiles on their faces, but most of the older ones looked as grim as undertakers in a town where nobody was dying. "What's the point of being obscenely wealthy if you're going to be fucking miserable?" I wondered.

The billionaires joylessly lifted their tired, gouty feet, roughly in time to the music. But on the far side of the stage I could see the waiters and kitchen staff who'd come out of the kitchen to dance happily and wave their hands in the air. The minimum-wage employees were smiling and happy, jumping around to Earth, Wind & Fire, whereas the billionaires looked miserable. And the billionaires weren't just joyless, I realized, they were angry. They owned the world, but they were perpetually dissatisfied. What was so broken in me that I aspired to be accepted by them and live how they lived?

There was Donald Trump. He had his name on gold-plated buildings and was the star of his own reality show. He had more than anyone could ever dream of, but as he stabbed his phone with his odd little orange fingers he looked like the saddest man on the planet.

The joylessness of the party finally broke me, so I walked off the dance floor and through the near-empty theater to leave. There was a song I'd started working on the day before, with a singer named Sylvia, and I wanted to finish it.

When Sylvia had shown up at my studio she told me that she'd been awake for thirty-six hours, but that she'd written some lyrics on the train on the way to my apartment. I'd recorded her, and I liked her lyrics, balanced halfway between consciousness and the apocalypse, but I hadn't had time to finish the song.

After taking a taxi back to my studio I flipped power switches and pressed buttons, bringing my equipment to life. I opened the Pro Tools session with Sylvia and listened to what I had so far: her vocals and some keyboards. I had planned to turn her performance into the core of a deep-house song, but after tonight and my febrile pursuit of hits and acceptance I was offended by drums and effort.

Sylvia's words washed over me:

If this be my last night on Earth
Let me remember this, for all that it's worth

I had been chasing after the gilded horrors of the world, when all I really wanted was this: this moment, with Sylvia's honest voice and some plaintive, repetitive chords. No matter what I did to destroy myself or betray my creativity and beliefs, no matter how aggressively I prostituted myself, music still waited patiently for me.

I sat alone in my small studio while the world brayed outside, and kept listening to Sylvia's voice:

If this be our last night on Earth
Remember us, for all that we were

52

NEW YORK CITY (1983)

New York City was everything, and it was only a forty-eight-minute train ride away from Darien. I escaped to New York as often as I could to see my favorite bands, to spot punk-rockers wandering into art galleries, to look at goth and new-wave T-shirts I couldn't afford.

By the end of my senior year of high school I had taken the train or driven to New York with my friends to see Fear at the Mudd Club, Echo & the Bunnymen at the Peppermint Lounge, Depeche Mode and the Cure at the Ritz, Bad Brains at CBGBs, Kraut and Agnostic Front at A7, and Minor Threat at Great Gildersleeves. The one club we still hadn't been to was Danceteria. I'd seen ads for its six floors of music in the *Village Voice* and the *New York Rocker*, and judging from those weekly newspapers I was sure it was the greatest place on earth.

It was one week before high-school graduation, and I felt safe and free. I was going to UConn in the fall, and until then I had nothing to do but play music, listen to music, and make enough money doing yardwork to buy a few records.

On the Saturday before graduation some friends (Dave, Jim, Chip) and I borrowed Dave's mom's station wagon and drove to Danceteria to see Mission of Burma and Bad Brains. As we left Darien we listened to a cassette I'd made of Mission of Burma songs; when it ended, we put on the Bad Brains ROIR cassette. The haunting guitar solo in "Banned in DC" was playing as I-278 rose out of Hunts Point, and suddenly Manhattan was in front of us, like an angel's dark tiara. This was the magic moment whenever we drove to Manhattan, when we realized that Connecticut was behind us and we were, in fact, going to New York City.

We parked near Danceteria and looked at our reflections in the car windows. We were going to the best nightclub in the world, so we'd dressed accordingly. Jim was wearing a Misfits T-shirt and a leather jacket. Dave was wearing a Devo T-shirt under a flannel shirt. And even Chip, who never wore anything other than old polo shirts, had put on a T-shirt with a picture of Mick Jagger as Frankenstein. I had a green sleeveless T-shirt that I'd written "ALIEN NATION" on in Magic Marker, and I'd tied a gold-and-red striped thrift-shop necktie around my head.

We didn't know if we were going to be let in — we were underage — so I pretended to be disaffected and British. I walked up the doorman and said in a terrible accent I'd learned from Monty Python and Benny Hill, "Yeah, are Mission of Burma playing tonight?"

The doorman looked at me, said, "Yup," and opened the front door. And we were in.

There was a schedule posted at the bottom of the first flight of stairs: Mission of Burma were going on in the basement at eleven, while Bad Brains were playing on the main floor at midnight. There was a new-wave video lounge on the third floor, and hip-hop and disco DJs on the fourth and fifth floors. It felt like we'd found four golden tickets and gained admission to a new-wave *Charlie and the Chocolate Factory* with black walls and sticky floors.

It was 10 p.m., so we decided to check out the video lounge. Kids dressed in dark gray and black were scattered around the room, sitting on cheap stools, while the VJ played Bauhaus videos. If Danceteria had been nothing but this, a room with skinny new-wave kids watching goth videos, we would still have been the happiest people on the planet. We had seen some new-wave and punk videos at the Rocks in Your Head record store on Prince Street and on the screen at the Ritz before bands performed, but MTV hadn't made it to Connecticut yet, so even a quick glimpse of a music video felt exotic.

We sat and watched "Third Uncle" and "Kick in the Eye" and "She's in Parties." And then the VJ played "Love Will Tear Us Apart." Joy Division were my favorite band of all time, and I didn't know that they'd ever made a video. We watched in rapt silence as the room disappeared and Ian Curtis sang one of the most beautiful songs ever written. It was a simple video, just the band playing in a long, empty loft, but it was the first time I'd ever seen him sing. By the end of the video I thought I was going to cry.

Still stunned that we'd been allowed into this miraculous place and that we'd seen an actual Joy Division video, we walked down the narrow stairs to the basement, where we waited for Mission of Burma to come on. I'd seen them at Pogo's in Bridgeport, and I'd taped some of their records from my relaxed Scandinavian friend Jacob's collection.

The basement wasn't crowded, so I went to look for the bathroom. Down a dark hallway, next to the men's room, was a door that said "Dressing Room." The Vatican Commandos had played a few shows in bars, but I'd never seen an actual dressing room before. I worked up my courage and gently opened the door. Six or seven people were sitting around a table at the far end of the room. Roger Miller, the guitar player, said in a friendly, booming voice, "Welcome to Burma headquarters!"

"What? Oh, I'm sorry," I said, trying to back out. This was a real band's dressing room, and I'd clearly crossed a holy line by daring to open the door and step inside.

"Hey!" said Peter Prescott, the drummer. "Come on in!"

I walked up to their table like a tremulous mouse.

"I'm Roger and this is Burma," Roger said, gesturing to the band.

"Hi, I'm Moby," I said. I wanted to be cool, but not knowing how much time I had with my heroes before somebody strong and official kicked me out, I blurted, "I just have to say how I love your band so much and I can't wait to see you play again."

"We have a show?" bassist Clint Conley said, laughing and pretending to look at his nonexistent watch.

"Damn, thanks for reminding us," Peter said.

They were talking to me. And being kind and funny. Was I allowed to laugh or respond? "Okay, I'm nice to meet you thanks see you on stage thanks!" I said, nervous and blathering my way back out the door.

I ran to the front of the stage, where my friends were standing. "I just met Mission of Burma!" I yelled.

"What?"

"Really! I went into the dressing room and talked to them in person!"

The band walked onstage, to mild cheering from the forty people in the basement. There they were, the same people I'd spoken with moments ago in their dressing room. "That's Clint Conley and Roger Miller and Peter Prescott!" I said to my friends, pointing. "And Martin Swope is the guy who does tape loops. I don't know where he is."

"Calm down, Moby," Chip said. "They're just people."

But he was wrong. They weren't just people – they were heroes who made records and went on tour. Chip and Jim and Dave and I were "just people," as we were in the audience. Mission of Burma were on a stage in New York City, so clearly they were far more than "just people." Their set was beautiful, and just as emotional and loud as the one I'd seen them play at Pogo's the year before. They ended with "Academy Fight Song" and walked offstage, with me yelling and banging on the stage, while the other members of the audience clapped politely.

My friends and I raced up the stairs, making it into Danceteria's main room just as Bad Brains walked onstage. "Hello, boys and girls," H.R., the singer, said, and then the band launched into "I." The crowd exploded, a hundred skinheads and punk-rockers moshing and joyfully beating the shit out of each other. We threw ourselves into the crowd, falling down, standing up again, pushing and being pushed, as Bad Brains sped through song after song.

I loved other hardcore bands, but nobody even came close to the ferocity and musicianship of Bad Brains. Doc the guitarist and Darryl the bassist were locked into a powerful groove, although they were hidden behind their swinging dreadlocks. Skinheads were diving, while H.R. did backflips onstage. Their set ended with "Pay to Cum," the first song we'd ever heard of theirs on WNYU.

As they walked offstage it dawned on me: this was the greatest night of my life.

"Should we go home?" Dave asked as the room emptied.

No, we shouldn't. We should live at Danceteria, find its DNA, and weave it into our own chromosomes. "Let's look upstairs?" I suggested.

We walked upstairs, past the video lounge, where the VJ was now playing a Roxy Music video, and into a hip-hop club. When the Clash had played at Bond's Casino in Times Square they'd had Grandmaster Flash open up for them. So now we loved hip-hop because one of our gods, Joe Strummer, loved hip-hop. The four of us stood shyly by the wall and watched the crowd dancing. We weren't familiar with any of the songs, but it was clear that something special was happening.

There'd been forty people watching Mission of Burma in the basement. There'd been a hundred moshing to Bad Brains. But there were even more people packed into this sweaty room, dancing and cheering for every song. They were black and white and Asian, male and female, straight and gay. The DJ played "The Message" by Grandmaster Flash, and I got excited because I'd heard it on the radio.

"This is 'The Message'!" I yelled to my friends. "I know this song!"

"Should we go upstairs?" Chip asked.

The floor above the hip-hop room was a gay disco. It was darkly lit and full of people and fog. We didn't know anything about gay culture, apart from kids in our high school saying we were gay because we liked Devo. The men and women were dancing and touching each other on the dance floor. The DJ segued into Donna Summer's "I Feel Love," and the crowd, maybe two hundred people, screamed in a way that I'd never heard people scream. It was a sound of joy and feral release, a message from a perfect planet far away beamed straight into my heart.

"Let's go," Chip said.

I couldn't. I moved into the room, toward the music and the strobe lights. It was late and my friends were tired and uncomfortable and wanted to go back to Connecticut. But I was home.

53

NEW YORK CITY (2007)

I was at the annual gala for the Museum of the City of New York, telling Ivanka Trump about my Valentine's Day. I tried to make it sound as normal as possible, mentioning dinner at Candle 79, cocktails at the Angel's Share bar on 9th Street, and gifts of earrings and a book of Sufi poetry, but leaving out my crippling panic attacks and the prodding role of my therapist.

I had met a wonderful woman named Nicole a few weeks before Valentine's Day, and as per usual, I started panicking after our first date. I wanted to end things and run away, but my therapist, Dr. Lubetkin, reminded me that unless I stayed and worked through the panic, I'd never get better. I kept going to therapy, but it didn't seem like I was making much progress. I'd been seeing Dr. Lubetkin for ten months, and liked him because he was good-natured and not afraid to tell me when I was being crazy. But I hated that he tried to get me to confront my panic, when every part of me wanted to flee.

"If you weren't crazy and panicking, what would you do?" he asked.

"I'd make Valentine's Day plans with Nicole," I said, defeated.

"So do that."

After Valentine's dinner and drinks Nicole spent the night at my sky castle. When she left in the morning the panic attacked me viciously, making my muscles ache and my teeth grind. I knew that the moment I broke things off with Nicole, the symptoms would abate. But Dr. Lubetkin had repeatedly told me that for cognitive behavioral therapy to work, I needed to stare down my panic, so for all of February 15 I tried to deal with it. The pain got worse and worse until finally, on February 16, I gave in.

I called Nicole, explained to her that I was having crippling panic attacks, and that even though we'd only been on two dates, I needed to end things. She cried, and I felt like the worst human being on the planet, just repeating "I'm sorry" over and over. I hung up and hated myself for once again hurting somebody. But my broken brain got what it wanted, and the panic was gone.

This had been my cycle for decades: date someone, have panic attacks, cut the relationship short, end the panic. I wanted to get close to someone and not be crippled by anxiety. Or at the very least I wanted to make choices in my life that weren't controlled by panic. I'd tried therapy and medication, but year after year the panic only got worse.

Sometimes to make myself feel better I talked about my dating life as if I were normal, as I was doing with Ivanka Trump now. I didn't know Ivanka very well, but over the last few years I'd run into her at fundraisers and parties and she'd always seemed pleasant and polite. She smiled kindly when I told her about my Valentine's Day itinerary, but I had no idea if she was humoring me or if she was actually interested in my emotionally redacted story. Her boyfriend had been out of town, she told me, so she'd spent Valentine's Day alone.

A tall, thin man came over and took Ivanka's arm. "Oh, Moby, this is Jared, my boyfriend," she said.

I'd met Jared before; he was the publisher of the *New York Observer* and I'd been to parties he'd thrown uptown. They went back to their table to rejoin Ivanka's dad, who looked like a bloated orange masseur in a tuxedo.

This event, the annual fundraiser for the Museum of the City of New York, was one of the most exclusive in the Manhattan social calendar, and the room glowed with money and candles. I was alone at the bar and feeling like a fraud, so I ordered another vodka and soda. The Trumps and the Bloombergs and the Clintons and the Rockefellers and the Hilfigers were all here, in black suits and evening dresses, making conversations at tables that had cost them more than towns in West Virginia.

A tall, beautiful woman in a black dress stumbled up to the bar and ordered a vodka gimlet. "They're all bitches," she slurred.

"Ha, what?" I said, not sure if she was talking to me or the drunken air.

"They're all bitches," she said, gesturing at the room full of soft money. "A year ago they were my best friends. Now they won't talk to me."

"Why not?"

"I got divorced, and now they're all afraid I'm going to fuck their husbands."

"I'm sorry," I said, uncertain what to say to this stranger.

"You're sweet," she said, looking at me like I was a lost child. "What are you doing here?"

"Oh, I'm with them," I said, pointing out my friends Celerie and Boykin, who were sitting with Senator Joe Lieberman a few yards away.

"You know, this is a fraud. The women are all terrified and the men are all impotent." She drank her gimlet bitterly. "Fuck them."

I looked at hundreds of immaculately dressed and perfectly pedigreed New Yorkers, drinking and laughing. I didn't see impotence and fear, I saw atavistic confidence, passed down from the *Mayflower* through New England governors and New York bankers and into this gilded room.

"My husband shot me," she said, gesturing to a scar on her arm.

She had my full attention.

"I was cheating on him, and when he found out he locked me in a room at our house in Amagansett and shot me. Cheers." We clinked glasses.

I'd been to dozens of events like this and the conversations had never previously gotten deeper than the price of a Rothko at auction or which crappy Hampton someone was going to for the weekend. I didn't know if this woman was older or younger than me; she just looked adult, well-bred, and like she'd been born knowing the difference between show jumping and dressage. When she'd walked up to the bar I'd thought she was pretty in a generic Upper East Side way, but now that she was being honest I could see how beautiful she was.

"Do you want to leave?" I asked.

"I should stay," she said, finishing her drink. "No, I shouldn't. Fuck them, let's go."

We walked out of the ballroom and down the long museum corridors, filled with costumes from the history of New York City: Revolutionary War waistcoats, ballgowns from the nineteenth century, powdered wigs, livery vests.

"How did you get your name?" she asked.

"Well, my real name is Richard Melville Hall, but my parents thought that Moby was a cute nickname for a baby related to Herman Melville. Forty-one years later, I'm still saddled with my infant joke nickname."

She laughed and we stepped outside into the cold air. "Richard Melville Hall," she said, as if she were tasting my name. "So you're a WASP?"

"My ancestors were on the *Mayflower*," I said, "but cleaning the toilets and scraping the barnacles off the bottom of the ship."

We got into the car I had waiting for me and I asked the driver to take us to The Box, as I didn't know where else to bring a fancy grandee from the Upper East Side. "So you're a cool musician. Why were you here tonight?" she asked.

I liked this woman and her unaffected honesty, so I told her as truthfully as I could. "I was born in Harlem, but I grew up poor white trash in Connecticut, ashamed that my family had no money.

Now, sometimes the beautiful people who wouldn't talk to me in high school invite me to their parties. So I go because it makes me feel like I finally have some worth."

"Trust me," she said, "you don't want to be friends with these people. You have more legitimacy than they'll ever have. You *make* things. They're just leeches. I should know – I'm a leech too."

"You're not a leech," I said.

"Thanks, but I'm a leech. The only creative thing I've ever done is hire a decorator."

We pulled up to The Box and walked inside, past the crowd of people waiting on the sidewalk. My friend Simon had opened the club a few weeks before, hoping it would be a degenerate *fin de siècle* place where uptown billionaires could mingle with downtown performance artists, and I was one of the investors. It had been an auto body shop when Simon rented it, but after a few million dollars in renovations it looked like a small, beautiful, and slightly run-down nineteenth-century theater.

One of the line items in the renovation budget had been the cost of taking brand-new wallpaper and distressing it so that it looked faded and old. I'd noticed that downtown developers were doing everything they could to make new buildings look like they'd been around for a hundred years. The Bowery hotel had just opened further up the street; it looked like a repurposed twenty-story garment factory from 1905. The truth was that four years ago, it had been a two-story gas station.

The host brought us to a table by the stage. We ordered $35 cocktails; even though I was an investor I still had to pay for drinks. "Um, what the hell?" my divorcée companion asked, looking at the stage, where an albino performer was fellating himself while a dwarf lip-synched to a Britney Spears song. The hedge-fund managers at the tables around us were cheering, thrilled to be in the presence of downtown art.

"It's the end of the world," I said calmly, finishing my drink.

We ordered more drinks and watched the rest of the show: top-less choreography to a Tom Jones song; a burlesque performer having sex with a statue of Jesus; a lounge singer doing backflips while wearing a silver thong and singing "Stairway to Heaven"; and finally my old friend Murray Hill, an old-school drag-king comedian who mercilessly insulted the audience while they laughed and spent more money.

"Well, that was . . . uh," my date said.

"You're right," I agreed.

We went upstairs to a curtained booth with one of The Box's other investors and some of his movie-star friends. When I fell in love with New York nightlife in the early 1980s, clubs had been full of artists, writers, and musicians – people who were broke and broken. Now it cost between $2,000 and $5,000 to rent one of these upstairs booths at The Box for the night. For that money you got a place to sit for a few hours and a bottle of champagne. This was the end of an age in New York, or maybe the beginning of a new one, in which buying art had been deemed a creative act.

A burlesque dancer from Nevada I'd met on the opening night of The Box came into our booth, sat between my new friend and me, and put her hands on our legs. She had short red hair and rhine-stones glued to her face; in her frilled brown leotard she looked like she'd stepped out of an 1890 vaudeville house. Someone had politely left a few hundred dollars' worth of coke on the table, and we all dove in like Cajuns at a crawfish dinner.

When the coke disappeared the dancer said to us, "You should take me home with you." It was only 3.30 a.m., but we left, stumbling down the narrow stairs and stepping out into the cold and quiet of Chrystie Street.

"Let's go to my house," the divorcée said. "My kids are with my husband in Bedford and I'm all alone." She lived in one of the legendary co-ops on Park Avenue, and the doorman let us in without batting an eye. I assumed that as an Upper East Side doorman he'd seen everything, and three drunks weaving through the lobby was nothing new.

We took the elevator to her apartment, and the dancer gasped as we stepped into a marble foyer large enough to raise elephants in.

"Let me show you around," the drunk divorcée said. She walked us through a walnut-paneled library, a formal living room with a grand piano, a full gym, and a restaurant-sized kitchen.

"I didn't know apartments like this existed," the dancer said, running her fingers along the marble in the master bathroom. "Can I live here?" She pulled us both onto the king-sized Hästens bed and we peeled off each other's clothes until we were all in our underwear.

These women were beautiful, and they wanted to have a threesome with me. But it felt rote, as if we were playing scripted parts: the debauched musician, the Park Avenue lady drinking away her sorrow, and the wide-eyed burlesque dancer from a small town outside Reno experiencing all that life in the big city had to offer.

There had been a time in my life when nothing would have been more exciting than a no-strings-attached threesome, but this just felt obligatory. The divorcée was putting up a brave and cynical front, but her eyes were full of sadness. And the dancer seemed far more excited by her proximity to wealth and fame than to the divorcée and me, two lonely and aging people.

Suddenly, even though I'd had five or ten lines of coke at The Box, I was very tired. I just wanted to rest, and the divorcée's bed was extremely comfortable. Apart from the sound of the divorcée and the dancer kissing, the bedroom was as quiet as a monastic library. So I closed my eyes.

I was startled awake by the sound of snoring. My snoring. The divorcée and the dancer looked at me, affronted. They were granting me a threesome, the highlight of every red-blooded man's life. And out of age, sadness, and defeat I'd fallen asleep.

54

DARIEN, CONNECTICUT (1983)

I had a girlfriend. And then I didn't.

I met Meredith at the Darien High School spring dance, when I begged the DJ to play "Blue Monday" by New Order. By the end of the song Meredith and I were the only ones dancing. She was going to Dartmouth in the fall, had strawberry blonde hair, and reminded me of Molly Ringwald. We started dating right after graduation; in July, only a few weeks later, we broke up.

I hadn't had sex since losing my virginity the year before to Victoria the new-wave ghost. I was headed to UConn in September, and as an almost-college student I assumed that having a girlfriend would mean having some sort of sex life. But in the three and a half weeks that Meredith and I dated we'd gone to the movies and gotten pizza, but only held hands and kissed a few times. So I was melancholy about being single, but cautiously thrilled by the possibility that someday I would have sex again.

The weekend after the Fourth of July I ran into my friend Paul at Johnny's Records, and he told me about a party that night near the Ox Ridge Hunt Club. "Come on, we're single, it's summer, let's get drunk and make out with girls," he said, as if describing a rudimentary and easily understood theorem.

Paul said he would pick me up at eight, so at seven I put on an Ultravox cassette and got ready. I'd recently come to love Ultravox and the New Romantics, even though my punk-rock friends ridiculed me for liking "gay synth-pop." I still loved Black Flag and the Circle Jerks, but Ultravox and OMD and the other New Romantics made beautiful music, wore old suits, and sang about Europe and broken hearts.

Most of my favorite synth bands were from Europe, so I'd started taking black-and-white self-portraits with a tripod and a timer at old churches and cemeteries. I used weathered stone crosses and moss-covered angels as my backdrops and did my best to make it look like I was in Germany or Scotland, or anywhere other than suburban Connecticut.

I'd never left the US, and I doubted that I'd ever be able to afford to go to Europe. But I knew that if someday I made it to England or Germany, I'd feel at home, since I'd spent so much time listening to sad European songs and fantasizing about gray skies over old cathedrals.

Tonight's party was at a 1920s estate near the border of New Canaan. The main house was brick, and in the back was a tennis court, a pool, and a guest house; in the front was an arched brick porte cochère.

At the beginning of senior year I'd made a new friend, Luke, whose dad worked for Shell Oil and had just been transferred from Houston to New York. Luke's new home also had a porte cochère, so the first time I visited his house I asked, "Can I leave my bike under the porte cochère?"

"The what?" he asked, in his thick Texas accent.

"Porte cochère?"

"How the hell do you know what it's called?" Luke asked, baffled by both the large stone canopy outside his front door and the French term for it.

I had grown up on food stamps and welfare, but I was still a Connecticut WASP. Expressions like "porte cochère" and "dressage" and "paddle tennis" were encoded in my hereditary lexicon.

Tonight's party was outside. We walked through the porte cochère and around the side of the house. Sixty high-school students were standing around the pool, so Paul and I filled plastic cups with beer and stood near them.

Looking around the party I realized I'd known most of these people since kindergarten or first grade. For the last twelve years I'd felt shunned and ridiculed by them – first for being poor, and then for wearing punk-rock T-shirts to school. I assumed most of them would go to Ivy League schools, graduate, move back to Darien, marry their high-school sweethearts, and step respectfully into their parents' J. Press shoes.

Paul went in search of a bathroom. While I drank my beer and stood awkwardly, Kyle Lapham walked over to me. Kyle – blond, six feet tall – was a lacrosse star who was headed to Duke in the fall. We'd been in preschool together, but hadn't spoken to each other since we were five years old. "Moby," he said, already sounding like the corporate lawyer he would probably become in a few years, "you probably don't like me very much. But I wanted to tell you that I know you've had a hard time in Darien and I really respect you."

"Thanks, Kyle," I said, truly taken aback. "I didn't even think you knew who I was."

He gave me a very grown-up, appraising look. "Moby, you know we're all intimidated by you and your friends," he said.

"Intimidated?"

"None of us have the courage to do what you're doing. I just wanted to let you know that I respect you."

Was Kyle making fun of me? Was he going to walk back over to his gang of tall boys and beautiful girls and say, "Ha, he fell for it! What a buffoon!"? I gave him an appraising look of my own. He was serious. And for a moment, at least, he'd challenged one of the foundations of my self-loathing.

"Thanks, Kyle," I said, sincerely. "That means a lot to me." We shook hands and he walked away.

A mix tape was playing in the pool house, segueing from Steely Dan to the Kinks to the Grateful Dead. Paul and I walked over to the stereo to see if we could put on the Police or the English Beat, the only two groups making new music that the preppy kids of Darien seemed to like.

As we flipped through our host's records, Lauren, a girl I'd known from my creative writing class, came into the pool house. She looked like a taller Audrey Hepburn, and had always seemed kind and bookish. "Hi, Moby, what are you doing?"

"Trying to change the music."

We went outside and talked, while Paul put a copy of *Special Beat Service* on the turntable. Lauren told me she was going to Europe for the rest of the summer, and then off to Yale in the fall. Which contrasted with my plans to watch TV and sneak in and out of New York on the train, before I headed to the University of Connecticut in September.

"Can I tell you something?" she asked.

"Of course."

She laughed nervously. "I feel silly now, but I've always thought you were cute."

I was confused. The foundation of my worldview had always been that in the world's eyes, and in actual fact, I was poor, loathsome, and unattractive. First Kyle, present and future captain of the universe, told me that he respected me. Now beautiful bookish Lauren said that she thought I was cute?

"Really?" I said. "Why didn't you say anything?"

"I don't know," she said. "I was nervous? I guess? And I heard you had a girlfriend?"

"No, she and I broke up."

"Really?" she said, smiling shyly.

"Really," I said, smiling shyly.

"Do you want another beer?" I asked, even though we were both holding full plastic cups of Rheingold.

We went back to the guest house to sit on the brown corduroy couch. Someone had changed the music on the stereo to Neil

Young. I didn't like most of the classic rock that got played on the radio, but I liked Neil Young. I never told my friends this, as he had long hair and looked like the hippies that punk-rockers were supposed to hate.

Lauren asked me what I was going to study at school.

"Philosophy, I think."

"Why philosophy?"

No one had ever asked me that before. "It sounds silly," I warned her. "I want to know what's really going on in the universe. Who we are and why we do what we do."

"Isn't that religion and anthropology?"

"Okay, I'll be a philosophy and religion and anthropology major. I'll graduate in fifty years and never have to get a job."

She smiled at me. And even though I wasn't drunk, I kissed her. She kissed me back, her mouth tasting like beer and strawberry lip gloss. After a few minutes of kissing I felt a surge of confidence. I reached my hand up under her shirt and touched her bare breast. I expected her to slap my hand away or tell me to stop, but she moaned softly into my ear.

The Neil Young album ended. Our drunk host came into the pool house to change the record. "Don't mind me, lovebirds," he said, full of beer and bonhomie. He put on the new David Bowie album, *Let's Dance*.

I hadn't loved *Let's Dance* at first. It didn't have the otherworldly atmosphere of *"Heroes"* and *Low*, or the dark mutant pop of *Lodger* and *Scary Monsters*. But the more I heard it, the more I liked it. When the song "Let's Dance" came on I stopped kissing Lauren and asked her, "Can we lie here and just listen?"

"Let's Dance" was a pop song, but underneath the Top 40 patina it had such longing and sadness. I'd heard it on the radio a few times, but lying on the couch with Lauren's head on my chest I suddenly felt how desperate and romantic it was.

I was leaving Darien, my weird home. Sometimes I'd loathed

this strange, hyper-affluent suburban town, but it was as familiar to me as breakfast. Even though being poor in a town of fifteen thousand millionaires had made me feel inadequate, I had to admit that Darien had also been a perfect little incubator. It was safe, but it was less than an hour from New York City. It was boring, but all my teachers had been progressive academics, encouraging me to write poetry and read Dostoyevsky and Arthur Miller. I never would have admitted it to my cool punk-rock friends, but I had an odd, soft love for Darien, and was grateful to have grown up here. But now I was leaving.

I was going to college in the fall, where I would become an adult. That could mean more nights like this one, where I kissed someone I liked, and got kissed back. Maybe I'd go to college and find my soulmate, someone who would be the embodiment of every romantic David Bowie and Cure song I'd ever fallen in love with.

"Let's Dance" ended. Lauren and I stayed in each other's arms, propped up by the giant brown pillows on the couch. Ultimately I longed to live in New York and make music and play concerts and teach philosophy and write books, but right now this warmth, this safety, this connection was all I wanted.

"How do you feel?" I asked.

"Perfect," she said, sighing like pale summer moonlight.

55

LONDON, ENGLAND (2007)

I held my hand up in front of my face, but I couldn't see my fingers. I reached into the total blackness and felt fabric over my head, and remembered: I was on my tour bus.

The night before we'd played a festival somewhere in France. After a long drive and a ferry ride across the English Channel, we'd ended up in a basement parking garage underneath Wembley Stadium in London. Tour buses were designed to be dark, but usually a few low-wattage lights were kept on. I'd never woken up in total darkness before.

I fumbled for my BlackBerry, and with the light of the screen found my way to the stairs. The bus was a double-decker, with twelve bunks and a big lounge on the upper level; the lower level housed a bathroom, a kitchen, and a smaller lounge. I made my way out of the bus and followed the signs through the parking garage to our windowless production office, where Sandy had set up his laptop on a folding table.

More curious than rancorous, I asked, "Sandy, why weren't the lights on in the bus?"

He looked up from his computer and considered the question. "Shit, I didn't know you were still on it. The generator broke, so some guys took it to get fixed."

"Is it daytime?" I asked. My BlackBerry thought it was 2 p.m., but since waking up I'd been in the lightless bus, the underground parking garage, the concrete warren of tunnels backstage at Wembley, and the windowless production office.

"Don't ask me," Sandy said. "I think there's daylight somewhere."

Sandy and I had been touring together steadily for almost ten years. When we first started touring together he'd been reserved but smiling and good-natured, even when we missed flights and our equipment caught on fire. But over the last couple of years, as our touring became more alcoholic and drug-fueled, he'd been looking increasingly worn and tired. "Do you have a schedule for tonight?" I asked.

He handed me a piece of paper. On top it read: "MOBY / WEMBLEY STADIUM." I'd played Wembley Arena before – twice – but this was my first time playing Wembley Stadium. Wembley Arena held fifteen thousand people, and I'd sold it out in 2000 and 2002, after releasing *Play* and *18*. The first Wembley Arena show had crystallized the strange and wonderful rise of *Play*. Afterward we'd had a party for a few hundred people backstage. British movie and TV stars had begged to be invited, Peter Hook from New Order had DJed, and I'd stayed up until 8 a.m., drinking and dancing and basking in the strange perfection of sudden fame.

Tonight: Wembley Stadium. Wembley Stadium held ninety thousand people. The biggest rock stars in history had headlined there: Queen, Guns N' Roses, the Rolling Stones. Tonight, for the first time, I would stand where Freddie Mercury and Mick Jagger had stood. But I didn't expect it to feel like much of a triumph – we were being paid to play a thirty-minute corporate set for a few hundred Nike employees and some marathon runners.

I wanted breakfast, so I went back to the bus and ate cereal and soy milk by the light of my phone. Then I thought about what I was going to do for the next few hours; we were going on at 7 p.m., and I had nothing scheduled until then. I considered going outside to see whether this early September day in England was sunny or not, but I was still hungover, so sleeping until showtime seemed more appealing. Bunks on tour buses are called "coffins," as they're small, dark, and cold. Curled up under a blanket in my bunk, I had a simple thought: *Maybe someday I'll fall asleep in my coffin and not wake up.* Comforted by that idea, I fell asleep.

At 7 p.m. we got onstage and played our thirty-minute corporate set in the rain. I was being paid well, but standing under a dark-gray sky in front of 89,000 empty, wet plastic seats was grim, even if it was Wembley Stadium. After we played the last song in our short set I said an overly loud "Thank you!" The nine hundred people who'd been getting steadily soaked clapped desultorily and hurried to the exits.

A few people from the record company and some friends of my British crew had come to the show. Afterward they came backstage to get drunk: even though we had played to approximately 1 percent of the stadium's capacity, it was still Wembley Stadium. After my seventh or eighth drink I tried to pretend that being onstage at Wembley Stadium had been a big deal. "Freddie Mercury and Axl Rose played on that stage!" I told Dan, my lighting director.

"Slightly bigger crowds," he noted dryly.

At midnight Sandy came to me and said, "Mo, we have to get going." We were booked at a dance festival near Manchester the following night, and the bus driver wanted to drive overnight to avoid traffic.

"Hey!" I said to the twelve people still hanging out backstage. "Come with us to Manchester!"

They were hesitant, until one of our road crew chimed in, saying, "We have drugs!"

I shepherded seven men and five women onto the bus. Gary, our laconic German driver, looked up from the magazine he was reading, rolled his eyes, and started the bus. I wanted to feel like a rock star, so I put on *Physical Graffiti*, while my guitar tech chopped up lines of coke on the downstairs lounge table. We rolled out of the parking garage and got on the motorway to Manchester.

Before the show I'd looked at my BlackBerry and seen an email from my aunt Jane, with my stepfather Richard and my aunt Anne cc'd. It was short, saying simply, "Hi, Mobes, just hoping you're doing okay."

I sent back a nonplussed response: "i'm good, why, what's up?"

As we got on the motorway I saw on my BlackBerry that my aunt had responded, but I was drinking vodka, listening to Led Zeppelin, and flirting with the women who'd joined us on the road trip to Manchester, so I ignored her email. We burned through a few bags of cocaine, and at 3 a.m. I went upstairs with a bottle of vodka and two of the women from the record company. We went into the upstairs lounge, and I put on *Felt Mountain* by Goldfrapp.

"Oh no, not this," one of the women said.

"You don't like Goldfrapp?" I asked, my drunken mouth tripping over the hard consonants in "Goldfrapp."

"I love Goldfrapp, but it's like fucking work," she said.

I put on a Massive Attack CD instead, and the three of us started taking off our clothes. One of the women pulled out a bag of ecstasy pills and gave one to each of us.

I told myself that even if I was selling fewer records and playing for smaller crowds, I could still find moments of happiness, so long as I had the trappings of rock stardom: the sex, the drugs, the double-decker tour buses, the hotel suites. Maybe I couldn't revive my fading career, but I could use the money I'd made to make sure that I had enough drugs and alcohol on hand so that someone would always want to hang out with me and pretend it was still 2000.

As the ecstasy kicked in on top of the vodka and the cocaine, we had sex. And somewhere around the time the sun came up, shining wanly as we sped past a field of English cows, I passed out.

I woke up alone, in the parking lot of the Lowry hotel in Manchester. The women were gone, the bus was cold, and I felt like gray death. There were empty vodka bottles on the floor next to some used condoms. And something smelled terrible.

london, england (2007)   325

I looked down at my naked body. There was shit on my legs and on my stomach. Either I had engaged in messy anal sex that I didn't remember, or somebody – possibly me, possibly one of the women – had shat the couch we'd had sex on. It smelled like an open sewer, and I had to fight the urge to vomit.

I pulled on my clothes, even though my legs and stomach were covered in drying shit. I had to get to my hotel room as quickly as possible so I could clean myself off and throw up. I stopped at the front desk and asked for my key. The bright-eyed receptionist handed it to me and said, "See you tonight at the festival!"

I tried to smile, but I felt like a corpse.

I took the stairs to the third floor – I didn't want to be caught in an elevator while smelling of shit. Once I was safely in my room I ran to the bathroom and threw up in and around the toilet. After emptying my stomach I got two bottles of water and one of grapefruit juice. I drank them in the shower while I scrubbed the shit out of my leg and stomach hair.

After ten minutes of scrubbing I still felt like I'd been poisoned, because, well, I had been. But I was clean. When I stepped out of the shower I still smelled shit. Oh. My clothes. I wanted to burn them or throw them out the window, but instead I took a plastic laundry bag, scooped them up, and dropped them in the garbage.

I took out my BlackBerry and, sitting naked on the bathroom floor, sent an email to Sandy: "too hungover, cancel any interviews today. also i need new clothes, can you get me jeans and t-shirt from gap?"

Looking at my other emails, I scrolled back to my aunt's reply from the night before. She had written: "Oh, Mobes, we thought you knew. Today's the tenth anniversary of your mom's death. We hope you're okay."

56

STORRS, CONNECTICUT (1983–4)

I'd spent my first semester at the University of Connecticut looking for the perfect college girlfriend, without any success. UConn was a university of twenty-five thousand people, so there were smart, beautiful women everywhere. But either they weren't interested in me or I was too shy to talk to any of them. So I studied hard and read Kant and Bertrand Russell and made friends with the few punk-rockers I met on campus.

One of my new punk-rock friends, Bethany, lived near me in southern Connecticut, and at the end of the semester she invited me to a dinner party her college-professor parents were throwing over Christmas break. Most of the guests were her parents' fellow academics, but Bethany was allowed to invite two friends: me and her high-school friend Jenny.

We sat down for dinner at a big dining table and drank red wine and ate pasta and spinach salad. "So, Moby," a professor at Manhattan College asked me, "you're a freshman at UConn? Do you know what you want to major in?"

"I think I'm going to be a philosophy major," I said.

The academics laughed, without malice. "So you want to get rich?" Bethany's dad asked, chuckling at his own joke.

"You do know that there isn't a less practical major than philosophy, right?" an NYU professor asked me, looking concerned.

"I could write books and teach?" I suggested sheepishly, to which they laughed again and shouted, in unison, "No!"

I smiled across the table at Jenny. She smiled back, and my heart stuttered. Jenny was blonde and wore black glasses, and looked like an intellectual Danish movie star. After dinner, with red-wine courage, I asked if she wanted to go to the movies the following night. She smiled and said, "Okay."

I picked Jenny up at her parents' elegant Tudor mansion in Greenwich. We'd decided to see *The Big Chill*, and tried to cram in a lifetime of conversation during the drive to the movie theater. I learned that she wanted to major in creative writing and teach and write fiction, and that she loved the Cocteau Twins. As Jenny talked I kept stealing glances at her. She had a relaxed beauty that made me want to wake up next to her and watch her eyes move under her eyelids while she slept, a beauty that made me think of faded sweatshirts and making babies while dogs slept in front of the fireplace. As the first preview started, for *Ghostbusters*, I thought that maybe I'd found my person.

For the next two weeks we saw each other as much as we could, going to movies and bookstores, and sometimes just kissing in front of the fireplace in her parents' living room after her mom and dad had gone to sleep. After Christmas break, when she went back to Connecticut College and I returned to UConn, we wrote letters or talked on the phone every day.

I'd ended up at UConn because it was a state school – the only college I could afford. It was a perfectly fine place, but I'd had my heart set on going to Kenyon College in Ohio. The admissions board at Kenyon had even sent me a personalized letter asking me to attend, but the cost of going to Kenyon was something my mom and I couldn't consider, as we were still on welfare and food stamps.

Jenny went to Connecticut College, which sounded like a state school but was actually small, private, and very expensive. It was in New London, about an hour away from the UConn campus in Storrs. Since neither one of us had a car, one weekend in early February she took the bus to visit me.

I got to the bus stop half an hour before she arrived, and waited with flowers and a forty-five-minute mix tape that I'd made for her, named "Under Blue Moon (I Saw You)," after an Echo & the Bunnymen lyric:

SIDE A
"Going Underground," the Jam
"Messages," Orchestral Manoeuvres in the Dark
"The Killing Moon," Echo & the Bunnymen
"Academy Fight Song," Mission of Burma
"Heaven," Talking Heads

SIDE B
"'Heroes,'" David Bowie
"Any Second Now (Voices)," Depeche Mode
"Vienna," Ultravox
"Ceremony," New Order
"Atmosphere," Joy Division

Jenny stepped off the bus, brushed a strand of blonde hair out of her eyes, and smiled at me. I hugged her and took her bag. We walked back to my dorm, making our way through the empty frozen fields that surrounded UConn.

My roommate had gone to his parents' house in Newtown for the weekend, so we had my tiny dorm room to ourselves. Normally I slept in the lower bunk, but I'd moved the bunk-bed frame out of the room and put the mattresses on the floor so that Jenny and I could sleep next to each other. I also spent a few hours before Jenny arrived cleaning up our filthy room. For forty-eight hours this was going to be our home, and I wanted her to be happy. Maybe in thirty years she and I would be telling this story to our kids: on our first real weekend together we slept on thin mattresses in a dorm room with a linoleum floor and concrete walls painted light green.

UConn didn't have a beautiful campus, but I still wanted to show

Jenny where I lived and went to school. After we dropped off her bag and had sex on the makeshift bed, I showed her the library, the buildings where I had my philosophy and anthropology classes, and then the dining hall, where we had dinner with my friends.

"Look at him!" Bethany said during dinner.

"What?" I asked.

"You can't stop smiling."

Jenny blushed. But it was true.

I knew that what I felt for Jenny was at least partly irrational – I had known her for only a month. But we'd communicated every day, and I knew her creative, brilliant mind. And she was so beautiful I couldn't stop looking at her. I couldn't imagine any reason not to spend the rest of my life with her.

After dinner we went to see a band play at one of the less offensive frat houses, and then danced to the new-wave DJ who played after the band finished. The DJ played the long remix of "Temptation" by New Order, and Jenny danced with her eyes closed, singing along. My girlfriend knew all the words to "Temptation." That was it. I didn't need any more evidence. She was my person.

Later, as we lay in bed, falling asleep, I wondered what our children would be like. Jenny was descended from David Hume and I was descended from Herman Melville, so I assumed our kids would be really smart and really WASPy. I let myself fantasize about the future: we'd finish college and then move to Boston, or maybe New York, get our master's degrees and then our doctorates. We'd live in a big city for a while, but then move to a college town, where we'd write books and be professors and make little progressive babies. I'd work on music in my spare time, but eventually spend more of it playing classical music, ideally at a piano by a leaded glass window. I'd play Bach and Debussy, while Jenny read Walker Percy books in a window seat as snow fell outside.

And we'd get old together. When she found her first gray hair I would remind her that she would always be beautiful to me.

Our children would give us grandchildren. And when we were eighty or ninety we'd have all our kids and grandkids and great-grandkids over for Christmas at our big house in some college town in Massachusetts. There'd be a fire in the fireplace, a tall Christmas tree, and a room filled with dogs, babies, kids, and adults. While our happy offspring were unwrapping Christmas presents, I'd look at her and say, from the bottom of my heart, "I'm still in love with you, Jenny."

It all seemed so nice and so possible. Jenny stirred in her sleep and mumbled something unintelligible. Smiling, I held her tightly while she slept.

57

NEW YORK CITY (2007)

The Island of Misfit Toys is the place in the *Rudolph the Red-Nosed Reindeer* TV special where the broken and unwanted toys go: a toy gun that shoots jelly, a train with square wheels. My mother and my grandparents were dead, and I didn't want to travel for Christmas, so I decided to host an "Island of Misfit Toys" holiday party at my sky castle on Central Park West.

I woke up early on December 25, at 10 a.m., and went for a walk through Central Park. I loved Christmas in New York, the only day of the year when the city slowed down to something approaching calm. I could see the limestone buildings on 5th Avenue and Central Park West through the leafless trees in the park, and the only sound I heard came from my shoes crunching on the fallen leaves and the dry winter grass.

I hiked up to Belvedere Castle and gazed across the park at my five-level sky castle. It hadn't fixed any of my problems, but nevertheless it was staggeringly beautiful. I walked back home to tidy before the guests started arriving.

At 2.30 p.m. I cued up a Johnny Mathis Christmas album on my iPod and looked around my apartment. It had turned bitterly cold outside, but the sun was shining through my leaded windows and I'd lit a cheery fire in the antique marble fireplace. Like an envoy from the past, Johnny Mathis sang "It's Beginning to Look a Lot Like Christmas." I looked at the pine boughs and holly leaves I'd put on the fireplace mantle, and I had to agree with Johnny: my apartment looked a lot like Christmas. It even smelled like Christmas because

I had a pot of hot cider (with cinnamon, nutmeg, and allspice) simmering on the stove.

At 3 p.m. a steady flow of friends and family started arriving, so I opened a few bottles of Veuve Clicquot champagne. At dusk we all went onto the west balconies of my apartment to watch the Christmas sun set over the Hudson River. I felt civilized in my sky castle, drinking champagne with other sophisticated New Yorkers as the sun peacefully vanished.

I hated the idea of anyone spending Christmas in New York alone, so I'd sent my "Island of Misfit Toys" invitation to everyone I knew who might not have plans. After the sun went down my apartment started filling up. Jonathan Ames, who had just signed a deal to produce *Bored to Death* with Jason Schwartzman, showed up with his extended posse of degenerate art stars; some eastern European organized-crime figures I'd met on tour came by with presents and cocaine; a few musicians I knew dropped by; and Era, a stripper I'd met recently, showed up with some other strippers and a few drug dealers.

By 7 p.m. all five levels of my apartment were full. My refined daytime guests had politely left, and as the drugs came out the earlier veneer of Upper West Side sophistication was stripped away from the party. Era took me by the hand and led me into one of the guest bedrooms, bringing a bottle of champagne and some crystal meth with her. She had grown up preppy in Westport, Connecticut, but now had jet-black hair, was covered with tattoos, and did naked performance art when she wasn't stripping.

We drank the bottle of champagne, inhaled the crystal meth, talked about childhood Christmases in Connecticut, and had meth-fueled sex on the guest bed. Era had to go to work at a strip club in the financial district – strippers can make a lot of money working on Christmas – so after we had sex, she hastily got dressed and headed downtown.

While Era and I had been in the guest bedroom, my party guests had chewed the meat of civilization off the bone. Someone had turned off my Johnny Mathis playlist, replacing him with a ghetto-bass DJ mix from the early 1990s. The mob bosses had invited more strippers and other organized criminals, all of whom were snorting lines on the small table where I normally kept the chess set my uncle gave me for my tenth birthday. And my friend Mangina, who was an amputee, was in the kitchen mixing cocktails in the top of his prosthetic leg. When he saw me, he yelled, "We're doing stump shots!"

I moved on from champagne and crystal meth to vodka and cocaine, because, well, it was Christmas.

My respectable friend Samantha came up the stairs, crying and clutching a bottle of vodka. "What's wrong?" I asked, pleased that the crystal meth and cocaine were keeping me from slurring my words. "Why aren't you upstate?"

Samantha was a tall blonde Park Avenue doyenne who had a hedge fund-managing husband and three perfect blonde private-school daughters. She and I had met the year before at a fundraiser for the Museum of Natural History; I'd invited her to my Christmas party, even though I assumed she was spending the holiday in Westchester with her family. She looked around at the mobsters, the strippers, and the throng of downtown degenerates filling my apartment, dancing to L'Trimm's "Cars with the Boom."

"Can we go talk somewhere?" she asked. I took her to the guest bedroom where I'd done crystal meth and had sex with Era. I shut the door and the din of the party disappeared, silenced by my apartment's stone walls and solid doors. "Do you have any coke?" she asked, much to my surprise.

"Hold on." I went back downstairs and got some coke from the girlfriend of one of the mob bosses. After we did a couple of lines Samantha told me why she wasn't upstate for Christmas. Her husband had disappeared three days ago. He hadn't called. He hadn't texted. And when she called the hedge fund where he worked, they told her that he'd been fired a year ago.

Early yesterday morning, 8 a.m. on Christmas Eve, he'd called. "I can't come back," he told her quietly.

"Where are you?"

"I'm in New Jersey, Sam. I'm not coming back." He told her that he now identified as a woman, was in love with a man in Newark, and was never coming back to her or their children.

Samantha had grown up on the Upper East Side. She'd gone to Spence and Yale and had married her husband after he finished Harvard Business School. Their married life, although chaste and platonic after the birth of their third child, had been picture-perfect. They'd vacationed in Palm Springs at her parents' winter home. They'd vacationed on Fishers Island at her parents' summer home. They'd vacationed in the Hamptons at their own summer home. They did the charity-ball circuit. Their oldest daughter was preparing to be a debutante, just as Samantha had been. And yesterday morning she had learned it had all been a lie: her husband was unemployed and smoking crystal meth at a motel in New Jersey.

Samantha had held herself together and spent Christmas with her kids at her parents' Beaux Arts mansion on 74th Street. After her kids had gone to sleep she'd taken a taxi across the park to my apartment. "Did I do anything wrong?" she asked, pleading, looking like a worried child. "Am I still attractive?"

"You're gorgeous," I said, truthfully. She was absurdly beautiful; she could have been Grace Kelly's sister. Samantha did another line of coke and kissed me.

I'd had twelve or fourteen drinks, plus a few lines of crystal meth and a few of coke. I was still looking dimly through my eyes, but I felt like my body was inhabited by an eternally hungry fallen angel living in a garbage bag full of alcohol and drugs. We pulled off our clothes and had sex on the bed where a few hours earlier I'd been snorting crystal meth and having sex with Era.

Afterward we sprawled on the bed silently. I felt like a glowing demon. It was Christmas, and I was high and drunk, lying naked next to a broken goddess. Samantha gathered up her clothes, kissed me gently, and said, "I need to get back to my kids."

I put on my clothes, swallowed the last dregs of the bottle of vodka she'd brought, and returned to the party. While Samantha and I had sequestered ourselves, the party had gotten even bigger. Louder. More unhinged. I looked around at the strangers doing drugs in my apartment and was filled with pride at the sweet hell I'd curated.

As I headed to the kitchen, my friend Genevieve, who'd recently moved to New York from Vienna, blocked my path. Looking around, she said, with horror in her voice, "You are chaos."

I put my hands on her shoulders and grinned. "That's the nicest thing anyone's ever said to me," I told her sincerely.

"It's not a compliment," she said, disgusted, and walked away.

But it was a compliment. I was proud to be chaos.

The world was terrible. I was worse.

In the kitchen I opened another bottle of vodka and pulled a knife out of a butcher's block. "Jonathan!" I yelled at Jonathan Ames.

"What?" He looked up from the table where he was sitting with one of the strippers. I threw the knife at him. Lovingly, because I loved Jonathan.

He screamed and held up his hand. I heard a sharp sound, like a hammer hitting a small nail. The point of the knife had bounced off Jonathan's Princeton college ring. He looked at me with horror, the blood draining from his face.

"No, Jonathan, it was nice!" I yelled. "It was 'cause I love you!" I picked up the knife again. He ran away from me, hiding behind Mangina and our elf-ear-wearing friend Reverend Jen. "Okay," I said, disappointed. "I'll put the knife away."

At midnight Era returned with one of her stripper coworkers. "You're back!" I yelled, over a Mötley Crüe song. When the ghetto-bass playlist had ended somebody had put on a hair-metal one.

"Here," she said, putting a filthy green Santa hat on my head, "I brought you a present." Taking my hand and that of her stripper friend, she led us into the master bedroom. We lit candles and did more crystal meth and had a threesome, getting glitter and menstrual blood on my California King bed and its 1,020-thread-count Millesimo sheets.

When we were done I walked out of the bedroom, naked except for the dirty green Santa hat. I wanted to see if the party was still going on and if Jonathan was still mad at me for throwing a knife at him. *He shouldn't be mad,* I thought. *I was chaos, and why would anyone be mad at chaos?* Also, his ring had saved him.

At the other end of the hallway, at the top of the stairs, was Ruth, a British journalist I'd invited to the party. She was dressed formally and was with her elderly British parents, dressed equally formally. I'd never gone on a date with Ruth, but I had a crush on her. She was erudite and kind and pretty. Apparently she'd read my invitation to a Christmas party at an elegant penthouse on the Upper West Side and assumed that I was hosting, well, a Christmas party at an elegant penthouse on the Upper West Side.

Instead she'd brought her parents into the second circle of hell, a bacchanal of strippers and drugs and Mafia bosses. And standing under an art deco chandelier there was me, the host and ringmaster, naked except for a soiled Santa hat.

I screamed, ashamed at my nakedness, and ran back into the bedroom, where Era and her stripper friend were waiting in the darkness, smiling.

58

STORRS, CONNECTICUT (1984)

During my second semester at UConn my friend Drew discovered LSD and started taking it weekly. It was cheap – only $5 a hit – and easy to get. During our first semester together he'd been a clean-cut freshman, trying to decide between poli-sci and history as his major. Now I would see him in the cafeteria, staring quietly at a patch of sunlight as it moved across towers of plates and plastic bins of Frosted Flakes.

I'd never done acid, but since Drew liked it, I decided to try it. One Tuesday afternoon I sat in his concrete dorm room, gave him $5, swallowed a tab of LSD, and picked up the Moody Blues album *Days of Future Passed*. For ten or fifteen minutes nothing happened, and I wondered if maybe I had gotten a dud dose. Then the shapes on the album cover slowly started moving. With a big smile, I told Drew, "It's working."

We spent the day wandering around the campus, studying the veins of marble countertops and watching newly sprouted grass poking through the snow, amazed at how this simple, inexpensive drug transformed everything. I felt light and happy; the world was showing me aspects of itself that were normally hidden in plain sight.

Around 8 p.m. Drew went to visit his girlfriend and I went back to my dorm room, ready for the trip to end. But it didn't. At midnight I was *really* ready for the trip to end. But it kept going and I started getting scared – the acid had been fun, but I wanted my old brain back. At 3 a.m. I took a shower, hoping I could wash the acid out of my system, but I was just hyperaware of each individual water droplet as it hit my skin. At 5 a.m. I decided that I was going to feel this way forever. I curled up in the bottom bunk of the bunk bed and fell asleep at dawn.

A few hours later I woke up, feeling almost normal. I took a deep breath, saw the melting snow outside my window, and something in my brain snapped. I didn't know whether I was having a flashback or whether I had gone crazy. I waited for my brain to feel normal again, but all day it felt like my mind had been taken away from me and replaced with something hard and foreign. At 10 p.m., at the end of the longest, strangest day of my life, I crawled back into my bottom bunk, terrified. I hoped that today had just been an awful day-after-taking-LSD experience and that in the morning my brain would go back to the way it had been.

But I woke up the next morning panicking: my brain was still broken.

After seven days of this I went to the school psychiatrist. He sat, stoic and professional, with his psychiatrist's sideburns and mustache, behind an institutional gray metal desk in a beige office. I told him that I'd done acid a week ago and that my brain hadn't felt right since. I didn't tell him I was having a panic attack, because I didn't know what a panic attack was. All I knew was that my brain had changed, and that I was terrified. I just wanted my old brain back.

The psychiatrist heard the word "acid," smiled thinly, and assumed I was another college acid casualty having some sort of flashback or LSD-inspired psychotic break. He wrote a prescription for perphenazine, a powerful antipsychotic, and said, "Here you go. This should help."

I took it as prescribed – and I felt worse. When I went back to the psychiatrist a week later, I told him that I still felt terrible. He said, "Okay, don't worry," and prescribed a stronger dose of perphenazine.

After another week of taking the medication and struggling through my school routines I had an allergic reaction to the perphenazine. On Friday morning I woke up feeling my usual despair and terror, but as the day went on I started to feel intense tightness and burning in all my muscles. By lunchtime my ligaments felt like they had been turned into scalding wires. And by the end of the day I felt like I was on fire.

I went to the emergency room at the college hospital, where they sedated me and put me into a metal-framed hospital bed. The next morning I woke up and admitted defeat. I was broken. My brain was broken. And the anti-psychotics had taken my wounded brain and made it worse. I still didn't know what was wrong with me – I just desperately wanted my old brain back. I dropped out of college, packed up my things, and moved home.

A few days after I left UConn my mom took me to a psychiatrist in Stamford. After talking with me for an hour, smiling kindly and calmly asking me questions, he diagnosed me. "You have an anxiety disorder," he said. "It's a rare and very unpleasant type called 'plateau panic disorder.' Basically you're having panic attacks that don't ever end."

"So it's not acid flashbacks?"

"No, it's not flashbacks, and you definitely don't need antipsychotics." He shook his head. "Whoever prescribed you perphenazine should lose his license."

I started crying, and apologized to him through my tears.

"It's not the first time someone's cried in my office, Moby."

"I just don't know what to do," I said. "I want my brain to feel normal again."

"It will, Moby. I promise." He took a deep breath before he continued. "To be honest, I don't know if what you're experiencing is from the acid, Moby. You might want to think about therapy. This type of extreme panic usually comes from buried trauma."

I'd been calling Jenny every day since I'd woken up with a broken brain. At first she had been incredibly sympathetic, but lately she'd sounded distant and almost annoyed when I reached her. After I got home from the Stamford psychiatrist's office I took my mom's phone to the wooden basement stairs for privacy and called her again.

"I need you," I told her. "Can you come home this weekend?"

She didn't respond.

"Jenny?"

She sighed and said quietly, "Moby, I'm sorry. I can't do this."

"What do you mean?" I felt vertiginous, like I was falling into a mine shaft.

She started crying. "I wish I could be there for you, but I'm at school. I can't do this."

"Are you breaking up with me?"

She cried harder. "I think so."

I went numb.

"Moby?" she asked. "Are you there?"

I still couldn't speak.

"Talk to me," she said.

But I couldn't.

"Moby? Talk to me!"

I managed to say, "I have to go, Jenny," and hung up the phone.

I rode my ten-speed bike – the same lime-green Schwinn I'd had since sixth grade – to a rundown local bar by the Noroton Heights train station. I didn't know where else to go. Since I'd started panicking I'd been drinking every day, as alcohol was the only thing that helped me to calm down. It didn't put my brain's synapses and neurons back in their pre-acid configuration, but it gave me a few moments of relief from the pain.

I showed the bartender my fake ID and ordered a beer. It was 6 p.m. on a Thursday and the bar was empty, aside from a few locals and some sallow-faced businessmen. There was a basketball game on the TV, but no one was watching it. I drank my beer and looked at my reflection in the mirror behind the bar.

I looked like a hollow ghost. I'd never been this scared. My brain had snapped almost a month ago, and despite what the nice psychiatrist said, I didn't know if it would ever get better. I quickly finished my beer and, defeated and despairing, ordered a second.

My friends were all at exclusive and expensive New England colleges, studying art history and French literature. They were meeting wonderful women, falling in love under oak trees, and thinking about the fascinating adult lives that were waiting for them. And I was an unemployed college dropout living at my mom's house. I had no career prospects, no money, no girlfriend, and – unless I was drunk – no respite from my unceasing panic attacks.

I wanted to kill myself. The only thing stopping me was that I didn't want the panic to win.

59

NEW YORK CITY (2008)

Hillary Clinton was talking to me, but I was too hungover to respond. We were standing on a balcony on the thirtieth floor of the San Remo apartment building on Central Park West. She was in a dark-blue power suit, and her silver-blonde hair was meticulously styled, falling just past her collar. I was swaying on my feet, unshowered and wearing a frayed gray sweater over an old Cramps T-shirt.

Hillary and I had known each other for a few years and had hosted a few fundraisers together. Every time we met up she asked my opinion on things and made a huge effort to be nice to me, but I never understood why. She had been a successful lawyer, a First Lady, and was currently a US senator. And I was a musician who with each passing year became more and more of an obscure *Jeopardy!* question.

Senator Clinton looked earnestly into my eyes as I tried to say something insightful about the state of American politics. I wanted to conceal from her that I was so hungover I could barely think.

"Oh," she said, filling my awkward synaptic-glue silence, "do you know Darryl from Run-D.M.C.? He's coming too."

I didn't tell her about the time in 1989 when I'd been DJing at Mars and had skipped the needle on a record while Darryl had been freestyling – that would have required using multisyllabic words. So, uncertain of my syntax, I managed to say, "Yes, I know him from back in the day." She gave me a warm smile, shook my hand, and headed back inside to the fundraiser.

The San Remo was a beautiful art deco building, a few blocks south of my five-level penthouse at the El Dorado – which I'd just sold. I looked up the street at my sky castle, bathed in the last light of sunset, and wondered what had gone wrong. I had planned on living there forever. I'd thought that as I approached the end of my life, I would walk my grandkids down the street to the Museum of Natural History. In my fantasy I would show them the giant blue whale (assuming it hadn't been replaced by an animatronic robot whale) and tell them about my first trip to the museum in 1968, when I stood underneath the whale and experienced open-mouthed terror and awe. My mother had tried to pull me away, but I couldn't stop staring at the belly of the giant creature.

But a week ago I had sold the penthouse to a Texan divorcée who was probably taking her actual grandchildren to go look at the whale. In addition to selling the sky castle I'd gotten rid of a lot of other things in the past month. I'd sold my sixty-acre upstate compound to a hedge-fund manager. CNN's Fareed Zakaria had bought some beachfront property I'd acquired in the Dominican Republic. I'd sold a house in Beverly Hills I'd only visited once. And I'd simply given teany to Kelly.

I'd originally bought these things to find happiness and legitimacy, but one night I'd been at a café in Tribeca, talking with my old friend Ashley, who I originally met at a Bible-study group in Connecticut. I was telling him about the headaches and hassles that came with owning all this far-flung real estate, and he asked a simple question: "Are you happy?"

I wanted to lie, as I normally did, and say, "Of course I am!" But Ashley had been guileless and honest with me through the years, even when he went through a painful divorce, so I answered truthfully. "No, I'm not happy," I said, defeated.

"So why not get rid of these things, if they don't make you happy?"

I wanted to explain that I had my houses and businesses to prove to the world that I had worth, and that I was no longer the poor kid from Connecticut who'd imploded with shame every time his mom had used food stamps at the supermarket. But I couldn't refute Ashley's simple logic, as I simply wasn't happy. The next day I called my lawyer and invented an acronym: MIGA, or Make It Go Away.

Now the only real estate I had was the same loft on Mott Street I'd lived in since the mid-1990s. I'd thought about selling that as well, but it was simple and pretty, it was where I made music, and it didn't make me anxious. And for now I was still alive and needed a place to sleep. I still wasn't happy after getting rid of my pointless real-estate portfolio, but I felt lighter, and less like an overcompensating Jay Gatsby.

A waiter strolling around the balcony on the San Remo offered me some pigs in a blanket on a silver tray. I'd compromised all my other ideals and standards, but I was still a militant vegan, so I politely said, "No, thank you, but could you get me a black coffee and a vodka on the rocks?"

He looked at me with alcoholic understanding and said, "I'll see what I can do."

Even though I'd had eight hours of chemically curated sleep, I was exhausted. The hangover made my teeth ache like badly rung bells.

Hillary Clinton left the fundraiser at 9 p.m., but I stayed for another hour, trying to flirt with a woman who worked for the Clinton Foundation and drinking glass after glass of the host's vodka. At ten I stumbled into a taxi and went downtown to the Highline Ballroom, where some vegans I knew were throwing an animal-rights fundraiser.

My friend Jesse Malin was performing when I arrived, so I walked onstage, stopped him and his band in the middle of a song, and took the microphone. "If anyone has any drugs," I said, looking out at five hundred confused faces in the crowd, "just meet me on the side of the stage. Thank you." I put the microphone back in the mic stand and said "Carry on" to the band, who stared at me with irritation and bewilderment.

I went to the bar at the side of the stage and ordered a Porkslap beer, while I waited for somebody to show up with drugs. Drinking Porkslap, even though it didn't contain actual pork, seemed ironic at an animal-rights fundraiser. But I wasn't drinking it to be ironic; I was drinking it because I'd had only seven or eight vodkas uptown and I wanted to get drunk.

After a few minutes a twenty-year-old boy in a Phish T-shirt and a light-blue hoodie walked over and cautiously offered me a joint. "A joint?" I said, vexed. "Pot is a seasoning, not a drug."

"Sorry," he said meekly, slipping back into the crowd.

Had I been rude to him? No, I reasoned, he'd been rude to me by offering me pot when I wanted real drugs. I was outraged. This was New York City, the land of Lou Reed and the New York Dolls, the island where sybarites came to be sybaritic, and nobody had real drugs?

I walked back onstage, fuming. Debbie Harry was performing and had just finished a song with Lady Bunny and Miss Guy. I took the mic from Lady Bunny and admonished the crowd. "I'm very disappointed with you," I told them. "You call yourselves New Yorkers, but no one here had drugs for me." A few people started laughing, and I scolded them. "I'm serious. I wanted drugs and you all let me down. You should be ashamed."

I handed the microphone back to Lady Bunny and stalked off the stage. A woman who worked at Angelica's Kitchen stopped me as I headed for the bar. "That was funny!" she said.

"I'm not trying to be funny," I told her. "I want drugs."

I went upstairs to the dressing rooms, where I found my friend Aurora smoking pot and drinking beer with some of the musicians who were playing at the fundraiser. Aurora was a burlesque performer who looked like a young Shirley MacLaine. "You look upset, Mo," she said.

"I wanted drugs and no one had drugs," I said, like a petulant seven-year-old, sitting down on a stained Ikea couch and draining my second can of Porkslap.

"You want coke?" she asked.

"Why, do you have any?" I said, my eyes brightening.

"No, but I want coke too."

"Okay, let's go find coke."

We asked bartenders, audience members, and the coat-check girl. Nobody had any (or nobody would admit to it). But then I asked some of the old roadies smoking cigarettes behind the stage, "Do any of you have drugs?"

"Follow me," a particularly old and grizzled roadie said, putting out his cigarette on a speaker box. Aurora and I followed him to a closet behind the stage. He had stringy gray hair down to the collar of the black T-shirt that covered his beer gut. He escorted us into the closet and closed the door behind us. "So what do you want?" he asked.

"Just some coke," I said.

He pulled a bag of coke out of his pocket. "One hundred dollars."

It was a very small bag of cocaine and I assumed it was terrible, as it was being sold to me by a man who looked like he'd spent most of his adult life in prison. But it was cocaine, so I didn't bargain. I handed him $100, he went back to work, and Aurora and I started doing coke off the back of my BlackBerry.

The cocaine was, in fact, terrible. It burned through my sinuses like pulverized salt and gravel. But it was cocaine, the most paradoxical drug: it seemed like the best drug when I was doing it late at night, and the worst at eleven the next morning, when I was anxious and grinding my teeth and trying to go to sleep.

"This coke is awful," Aurora said, as she finished her third line.

"I know," I said, cutting a fourth line on the back of my phone. "It's awful, disgusting cocaine, and I love it." I'd started doing cocaine only two years earlier, but I already felt like getting drunk without cocaine was a horrible compromise.

The roadie came back into the closet. "Moby, I feel bad that I charged you so much," he said. "Here's another bag of coke."

"Thank you so much," I said. "Will you do a line with us?"

I cut him a line on the back of my phone. "I've never done coke off a phone," he said, leaning down to snort the powder.

"Phones are clean and smooth – perfect for cocaine," I opined.

"You know," he said, "the last time I saw you was in 1999, at the Virgin Megastore."

"You were there?"

"Yeah, I loaded in the P.A.," he said. "So how've you been?"

I laughed. And then I laughed harder, even though Aurora and the roadie weren't laughing.

What could I say? How had I been? My narcissism, abetted by the cocaine, made me want to spend the next five hours telling him everything: how after playing that show in the basement of a record store I'd sold tens of millions of records, toured the world, dated movie stars, made millions of dollars, and managed to screw everything up – my life, my career, my friendships. I wanted to tell him that not a day went by without me thinking about killing myself, and the final punctuation mark on my failing life and career was this very moment, doing rotgut cocaine in a cramped closet with a roadie.

"Well," I said, "it's been a strange few years."

After consuming most of the two bags of coke, Aurora and I left the closet and went to the bar to order more Porkslap. I saw my friend Johnny Dynell and ran over to hug him. Johnny looked like a 1950s Latino pop star and had been Andy Warhol's favorite DJ in the 1980s. He and his wife, Chi Chi Valenti, had thrown some of the best parties in lower Manhattan, from "Gray Gardens" to "Night of a Thousand Stevies."

"Moby!" he said, grinning. "Come with me! You need to meet the hippies!"

After ten drinks and an equal number of lines my teeth were grinding, my nerves were singing like high-tension power wires, and I was filled with God's own love and chaos. "I want to meet the hippies," I said deliberately.

Johnny took my hand; I took Aurora's; we walked onto the middle of the dance floor. Another drag-queen band was playing onstage, and on the dance floor a circle of Burning Man hippies were doing interpretive hippie dances. "Hippies!" Johnny yelled, by way of introduction. "Moby!"

"Moby!" they yelled, and pulled Aurora and me into their dance circle.

"Wait!" I shouted. "I need a drink." I ran to the bar and ordered two vodkas, one for me and one for Aurora. Back on the dance floor, I drank my vodka and lurched around with the hippies, while the band played a heavy-metal version of Juice Newton's "Queen of Hearts." I yelled, "I love this song!" The room was spinning and I was surrounded by twenty hippie dervishes who looked like they'd just left an audition for a Broadway revival of *Hair*.

I'd gotten past my childhood resentment of hippies; as I'd gotten older I'd decided that most of them were fairly harmless and well-intentioned. The song ended, the band said, "Thank you, good night!" and the hippies and Johnny and Aurora and I all collapsed onto the floor in a heap of human flesh reeking of vodka, cocaine, and patchouli.

"Do we have more coke?" I asked Aurora.

She looked in her purse and pulled out a plastic bag with a little bit of white powder at the bottom. "Just a bit," she said. I took the bag, poured the rest of the cocaine on the back of my phone, and cut myself a line.

"Moby, you shouldn't do that in public," Johnny said, as the Highline's lights came on. The fundraiser was over and the audience were walking around us on their way to the exits.

"But I want to," I said, doing my line and handing the phone to Aurora.

"I don't know," she said.

So I took my phone back and did the rest of the cocaine, while Aurora and Johnny looked around nervously.

"Uh-oh," Johnny said, spotting a security guard heading in our direction. He was wearing black from head to toe, and from my vantage point on the floor he looked like an eleven-foot-tall stormtrooper. "I don't care who the fuck you are, you can't do that shit in here!" the security guard yelled at me.

"Oh, it's okay," I said magnanimously. "I'm all out of coke, so I won't do any more."

He pointed at the exit. "You and your friends, leave!"

He was mad, but my veins were singing with vodka, Porkslap beer, and cocaine and I felt nothing but love for everyone, even this angry stormtrooper. "Do you want a hug?" I asked earnestly.

"Get the fuck out!" he yelled in my face.

As we headed for the door, one of the hippies said, "Moby, you should come with us on our bus."

The hippies led us around the corner to their brightly painted school bus. "Like the Partridge Family," Aurora said.

"It's our Furthur," one of the hippies said, smiling at the battered vehicle. We piled onto the bus, and one of the hippies started playing records in the makeshift DJ booth at the back. The seats had been removed from the inside of the bus and the ceiling was painted with hieroglyphics and cartoons.

As we drove up 10th Avenue, the DJ played my song "Go," and the hippies cheered. "Moby Go!" a British hippie said. "Wicked tune!" The bus stopped for a red light near the Lincoln Tunnel and everyone happily fell over.

"Where are we going?" Aurora asked.

"Harlem!" the hippies yelled.

"Harlem? I was born in Harlem," I said. Changing the subject, I asked, "Does anyone have any drugs?"

"Sure, we've got pot," a young Asian hippie said.

"No, real drugs," I said, as if I were talking to a child.

"Only organic drugs," he said indignantly.

"Beer?"

"Just pot."

I pouted. Pot was my least favorite drug. Cocaine, vodka, ecstasy, crystal meth, tequila, champagne, cheap beer: they all sped me up and made my synapses fire like manic speedboats. But when I smoked pot I felt like someone had shellacked my brain with glue and molasses. I pulled Aurora aside. "Roar" – her nickname – "they don't have beer or drugs. I think we need to go."

"But the hippies are so cute! Come on, let's smoke pot with them." She tried to pass me a joint.

The bus stopped in front of an abandoned brownstone at 160th Street, near the West Side Highway. I said to the hippies, "Thanks for the ride, but we have to go. I need vodka and real drugs."

They looked crestfallen, but hugged us as we said goodbye. It started raining as we walked away from the hippies and their iron-ically drug-free bus.

"You were born in Harlem?" Aurora asked.

"168th Street, near here," I said. I was still high, but starting to come down. "Can we go see where I was born?" We walked west as the rain picked up.

I was born in Harlem at the Columbia Presbyterian Hospital on September 11, 1965. The only other time I'd been there was in 1997, for a study on panic attacks. I'd agreed to be a part of the study to see if the psychiatrists could help me with my unrelent-ing panic attacks. The first part of the study involved a ten-page questionnaire about anxiety and lifestyle. I'd answered the ques-tions honestly, except for one: "How many drinks do you have in a month?" I'd lied, checking "40–50."

When the doctor reviewed my responses he said, "Forty or fifty drinks a month? You might be an alcoholic." I didn't tell him the truth, which was that I was having forty or fifty drinks a week, or somewhere upward of two hundred every month. That was a decade ago; now I was up to around a hundred drinks a week, or four hundred a month.

At the end of the study the doctor confirmed what I'd been told in 1984: I had a severe plateau panic disorder, which meant that to some extent I was always panicking. I also had episodic spikes of panic, but he told me that because of my disorder, I was never not anxious. "Which might explain your drinking," he said, clearly worried. "At some point you might want to get help."

Aurora and I looked up at the gothic facade of Columbia Presbyterian Hospital. It was 1 a.m. on a rainy Tuesday night; the streets around the hospital were wet and empty.

"You were born here?" she asked.

"That's what it says on my birth certificate."

"It kind of looks like a prison."

As we looked at the hospital I spotted a pair of orange stripper shoes on top of a plastic garbage bin. "Roar, look," I said in awe. I picked up the shoes. They were bright orange and had shiny silver heels. Even though they'd been in the garbage, they weren't very dirty. "They're my spirit animal," I said, taking off my sneakers and putting on the glittering orange shoes. Tottering around the sidewalk in my glowing orange stripper shoes, I asked, "Should we head downtown and find sex and drugs?"

Aurora suddenly got serious. "You were born here. What would baby Moby say to you?"

I stood, wobbling in my high heels, and looked up at the hulking gothic building where I'd been born. The night was young, but I'd already had a dozen drinks and a dozen lines of bad cocaine. The day before I'd had a session with my therapist, Dr. Barry Lubetkin, in which I'd told him that I was getting rid of all my unnecessary property. "Are you going to kill yourself?" he asked me bluntly.

I was taken aback. "I don't know. Why?"

"People sometimes get rid of their stuff before they kill themselves."

I knew that therapists had to report you to the police if they thought you were suicidal, so I laughed and said, "Look at me, I'm doing great!" I didn't want to be institutionalized.

I looked at Aurora and seriously considered her question. What would baby Moby say to me as I stood on the sidewalk, drunk, high, wearing orange stripper shoes and torn apart by hangovers and depression and panic attacks?

"I don't know – 'Stop hurting me'?"

60

DARIEN, CONNECTICUT (1984)

I loved animals. But I also loved eating them.

When I was growing up our house was full of rescued dogs, rescued cats, rescued mice, rescued gerbils, rescued lizards, and even rescued lab rats. It had also been full of meatloaf, hamburgers, hot dogs, salami, and chicken nuggets. I loved our rescue animals unconditionally, even when they bit me or peed on me. When I was very little my mom had taught me that if a gerbil bit me or a mouse peed on me, it was because they were scared. She explained, "Wouldn't you be scared being held by a thing with giant teeth that was a few hundred times bigger than you?" I agreed that I would.

In 1975 I'd been walking past the Darien town dump when somehow a tiny mewing sound cut through the noise of traffic and dump trucks. I walked over to a stained cardboard box, where the tiny mewing was coming from, and opened it. Inside were three dead kittens and one tiny gray one, barely alive, not much bigger than a finger. Someone had poured beer on them, and the barely alive kitten was mewing pitifully and blindly, as his eyes hadn't opened yet. I picked him up as gently as I could, wrapped him in my T-shirt, and rushed home.

My mom and I took him to the local vet, who examined him and shook his head sadly. "He's very sick," the vet said. "In fact, I'm surprised he's alive. I can give you some medicine for him, but don't get attached, because he probably won't survive." We brought him home and set him up in a clean box that my mom had lined with old T-shirts. We gave him warm milk and medicine, and for some reason that we could never remember we called him Tucker.

George, my grandmother's cranky old dachshund, walked over to see what sort of tiny mewing creature was now living in his house. My family had told me that when George had been a puppy he had been friendly, but now that he was elderly, he growled at my mother and me, and barely tolerated my grandmother.

Cranky George looked at tiny mewing Tucker and lay down next to him. Tucker stopped mewing. A minute later he started making the tiniest little baby-kitten purr. And in that instant old, cranky George became Tucker's mom. For the next few weeks he didn't leave Tucker's side, and Tucker didn't die.

As Tucker grew up he followed me around the house, played with me, and met me every day when I came home from school, like the little brother I never had.

Growing up I'd known only one vegetarian, a girl in my high school, and I thought she was absurd. At one point I was arguing with her about vegetarianism, and she asked me, "If you love animals, how can you eat them?" I didn't have an answer, but it seemed like a nonsensical question. Everyone ate animals. And as far as I knew, everyone had always eaten animals. Eating animals was woven into the fabric of humanity, like cars or television. So even though I loved animals, generally more than people, I kept on eating them.

After I dropped out of UConn, Tucker knew something was wrong, and he tried to take care of me as best as he could. But even with his ministrations the first month of being a college dropout was horrible. Every morning I woke up panicking, and the only time my anxiety waned was when I drank beer or vodka. My friends were all off at college, so I didn't have anyone to hang out with, and I couldn't get a job because the anxiety was so intense and unceasing.

Most days after breakfast I put a Joy Division or Echo & the Bunnymen cassette in my Walkman and rode my Schwinn ten-speed to the beach or a local park. There I would sit on a bench, trying to write in my journal, wondering when the panic would abate even a little bit. But day after day the anxiety held my brain in its horrible talons.

I found a bar called The Beat, in Port Chester, New York, twenty minutes from my mom's house, and started spending most of my nights there. It was a dive bar run by two local artists – and the only place nearby where the DJs played new wave and punk rock. I made some friends there who weren't at college for a variety of dysfunctional reasons. Allard, a Canadian who looked like Ian McCulloch, lived with his parents in New Canaan, after being kicked out of art school for drawing ears on the walls. "The walls have ears!" he told me the night we met at The Beat. "Get it?" Melissa was a nineteen-year-old new-wave bassist with baby-blue hair who'd left Hampshire College to live in Greenwich and take care of her sick mom. And Brock was a tall stoner from Stamford who'd dropped out of Boston College with the grand ambition of being a drummer.

I befriended a few other lonely suburban misfits at The Beat, but Allard, Melissa, and Brock became my closest friends. Since Melissa played bass, Brock played drums, and Allard looked like Ian McCulloch, we started a band. We were all obsessed with sad, self-pitying music from the north of the UK, so even though we were Connecticut teenagers, we did our best to look and sound like the Smiths and Aztec Camera.

Having friends and playing music helped loosen the grip of the anxiety; by the beginning of the summer I was able to look for a job. I'd seen an interesting ad in the *Stamford Advocate* help-wanted pages: "Arts & crafts store looking for part-time sales help, creativity a plus." After filling out an application and being interviewed for a few minutes I was hired at $3.25 an hour to work at Feats of Clay in the Stamford Town Center mall.

then it fell apart

The owner of the store, Jimmie, was an old hippie who seemed even more anxious than I did, largely because no one came into Feats of Clay. It was 1984, so people went to the mall to buy bright clothes that would make them look like Molly Ringwald or Eddie Murphy. People wanted Madonna T-shirts, not dusty tribal drums from Rwanda and hand-carved chess pieces from Ecuador. Jimmie paid me under the counter, and I worked three days a week, dusting the handmade things from South America and Africa that nobody wanted to buy.

One day Melissa and Allard came to the mall to have lunch with me at Sbarro, in the mall's food court. I ordered pizza with sausage and pepperoni, while they ordered pizza with peppers and onions. "Are you trying to lose weight?" I joked. They were both already as skinny as pencils.

"Last night we saw this British animal movie," Allard said.

"And now we're vegetarians," Melissa said.

I paused and waited for the punchline. When it didn't come, I said, "What?"

"We're vegetarians," Allard said again.

"What does that mean?"

It was their first day as vegetarians, so they had to think about how best to answer the question. Melissa shrugged and said, "No more meat, I guess."

I laughed at them and told them they'd be eating meat again in a week.

After work I borrowed my mom's Chevette and drove to the Burger King in Norwalk, where I ordered my usual: a Whopper, medium fries, and a chocolate shake. I sat in the parking lot, eating my Whopper, and thought about the question I had been asked in high school: "If you love animals, how can you eat them?" I wanted to sit down with Allard and Melissa and the girl who'd asked me that question and yell at them, "Because everybody eats animals!" But I knew it was a paltry defense.

At UConn I'd planned on being a philosophy major, and before I dropped out I took an introductory philosophy class. The professor, Dr. Fink, told the class about the is–ought fallacy. In short, justifying something just because it had been part of the status quo for a long time was logically indefensible. He'd asked us to think of examples, and we'd come up with slavery, children working in factories, women not being allowed to vote, spraying DDT on vegetables, and lead paint. They were all noxious aspects of history that at one point had been defended with logic that boiled down to "This thing exists, so it should continue to exist, even though we know it's bad and wrong."

I finished my Whopper, even though suddenly it wasn't as delicious as it normally was. I drove back to my mom's house, where Tucker was waiting for me on the orange-carpeted stairs. I sat down to play with him, moving a pen along the edge of the stairs while he stalked and attacked it.

I loved Tucker. And I knew, to the depths of my being, that I would do anything I could to keep him from pain, or even sadness. I looked at his gray-striped face, as I had thousands and thousands of times. He had two eyes, a central nervous system, an unbelievably rich emotional life, and a profound desire to avoid pain and suffering. And as he wrestled with my pen, I realized that every animal with two eyes and a central nervous system had an unbelievably rich emotional life and a profound desire to avoid pain and suffering.

In that instant I knew that I couldn't be involved in anything that caused an animal to suffer. I called Allard.

"Hello?"

"Okay, don't feel smug, but I'm a vegetarian now too."

61

MIAMI, FLORIDA (2008)

When I first met my friend Matt he was a junkie working at The Beat in Port Chester, New York. Over the decades I'd known him he'd struggled with heroin addiction and homelessness. His addiction got to such a bad place that after shooting up with a dirty needle in his twenties, he had his leg amputated. He'd ignored the infection as it spread, just self-medicating the pain away with heroin. By the time he made it to an emergency room, his leg was so gangrenous that they had to cut it off.

But a few years ago he'd kicked heroin. He met a wonderful woman and was now happy, sober, and married, living in Miami with his wife and three Boston terriers. I'd booked a DJ gig in Miami so I could fly down for the weekend of his fortieth birthday party. I wanted to be there for Matt – I loved him and I was proud of him for beating his addiction and not dying.

My plan was to DJ on Saturday night, get a good night's sleep at my hotel, and wake up early for Matt's birthday brunch, before flying back to New York. I was staying by Biscayne Bay, and after I checked in I walked to the hotel's small beach to jump in the water – where I promptly stepped on a jellyfish. At first it stung a little bit. Then it felt like my foot was being bathed in acid, while somebody held a blowtorch to it. As the pain kept escalating, I hopped around the hot sand, wondering what to do.

I'd read somewhere that peeing on a jellyfish sting helped, but I was on a beach full of glamorous fashionistas, and I couldn't just start peeing on myself. I hobbled up the beach and went into a bathroom stall, where I held my foot over the toilet and peed on it. It brought the pain down from unbearable to just run-of-the-mill excruciating.

I limped back to my room and alternated between peeing on my foot and washing it in the stylish white-tiled shower. I asked the Internet what to do, and it said that I should get some hydrocortisone cream for my foot. I texted Sandy, my tour manager, who bought some cream at a nearby Rite Aid. I slathered it all over my pulsing, wounded hoof and then planted myself in an Eames chair next to the orange lucite desk in my room, watching CNN to distract myself from the greasy pain.

I was scheduled to DJ at midnight, so at 11 p.m. Sandy and I headed to the venue, my foot slathered in hydrocortisone cream and stuffed into my sneaker. I could barely walk, but I didn't need to walk or run to DJ. I just needed to be able to stand behind the Pioneer mixer and occasionally wave my hands in the air. I thought that vodka would help with the pain, so backstage I opened the bottle of Stolichnaya that was in my dressing room.

I was scheduled to DJ after Princess Superstar, a friend of mine who had been sober for years. We'd known each other since 2002, when she rapped on one of my songs, but now whenever I saw her she made a point of letting me know that I was an alcoholic who needed help. Princess Superstar visited my dressing room, wearing silver shorts and a hot pink shirt, and saw me sitting on a gray metal folding chair, drinking vodka by myself. She looked at me sadly and shook her head.

"I hurt my foot," I said, by way of explanation.

"Whatever, Mobes," she said, and went onstage to start DJing.

After three or four drinks, and two Vicodin from the promoter, my foot felt much better, and I thought I might be able to walk without pain. I did a gentle hop and realized that the vodka and pills had actually made the pain disappear completely. I felt smug: if I'd been sober like Princess Superstar, I would have still been hobbling around.

I walked to the stage to watch her DJ and to check out the crowd. In the early 2000s, when I'd performed or DJed in Miami the venues had been large and sold out, with lines of people trying to get in. But now it was 2008, and the club was small and only a third full. A few people were dancing to Princess Superstar's set, but the room and the crowd felt listless. I went back to the dressing room to sit alone and drink.

"Mo?" Sandy poked his head into the room. "Do you know a Constantin?"

Constantin? I didn't know any Constantin.

"From eastern Europe?"

Oh. *That* Constantin. The promoter/mobster who'd unsubtly threatened my life when I'd had the flu during the *Animal Rights* tour. "He's here?" I asked tentatively.

Constantin and his coterie of four models, two fellow crime bosses, and two black-suited security guards filed into my tiny dressing room. "Moby!" he boomed. "My good friend!" He gave me a bear hug and introduced me to the models and the eastern European crime bosses. The models smiled, almost shyly, and the crime bosses just nodded their heads. "After you DJ you come out with us! To my club! I own club here!" He reached into his pocket and handed me a bag of cocaine, saying conspiratorially, "For your show."

"Okay, see you after," I said, as they trooped out of my dressing room. I'd done cocaine after DJing, but never before. Well, I was in Miami, a city built on cocaine, so why not see what doing coke before DJing was like?

I did a few lines on the back of my BlackBerry and washed them down with a few more shots of vodka. The cocaine made friends with the alcohol and Vicodin in my bloodstream, and I felt great. Electric. Suddenly I couldn't wait to DJ. The club might be only one-third full, and I was walking around on a swollen, blistered foot, but tonight was going to be amazing.

I did some more cocaine, wondering why it had taken me so many years to do drugs *before* a DJ gig, and thought about the records I was going to play. This was a golden age for dance music, or so I'd just decided. I did another line and had another shot of vodka.

Every age was a golden age for dance music, I thought, but this was the most gilded. Or gelded. No, not gelded. I did another line of coke and thought about "gilded" and "gelded" – how I loved one, but not the other. I took a moment to savor the way cocaine dripped down the back of my sinuses and into my throat. Some people complained about this, saying it tasted like toxic chemicals, but I loved parsing the different flavors on my tongue. My cokehead palate could taste the cocaine itself, the baby powder, the kerosene, and some other mystery chemicals that had attached themselves to the white powder as it made its way out of South America.

"Time to play," Sandy said, interrupting my party of one. I marched proudly onto the stage.

Standing next to Princess Superstar, I put my arm around her. "Isn't this great!" I yelled.

She looked at the mostly empty club and raised her eyebrows. "It's all yours," she said dispiritedly, stepping away from the equipment. The night was anemic, but I knew I was going to save it. Constantin and his posse of criminals and models were in a booth near the stage. I heard him yell "Moby!" so I waved to him, deciding that he was my new best friend.

I started my set with a remix of an old Fatboy Slim track and proceeded to play my favorite records of 2008 – Loops of Fury, deadmau5, Miles Dyson – and even some remixes of my older tracks, like "Natural Blues" and "Porcelain." My foot was greasy but pain-free, so I danced behind my equipment like a crazy person.

"Can you bring the vodka bottle from backstage?" I yelled to Sandy. He fetched it, and I held it high in the air before drinking straight from the bottle. The small crowd cheered, and I felt like Ozzy Osbourne, if he had been playing other people's records in a small club in Florida.

then it fell apart

I wanted to hear Underworld's "Born Slippy," one of the most iconic and beautiful dance tracks ever recorded, but I also wanted to do more cocaine. I ducked down behind the DJ booth and did two lines of coke off the back of my phone. After the second I looked up and saw Princess Superstar on the side of the stage. She shook her head in disgust and walked away.

I shrugged, stood up, and played "Born Slippy." The small crowd cheered, and for a moment the air felt like sunlight. I saw some old ravers hugging each other in front of the DJ booth. I held up my hands, blessing them, blessing all of us. Then I grabbed Sandy and yelled "Ecstasy!" in his ear.

He understood. I wasn't saying, "This is ecstatic," I was saying, "Get me some ecstasy."

He looked like he was going to quit, but then he shook his head, walked offstage, and came back a minute later, saying, "It's your funeral." He handed me two pills. I washed them down with vodka.

I segued into "Good Life" by Inner City, and realized I had everything I needed: a central nervous system flooded with alcohol and drugs, and my favorite records played as loud as an exploding 747. As I danced with my eyes closed I could almost hear the chemicals grinding their way through my body. I reflected on how the word "good" was descended from "God." In many languages, "good morning" was the descendant of "God morning."

And then I thought, *I'm descended from God*. Or maybe I was improving on God. Since God gave us the ability to feel transcendent joy, I wasn't usurping God's place in the cosmos, I was just taking what He had started and helping it along with alcohol and drugs and deafening techno. Why would God give me a brain that responded so well to alcohol and drugs if I wasn't meant to bathe it in alcohol and drugs?

No matter what the answer, I realized that I was impermanent. Music was impermanence defined, as it was just air molecules pushed around for a millionth of a second. Then I remembered that

I was onstage, DJing in a nightclub, and I opened my eyes. I cued up a remix of "Infinity" by Guru Josh. When its gorgeous instrumental break kicked in and the crowd cheered, I felt something beyond joy. I was having an out-of-body experience, but in my body. The eternal and the divine were revealing themselves through my broken, flawed, dying cells.

I followed up "Infinity" with a new Zodiac Cartel record, and I yelled. In the early rave days I'd screamed and shouted onstage all the time. I'd been sober then; I'd been challenging the void, defining myself by trying to fill the universe's emptiness with joyful noise. But now I yelled with the void. I was part of the deafening darkness. And I loved it.

My set ended and the next DJ, Wolfram, started playing. "Great set," he said. I hugged him and told him I loved him.

Constantin was waiting by the backstage area with his entourage of models, criminals, and security guards. "Let's go!" I yelled. And then, "Do you have more drugs?"

We piled into a stretch limo Constantin had waiting by the exit. Nestled on the backseat among the tall models, hulking eastern European criminals, and oversized security guards, I felt like an adopted baby elf. Somebody put on a generic techno mix and handed me a bottle of vodka. "Great set!" someone was saying to me. I turned to my left: it was Yasmin, one of the models. Her smile was wide and her pupils were dilated.

She understood. She was African American and beautiful, and I instantly wanted to spend the rest of my life with her. I took her hand. "I think I love you," I said. She laughed merrily.

We got to Constantin's club, which was dark, generic, and far more crowded than the club where I'd just played. He took us to the VIP room, which was populated with older foreign men and young, skinny models. It was gross, but so was I, and who cared? This was humanity, and humanity was nothing if not beautiful and repulsive.

A waitress appeared with a silver tray covered in cocaine. We all hungrily snorted as much and as quickly as we could – and soon every last flawed, divine granule was in somebody's nose. The waitress quickly returned with bottles of Russian vodka in buckets of ice. This was the worst place I'd ever been, everything I'd always claimed to hate, and I loved it.

"Did you go to school? I asked Yasmin, the model I'd fallen in love with in the limo, noticeably slurring my words.

"College?" she slurred back.

"Yes."

"For a little while." She looked troubled that I might be asking about something serious. "Did you?"

"I was a philosophy major," I said. She smiled vaguely. "But this" – I gestured at the expensive debauchery surrounding us – "is my dissertation." As I said it I discovered that "dissertation" was a hard and fun word to say when you were as drunk and high as I was. So I said it again, slurring and stumbling over the sibilance: "Dissertation. Dissertation." I leaned over to Yasmin and told her, unnecessarily, "I'm drunk."

Constantin came over and announced, "At dawn we go on my boat!"

"When is that?" I asked, as we might have been in this hermetically sealed VIP room for thirty minutes or three hours.

He looked at his watch. "Ha! Is now!"

We stepped outside. I was surprised to see that it was daytime. I shouldn't have been, as I couldn't remember the last time I'd gone to sleep when it was still dark outside. As we all got back into Constantin's limo, I gripped Yasmin's perfumed hand with my bony fingers.

Constantin's boat was surprisingly big, with bedrooms, a dining room, and a hot tub near the back. It should have been tacky, but somehow, through the prism of cocaine and ecstasy and vodka, it looked beautiful. "Can I drive?" I asked Constantin, as we stepped onboard.

"Ha ha, no!" Constantin said. He gestured at the security guard behind the wheel of the boat. "He drive."

I tried to adopt a serious tone, which was somewhat undercut by my swaying and slurring. "I grew up on boats," I told him.

"Is okay, just party," he said, putting his arm around me.

As we headed out, I asked, "How fast does it go?"

Constantin smiled and lifted his thumb in the air, the universal boat hand sign for "Go faster." For a big boat it went very fast.

The soft, pink Miami air blew into my face. I squeezed Yasmin's hand and she squeezed back. She was part of my dysfunctional family. So was Constantin. All the people on the boat were my children, I decided, and I loved them all. Even outside the club, I felt like God.

"You know what's fun?" I asked Constantin. And I jumped over the edge of the speeding boat.

I hit the water hard, bouncing a few times. And then I just floated, looking up at the baby-blue tropical sky. The world was gentle. The sky was gentle. The water was gentle. My phone was probably ruined. But I smiled into the sky.

I heard the boat coming back around to me. Constantin and the models were all standing at the rail, looking angry and worried. "I'm okay!" I yelled, and started doing backstroke away from them.

"Moby!" Constantin yelled. "Get on boat!"

"No," I laughed, swimming away from the boat. "Just leave me here!" I wanted to swim, and then float, and then die. I would sink into the sea and finally be gone. "Just let me die," I said to myself. But when I looked at the boat they all looked so concerned. They were my new family, and I was their new father, and they looked worried. So I swam back to the boat.

Constantin shook his head. "Man, you fuckin' crazy."

I wasn't crazy; I just wanted to claim my birthright and die. "No, I'm happy," I told him.

My hotel had a dock, so they dropped Yasmin and me off there.

then it fell apart

We stumbled up the beach to my room, took off our clothes, and got into the shower. "This water feels like oil," I said, because somehow it did. I dried Yasmin off and she lay down on the bed.

I knew we weren't going to have sex: it was too late and I was too ruined. "I want to ask you a question," Yasmin said as she got under the sheets. She looked at me earnestly. "Do you know Stephen Colbert?" And then she passed out.

I realized I was going to be hungover soon, so I took my usual end-of-night cocktail of Xanax and Vicodin, lay down next to Yasmin, and closed my eyes.

The phone next to my bed started ringing. The sun was blazing through the white curtains, I was alone, and I felt like I'd been violated by demons. But I was still alive, which vexed me.

"Hello," I croaked into the phone.

"Mr. Hall," Sandy said, "your car is here."

This confused me, until I remembered that the whole reason I had come to Miami was Matt's birthday brunch. "Okay, Sandy, thanks," I said, almost feeling guilty that over the last nine years he had gone from being my tour manager to my nanny. I stood up and discovered that I was still drunk and high enough to be unstable, but sober enough to be in pain.

I saw a note on my pile of wet clothes. It was from Yasmin and it said, simply, "Bye."

I stuffed my clothes and my computer into my backpack and staggered to the lobby. Once again I was stumbling out of a hotel in pain and hoping to die. I didn't want the glamorous existential dissolution that I'd longed for in the ocean; I just wanted an end to this sickness and agony.

Sandy was waiting for me in the lobby. "Rough night?" he asked me for the five hundredth time. Or maybe the thousandth time.

And for the five hundredth time, or maybe the thousandth time, I just shook my head.

We walked to the limo. Sandy was usually unflappable, but he looked angry. "I'm not sure I can keep doing this, Moby," he said.

I understood. I wasn't sure how long I could keep doing this either. I didn't feel capable of having a conversation, so I leaned my head against the cold, black leather headrest and closed my eyes. When the limo arrived at the restaurant where Matt was having his birthday brunch, I meekly told Sandy, "I'll be about an hour."

Matt, his beautiful wife, and a few of his friends were sitting at a table outside. There was a soft, salty wind blowing in from the Atlantic Ocean; the restaurant was full of happy people eating pancakes and drinking mimosas on a Sunday morning.

"Happy birthday," I said to Matt as I collapsed into a chair. And then I needed to throw up. I tried to run to the bathroom, but I didn't make it any further than the edge of the restaurant's deck. I vomited in some potted plants.

I went back to the table, wiped my mouth, and ordered a screwdriver and a cup of black coffee. "I had a weird night," I said to Matt and his friends, who smiled nervously at me.

Matt looked at me. He had been a bottomed-out junkie for years. He'd lost everything to his addiction, including one of his limbs. "I'm worried about you, Moby," he said.

62

NEW YORK CITY (2008)

My problem wasn't drinking and drugs, I decided – it was daylight.

After selling the sky castle on Central Park West I had moved back to the loft on Mott Street I'd had since 1995. I had spent years acquiring more impressive properties, but the Mott Street loft was the only place that had ever felt like home. The problem was that it had a ceiling full of skylights. This made it more beautiful, with sun and shadows playing on my empty white walls, but it made it hard to sleep during the day.

I was out six nights a week, not going to bed until seven or eight in the morning. In the winter this was fine: I put on an eye mask and stayed in bed until 5 p.m., while people trudged through the cold and dirty snow. But now it was summer, the gray clouds of winter had burned off, and even with a mask on I was fighting the pitiless daylight. As much as I loved my loft, I thought I'd be better off living in a basement apartment with no windows, avoiding seasons and daylight entirely.

The week before I'd been in the bathroom of a bar on Ludlow Street, doing cocaine with a few best friends I'd just met. When I told them of my plan to live in a basement and never see the sun, one of my new best friends told me that he knew somebody selling a bar in Brooklyn. In fact, he said, he wasn't just selling the bar – he was selling the whole building. And, he informed me with a cocaine grin, it had a windowless basement.

The next day I called the owner and took the L train to Bushwick to see the building for myself. A decade earlier Williamsburg had been the new frontier, and Bushwick had been the unknown world at the edge of the map. But the steroidal gentrification of Manhattan had pushed people into the slippery diaspora of the outer boroughs.

I normally would have taken a limo to check out this bar, but I hadn't been on the L train in almost twenty years, and I wanted to see how much it had changed. When I moved to New York in 1989 and lived on 14th Street, the filthy L train had been my lifeline. I took it west to go to my studio at Instinct Records on 8th Avenue, and I took it east to visit my friends who had become pioneer home-steaders in the new hipster country of Williamsburg. The last time I'd been on the L train was in 1992, when I took it to a rave deep in Brooklyn. Other than being somewhat cleaner, the L train in 2008 wasn't much different to how it had been in 1992. But I was.

Sixteen years ago I'd been bright-eyed, sober, and in love with the nascent rave scene. Now I'd lost most of my friends, I was suicidal, and I was looking to buy a bar where I could drink myself to death. In 1992 I'd assumed that by 2008 I would be married and living in a farmhouse somewhere upstate with a kind, loving wife and lots of kids and dogs. Now all I wanted was to live in a basement and avoid the light until I died.

When I'd spoken on the phone with the man who owned the bar he had been forthright about why he was selling his lightless paradise. He was a film producer who had bottomed out on liquor and drugs, and he was selling the bar because he was newly sober – and because after a decade-long coke binge, he was broke.

I'd considered sobriety, and I was having a harder and harder time avoiding the evidence that the way I was living was destroying me. I'd even made a couple of exploratory trips to AA meetings, but although the war stories I heard were remarkable, I was confident that I wasn't a real alcoholic. I was, as I told myself and anyone who would listen to me in a bar at 3 a.m., an alcohol enthusiast.

Alcohol had never failed me. It was inexpensive, ubiquitous, and dependable. If drinking was killing me, that wasn't the alcohol's fault but the world's fault. The world had promised so much, but it had turned out to be cruel and dishonest.

I got off the L train at the Bushwick stop, walked a few blocks, and met the bar's current owner. He was smoking a cigarette and was stooped in a defeated posture that I'd seen in people standing outside the handful of AA meetings I'd been to. We shook hands and he unlocked the front door of his bar. "I spent a lot of days in this place . . ." he said, his voice trailing off.

The building was a small tenement, with two above-ground stories, a street-level bar, and a basement that was the owner's former coke den. I wanted to hide my enthusiasm, but I also wanted to buy the bar on the spot. It was hidden away in an industrial neighborhood and sandwiched between warehouses on a street that I knew would be completely empty after 6 p.m. And it felt right. The current owner might have bottomed out here, but he had good taste.

The upstairs levels were clean and modern; I thought I could even let some of the animal-rights organizations I worked with use them as offices. The street-level bar was simple and tasteful, with an old wooden bar against one wall and custom-made booths on the opposite wall.

And the basement coke den was perfect. Painted black, it had a DJ booth in one corner, a small bar in another, and overstuffed couches against the windowless walls. It seemed like a place where people could stay for twelve or twenty-four or ninety-six hours, scrubbing their brains of any awareness that the outside world had ever existed.

"I'm a bad bargainer," I said, "but I really want to buy your bar."

"Well, let's go talk." We left his bar and walked to another, Northeast Kingdom. It was full of beautiful hipsters, using their trust funds to live in urban squalor. When I was growing up poor I assumed that rich people wanted nothing more than to look and feel rich. And now the children of affluence were using their parents' money to look like they'd grown up on welfare.

I ordered a beer; he got a club soda with a slice of lime. "I'm curious," he said. "Why do you want to buy my bar?"

I wanted to tell him about my pretentious and ostensibly lofty reasons. I wanted a place to ride out, as E. M. Cioran had described it, the curse of life. I needed welcoming darkness: teany had been lovely, but too bright; my loft was beautiful, but also too bright. I couldn't stop thinking about how living in a world without light was going to solve all my problems.

I even had a name picked out for the bar. I'd call it Slow Dive, but on the neon sign the "v" would be intentionally left dark, or painted over: "Slow Di e." Everything inside would be dark and soft, like a womb. This would be a rejection of the actual post-womb world that had turned out to be jagged and noisy, demanding and disappointing.

Instead of unloading my brainpan of issues and garbage on this friendly, newly sober man, I just said, "I think it would be really fun to own a bar."

"You know, in the beginning it was really, really fun," he said, staring at his club soda. "But by the end it got really dark."

I didn't tell him that, for me, darkness was actually a selling point.

Over the past two decades I'd made money and had success. But I knew I wasn't a sexy rock star, I was human garbage. I had been born worthless, for why else would my father kill himself and leave me? And I had grown up worthless, for why else would my mother run into the arms of terrible men? The parties and promiscuity and platinum records hadn't changed the essential facts: I was inadequate and unlovable. And it was time to stop pretending otherwise.

63

NEW YORK CITY (2008)

It was September 11, 2008, and I was forty-three. Birthdays had never been important to me, and for a few years after September 11, 2001, I'd stopped celebrating my birthday altogether. But since it was now seven years since 9/11, I thought it wouldn't be too distasteful to celebrate turning forty-three.

I started my birthday night drinking in Brooklyn with my ex-girlfriend Janet and her new boyfriend. Janet and I had met at a Bible-study class in Connecticut in the late 1980s and had dated in 1989, when she was a student at Barnard and I was an aspiring DJ living in an abandoned factory. We had reconnected a few weeks earlier, after running into each other at a coffee shop on Broome Street. She still had long curly hair, and somehow looked as young and pretty as when I first met her.

After my second beer I awkwardly asked, "How's your faith, Janet?"

She looked uncomfortable. "I don't know, Mo. How's yours?"

"I don't know either. I still pray, but I don't know."

"Do you still go to church?"

I laughed. Aside from being a spectator at a couple of AA meetings in church basements, my last time in a church had been for my grandmother's funeral in 1998. I wanted to talk about balancing the spiritual with the secular, but Janet's new boyfriend seemed uninterested. Understandably – he was a young hip writer, and no self-respecting erudite hipster in a Brooklyn bar with dark wood beams and trendy exposed lightbulbs wanted to talk about God.

It made me sad – not that Janet and I couldn't talk about God, but that I was so unmoored. I'd come to see my early, rigid Christianity as being dogmatic and tribal, but at least it had been something. In 1995, when I accepted that I was no longer a Christian, I moved on to what I thought of as agnostic secularism, embracing the universe's complexity and impermanence. The problem was that I'd fallen in love with the world, especially the sex and alcohol and fame, and I was heartbroken that it wasn't proving to be permanent.

Late at night I paid lip service to the idea that life was as evanescent as a Nietzschean sand painting, but I really wanted the universe to laud me and my existence. The week before I'd been in Los Angeles. As I was leaving my hotel the receptionist asked, "Do you need validation?" She was asking if I wanted the hotel to stamp my valet-parking stub, but for a second I got excited, thinking she was offering to give meaning to my life.

"Do you want another drink?" Janet's boyfriend asked me.

"Of course," I said.

I had agreed to DJ a birthday party in a loft around the corner from the bar where we were drinking. Some Virgo acquaintances thought that having one big Virgo birthday party would be fun, and also a good way to get me to DJ for three hundred of their friends for free.

I plugged in my USB sticks and played some old house-music tracks, even getting a muted cheer from the hipster crowd when I played the "Woodtick" mix of "Go." It was 2008, which meant that "Go" had been released eighteen years ago. I was old. And drunk. I had another beer and played another house-music record. Suddenly everything seemed flat – the hipsters, the lights, the levity – as if life was just a staged photograph in a bad design magazine. I was sad, but underneath my sadness I was angry and disappointed. I'd been given the kingdom, and I'd squandered it.

I stopped the house record I was playing. The party cheered, assuming that something big and dramatic was going to happen.

But I didn't want big and dramatic; I wanted quiet and sad. After a few seconds I played "Going to California" by Led Zeppelin. Some of the hipsters cheered, assuming that this was going to segue into a Zeppelin/techno mashup. But I just wanted to hear "Going to California" in its entirety. So I closed my eyes and drank my beer while I listened to this delicate, yearning ballad in front of three hundred increasingly confused hipsters. It ended, and the crowd looked at me expectantly. So I played it again.

Karim, one of the other DJs, came over and tapped me on the shoulder. "Is everything okay?" he asked.

I smiled at him with tears in my eyes. "Isn't this song beautiful?" I said.

He looked at the restive crowd, whose loud loft party had been stopped in its tracks by an old drunk playing Led Zeppelin. "You mind if I play?" he asked.

"Just let this finish," I said, putting my hands on the controls to keep him from stopping the plaintive music. As I closed my eyes and listened to Robert Plant sing the last mournful lines I could feel the tears running down my cheeks.

The song ended. Karim played an LCD Soundsystem song about how great nightlife in New York had been in the 1980s and 1990s, and the crowd cheered. My friend Carrie-Anne tapped me on the shoulder. She was a commercial real-estate agent with short blonde hair who looked like a glamorous newscaster. We had met a few years earlier, when she rented me a commercial space on Elridge Street that I'd wanted to use as an office.

"Happy birthday?" Carrie-Anne asked.

I smiled at her sadly. "Wasn't that song beautiful?" I said.

"I'm not sure they thought so," she said, gesturing at the rest of the party.

"Let's go," I said. We walked to the street and got a taxi back to Manhattan.

"Where are we going?" she asked.

"The Box." The Box hadn't become the egalitarian Weimar-esque mix of downtown performance artists and uptown money that I'd hoped it would be, but as the owner of a minority stake I still went there almost every night. We bypassed the line out front, and once inside I looked around for people I knew.

I had wanted The Box to be my debauched, kindhearted home, full of creative performance artists. But tonight it was full of entitled finance workers. Then again, I'd wanted New York City to be my debauched, kindhearted home, and it too was now full of entitled finance workers. I looked at Carrie-Anne and said bitterly, "Fuck this place."

"Do you want to leave?"

I did, but I also wanted a drink. The line at the bar was three deep, but I found a space and tried to squeeze through. A tall young finance worker in a thousand-dollar suit was talking to another tall young finance worker in a thousand-dollar suit, blocking my access to the bar.

I tapped him on the shoulder politely. "Excuse me, can I get through?"

He ignored me.

I tapped him again, increasingly vexed. "Hi, can I get a drink?"

He looked at me with haughty disdain and said, "Fuck you." Then he went back to his conversation.

This was the wrong thing for him to have said. I grabbed his shoulder and turned him around. Losing my cool, I yelled at him, "You come into my bar" – I might have been exaggerating my ownership – "and say, 'Fuck you'?"

"Yeah, fuck you," he said, and pushed me.

I stumbled backward, my self-pity transmuting into rage. Suddenly I saw him as everything I loathed and feared: the confident finance workers taking over New York; the hipsters with the temerity to be younger and cooler than I was; the terrible men my mom had dated. So I punched him in the face.

I wasn't usually a violent person, but I'd been taking kickboxing lessons on and off for the past few years and had (unfortunately) learned how to throw a punch. He crumpled to the ground, people quickly backed away from the barroom violence, and security guards ran over to us. His fellow finance worker tried to attack me, but a guard held him back.

"Moby, what happened?" the head of security asked me.

"This yuppie piece of shit attacked me," I said, somewhat over-stating the severity of his assault.

The security guards picked up the guy I'd punched, who was now yelling, "Fuck you! I'm going to fucking sue you!" He gestured at the security guards. "And you! And everyone here! I'm going to fucking ruin all of you!"

"Okay, American Psycho, party's over," the security chief said. The guards frog-marched the two Wall Streeters out onto the street.

After they were gone, Carrie-Anne said to me, "Did you really just hit that guy?"

Suddenly all my anger and bravado deflated like a scared balloon. "Fuck," I said. "I'm sorry."

"No, it was awesome."

"It was?"

"Kind of."

We ordered drinks and looked at the crowd. It was as if the guy I'd punched had been cloned before he got ejected: it was a sea of dudes in thousand-dollar suits talking loudly in the way only confident finance workers could. The same people who'd made me miserable as a child had taken over The Box, and New York City, making me feel small and terrible as an adult.

I finished my drink. "Let's go," I said to Carrie-Anne. We walked up the street to the 205 Club, where my new assistant, Alex, and some of his friends from DFA Records were DJing. I'd gone through a number of assistants in the last few years; they usually quit when they realized their main job responsibilities were making sure I had enough alcohol in my house and coming up with excuses for me when I had to cancel plans due to being hungover.

Alex and his friends were tall and handsome, and had grown up listening to hip-hop on the Upper West Side. But a few years ago they had discovered old disco, and had ditched hip-hop to become disco evangelists.

"Disco?" I asked him when he started working for me.

"Disco!" he answered, as if good-looking twenty-five-year-olds listening to old Sylvester records in 2008 was the most normal thing in the world.

We reached the entrance of the 205 Club, where Carrie-Anne said, "Happy birthday, Mo, but I have to head home."

"Really?"

"You look so sad," she said, touching my face. "Yeah, I have to be up at seven. And it's 2 a.m."

I hugged her good night and walked inside the club. I'd had a dozen drinks, and I was unsteady on my feet, but the two-second fistfight at The Box had woken me up. Alex and his DFA friends were DJing in the basement, so I headed downstairs.

I did a shot of vodka at the bar, and then ordered a vodka and soda. Clutching my drink I walked across the small dance floor and into the DJ booth. "Happy birthday, Moby!" I said, slurring, to the young, cool DJs. Jacques Renault gave me a drunken hug and went back to DJing.

I finished my vodka and soda, ordered a tequila, and took it upstairs to the quieter lounge. It was brighter there, and with the better lighting I could see that everyone else in the club was young and stylish in ways that I had never been. I drank my tequila, feeling awkward and hoping that someone would recognize me and talk to me. But no one did.

I ordered another tequila and went back downstairs, where I stood in the back of the DJ booth, hoping some of the DFA crew's youth and attractiveness would rub off on me. But they were busy

DJing and the crowd was too busy adoring them to notice me hovering behind them in the shadows.

I went back to the bar and ordered another tequila, drank it at once, and ordered another. The bartender eyed me warily. "Dude, are you sure?"

"It's my birthday!" I slurred, trying to look happy.

I took my new drink onto the dance floor and realized that with the twelve drinks I'd had before arriving at the 205 Club, and at least six more in the hour that I'd been here, I was very drunk. I was accustomed to being drunk, but I rarely got to this point: my vision was blurry and I was having a hard time standing.

I tried dancing with a young, beautiful woman who ignored me. I tried dancing with a different young, beautiful woman, who also ignored me. "It's my birthday!" I tried to say to her, realizing dimly that I had just yelled a few slurred syllables over the loud house music. Trying as hard as I could to enunciate clearly, I said, "Will you kiss me?"

"Ew, no," she said, and turned away.

I finished my drink – my twentieth? – and fell down. The floor felt good. I lay there for a second with my eyes closed, feeling the kick drum thump through my back. Then some hands pulled me up, aggressively. They were connected to two bouncers, who dragged me to the staircase.

My assistant Alex ran over to intercede. "Hey, that's Moby! He's my boss!"

The bouncers looked at me like I was drunk garbage. Which I was. "So?" one of them asked.

"Happy birthday, Alex," I slurred.

Alex just stood there, watching helplessly as the bouncers dragged me up the stairs and threw me onto the sidewalk. I wanted to put them in their place and yell, "Don't you know who I am?" like the self-entitled aging celebrity that I was. But they'd already gone back inside, and I was alone, lying on the sidewalk on Stanton Street.

With great effort I stood up, realizing again that I was extremely drunk. I was only a few blocks from my apartment, so I stumbled west on Stanton. As I crossed the Bowery I tripped in the middle of the crosswalk, falling down and scraping my hands.

When I reached my building I decided that I needed to listen to music and write down some new ideas for the record I was working on. I sat on the sidewalk, leaning against the old brick loft building I'd lived in since 1995, and threw up in my lap. I wanted to go inside and clean myself up, but standing up seemed like too much work.

I lay down on the sidewalk, covered in vomit, and played a Joy Division song on my phone. Ian Curtis started singing, and I started crying. Not the quiet, restrained crying of earlier, when I'd been listening to "Going to California" with my eyes closed, but sobbing.

I heard people walking by, so I turned my face to the building to keep them from seeing me crying and covered in vomit. I held my phone to my ear and Ian Curtis sang to me from the tiny speaker.

64

DARIEN, CONNECTICUT (1985)

The ATM wouldn't let me take out any money because I had only $18 in my savings account.

Maybe being broke was hereditary. Aside from my grandfather, I didn't know anyone in my family who hadn't been poor. I had relatives who'd come across on the *Mayflower*, but they weren't the ones who went on to become bankers and governors. Now I was honoring my impoverished hereditary line by being a twenty-year-old adult with $18 to my name. It was cold and starting to rain, so I held a newspaper over my head as I walked across the street from the bank to the Darien train station.

I had started DJing at The Beat at the end of 1984, when Tom, one of the owners, had given me a DJ slot out of pity – and because I was spending more time at The Beat than any of the actual employees. At first Tom paid me $20 to DJ from 10 p.m. to 4 a.m. on Monday nights, but a few weeks ago he'd given me a promotion. Now I was getting $25 a night, and DJing Wednesdays as well as Mondays. Tom also gave me a key to the bar and offered a quid pro quo: if I cleaned and maintained the sound equipment, he'd let me keep my records in the DJ booth and allow me to practice DJing in the afternoon.

Port Chester was five stops away on the Metro North train. To avoid paying the $1.25 fare all I had to do was stay away from the conductor, or hide in the bathroom. The local train in the middle of the day felt like a refugee camp, with exhausted maids, gardeners, and barely employed poor white trash like me all hunching our shoulders and hoping that nobody would look at us too closely. Occasionally I'd take the train during rush hour and sit among the rich businessmen commuters who carried themselves erect and loud, spraying the world with their confidence.

The train pulled into Port Chester and I stepped onto a platform that was as wet and gray as the low sky. I went down the stairs and under the old iron train trestle, walked to The Beat, and let myself in.

The Beat was a dive bar in a neighborhood of burned-out buildings, empty parking lots, and vacant storefronts. It had a black tin ceiling, chipped tiles on the floor, a long wooden bar on the left side, cigarette-stained paneling on the right, and a smattering of old tables and chairs. When the new owners, Tom and Fred, took it over, the only changes they made were to make a tiny dance floor in the back and to build a plywood DJ booth next to the men's room. The Beat smelled like cigarettes and a century's worth of vomit and spilled drinks, but after I dropped out of UConn it became my second home and my refuge.

The bar held only forty-five people, but the other oddballs and dropouts who hung out there had become my surrogate family. Some of the other regulars were students at SUNY Purchase, an art school a few miles away. But most of them were people who needed a dim refuge from the normal world: musicians who were too shy to play a show, artists who never seemed to finish a painting, and alcoholics and drug addicts who found the outside world too painful.

Allard, Melissa, Brock, and I had played our first show here two weeks earlier. We'd finally decided on a name, Caeli Train. It had no literal meaning, but to our Connecticut ears it sounded like a vaguely Celtic name that a band on Postcard Records would have. For our show we'd set up our equipment on the tiny dance floor in front of the plywood DJ booth. All four of us wore black, and Melissa and I wore little fishermen caps, as we'd seen pictures of Ian McCulloch and Roddy Frame wearing them. Twenty of our friends came and clapped politely between our delicate alternative-rock songs.

After we finished playing our show I did my regular Monday-night DJ set. As I played a remix of "Confusion" by New Order I noticed that the small audience was more enthusiastic about my DJing than my indie-rock band.

In addition to DJing two nights a week at The Beat I was also making $50 a week as the DJ at an all-ages club in Greenwich called The Café. Which left me confused as to why I was so broke, as I was earning $100 per week from DJing. Even though I was giving my mom some money for food and utilities, I should have been able to keep more than $18 in the bank.

I poured myself a Coke from the soda gun behind the bar and got some rags and cleaning products to wipe down the DJ booth and sound equipment. The rags turned black almost immediately, as the DJ booth was covered in dust, nicotine stains, rat poop, and a disconcerting number of dead cockroaches. After a half-hour of cleaning I took out some of my hip-hop records to practice DJing.

I still loved my old punk-rock records, and I adored the Smiths and the Chameleons and the other sensitive British groups. But the more I DJed, the more I found myself excited by the hip-hop and dance-music producers who were rushing to create the soundtrack to the future. I tried to share my enthusiasm with my rock friends, playing them new and remarkable twelve-inch singles by Mantronix and Schoolly D and Doug E. Fresh, but they were indifferent.

I even tried being a Socratic dance-music syllogist, arguing to my friends that since New Order loved dance music, as evidenced by "Confusion" and "Blue Monday," and we worshiped New Order, shouldn't we also be open to the music that New Order revered? My entreaties fell on deaf ears, although Melissa did admit in a private moment to liking Schoolly D's "P.S.K. What Does It Mean?"

I took out two copies of Run-D.M.C.'s "Sucker M.C.'s" and cued them up on the now-clean Technics 1200 turntables. I'd heard hip-hop DJs on Kiss-FM and WBLS playing two copies of the same record, scratching and cutting back and forth flawlessly, and I wanted to learn to do that. I'd even read an interview with Grandmaster Flash, in which he talked about reading the record "like a clock." I had no idea what he meant, but I was determined to figure it out.

I got the two copies of "Sucker M.C.'s" playing at the same tempo and tried to go back and forth between them. I played the instrumental version on the left turntable and tried scratching in the intro to the vocal version on the right turntable. Most of the time it was a rusty train wreck, but now and then it sounded semi-professional. I was proud of my progress; when I had started DJing the year before I couldn't match the beats when mixing between one record and another, but now I successfully beat-matched almost half the time.

I kept the instrumental version of "Sucker M.C.'s" playing on the left turntable and put a copy of T La Rock's "It's Yours" on the other. It took me a few minutes to change the tempo so that "It's Yours" matched "Sucker M.C.'s," but once I had it I played the T La Rock track over the Run-D.M.C. instrumental and it sounded good. I had to keep speeding up and slowing down the T La Rock record with my hand to keep it in time, but when the two tracks synched up they almost sounded like they were being mixed by a real DJ.

I still couldn't believe how lucky I was to get a job as a DJ. I'd done so many terrible jobs in high school and since dropping out of UConn – stuffing envelopes in an insurance company, washing dishes in a Macy's restaurant, selling arts and crafts, caddying – but now I was getting paid $100 a week to play music.

I pulled out a copy of "Shout" by Tears for Fears, as it was the same tempo as a lot of hip-hop tracks, and played it over the instrumental of "Sucker M.C.'s." It was a bit odd to combine emotional new wave with electronic hip-hop beats, but somehow it seemed to work. Then I tried out a trick I'd heard a DJ do on Kiss-FM, where he scratched part of the record while it was playing, not even

then it fell apart

cueing up a particular sound. I hadn't wanted to try it out when I was working, because it had the potential to go terribly wrong. But I was in a cold and empty bar in the middle of the afternoon, and no one was listening. While "Shout" was spinning, I put my hand on "It's Like That" and scratched a sixteenth-note pattern with the kick drum. It wasn't just okay – it sounded *good*.

I smiled to myself and looked up. I was happy playing music at 2 p.m. in an empty bar, or even for the twenty or thirty drunks who hung out at The Beat when I DJed. But someday I wanted an audience. It didn't have to be big – I just wanted someone to notice me.

After seventeen years of being on the road I finally admitted to myself that I didn't enjoy touring. Not that I could complain to any of my friends with real jobs, as it was hard to elicit sympathy for traveling around the world and being paid to stand onstage and play music.

In the early 1990s going on tour had been novel, and I had been an enthusiastic evangelist for the nascent rave scene. And then for a few years, after the success of *Play* and *18*, it had been exciting, a perpetual road-trip party with huge concerts, unceasing drunkenness, and almost effortless promiscuity. But lately touring had turned into a routine, one in which I played in smaller venues to smaller audiences who just wanted to hear older songs.

Even though I didn't want to tour, I still wanted to play music. So I started playing bass in a bar band with some friends: Aaron, a dreadlocked drummer whose mom had been Led Zeppelin's publicist; Daron, a handsome, erudite journalist from Massachusetts who played guitar and harmonica; his wife Laura, the creative director of moveon.org, who sang like a lusty demon; and a rotating trio of glamorous backup singers. I had played with Laura and Daron a few times before (for example, at the David Lynch Weekend in Fairfield, Iowa).

Inspired by Bertolt Brecht and Georges Bataille, we called ourselves the Little Death and did our best to sound like a blues cabaret band playing at a roadhouse in 1945. When we performed we wore old black suits and dresses, looking like gun molls and crooked Bible salesmen from a Flannery O'Connor story.

Lizzie Grant, whom I'd tried dating a couple of years ago, was one of our original backup singers, but she left the group to pursue her own career as Lana Del Rey. The band started as a lark, just a way for some friends to drink beer in a rehearsal space on Ludlow Street. But after we played a few shows at small bars on the Lower East Side we realized that we were actually good. David Lynch came to some and became a fan, while John Waters gave us a one-line endorsement that we cherished: "You're like Ike and Tina Turner, minus the beatings."

With the election less than a month away, and Laura and I knowing some of the movers and shakers in progressive politics, we got invited to play a fundraiser for Senator Kirsten Gillibrand in Hudson, New York.

"Have they heard the lyrics?" I asked. One of our songs had the refrain "I'm a mean, mean woman / I like to argue, fuck, and fight."

Daron laughed. "Maybe we could change it to 'Hug, vote, and snuggle'?"

The rest of the Little Death were driving upstate to Hudson in a van, but I decided to take Amtrak, as I loved the train ride by the Hudson River. I made a peanut-butter-and-jelly sandwich at my loft on Mott Street, put it in a paper bag, along with a copy of *The New Yorker*, and sat on the left side of the train so I could watch the sun set.

As the train headed further north out of the city the autumn leaves turned brighter and brighter shades of orange, yellow, and red. I hadn't gone out drinking the night before, so I felt great. I put on a CD I'd burned of some of the music I was working on for my next album, and listened as the last bits of daylight spilled over the mountains on the other side of the Hudson River. There was one song I'd written the week before, "Wait for Me," that I really liked. It was sad and delicate, built around a lonesome piano arpeggio, and I wanted it to be the lead track on my next album.

As the train pulled into Hudson station I felt clean and civilized. It was the middle of October, and the cold, clean air smelled like fallen leaves and campfires. We had an hour before the show, so I went to the venue and sat backstage with Kirsten Gillibrand and some other New York Democrats. "How are you feeling about the election?" I asked her.

"Hopeful?" the senator asked, with the same timorous note that we all had. After two hundred years of white presidents, and eight years of Bush and Cheney, the thought of having a smart, young African American president seemed dream-like but desperately necessary.

I had worn my suit on the train, but Daron and Aaron changed into their own black southern gothic suits while Laura and the singers put on their Eudora Welty mourning dresses. At 8 p.m. the house lights went down and we got ready to go onstage. "Daron," I said, before strapping on my bass, "let's shotgun beers."

We laughed and each shotgunned a Bud Lite like the frat boys we never were.

"Classy," I said, crushing the cold aluminum can as I burped. I didn't want to stop drinking just because we were performing, so I brought six beers onstage with me. I loved playing dark rhythm and blues with the Little Death, but I also loved that some of our songs were simple enough for me to play bass and drink beer at the same time.

By the time we played the last song in our hour-long set I'd had seven beers. I took the mic from Laura. "Everyone has to vote," I said drunkenly, "because Republicans are fucking subhuman devils and need to be fucking destroyed."

I looked over at my new friend, Senator Kirsten Gillibrand, hoping she'd smile and applaud my progressive courage and profanity. But she looked horrified, and was hurried out of the venue by her entourage.

Laura took the microphone. "Sorry, Moby sometimes has alcoholic Tourette's," she said.

then it fell apart

I took the mic back. "I'm not an alcoholic," I said with fake umbrage, "I'm an alcohol enthusiast."

We walked offstage, drank the rest of the backstage beer, and then got a ride in a minivan to a local bar. The rest of the band left early to drive back to New York, but the promoter had booked me a room at a local B&B, so I stayed in the bar and did shots of tequila with the locals.

A band was performing, doing nostalgic cover versions of Hudson Valley classics like "Rainy Day Women #12 & 35" and "The Weight." At midnight I stumbled onstage, borrowed a guitar, and tried to play "Purple Haze" with them. I'd learned the song in ninth grade with my guitar teacher Chris Risola and had played it enough times that even drunk I could get through it without too many mistakes. I did a long, sloppy guitar solo, and after the song I took the lead singer's microphone. "If anyone has cocaine they can give me or sell me," I said, repeating my tactic from the Highline Ballroom, "meet me on the side of the stage."

As I stepped offstage a bearded guy in a motorcycle jacket nodded at me and led me to the men's room. "A hundred and fifty dollars," he said, handing me a small bag of white powder. I knew I was being egregiously overcharged, but it was cocaine, so I thanked him profusely.

I did the bag by myself in a toilet stall, and left the bathroom feeling like a superhero. I tried to jump back onstage with the band, but I slipped and fell onto a table covered with glasses and beer bottles. I knocked it over and tumbled into a pile of broken glass, but hopped up unscratched. "The liquor gods protected me!" I yelled, my arms triumphantly raised over my head.

At 5 a.m., after more tequila and more cocaine, a doorman from the bar escorted me to my quaint bed-and-breakfast off the main street. "What a great night!" I shouted outside the little house.

"Dude, ssshhh," he said. "This is a small town."

"Should I move here?" I asked earnestly.

"Might be too quiet for you," he said, and walked away.

My room had floral wallpaper and a copy of F. Scott Fitzgerald's *Tender Is the Night* on the bedside table. I got into bed and tried to read, but the words kept moving, so I gave up after one or two sentences. The cocaine and beer and tequila were churning through my body like angry fish, so I tossed and turned for a few hours without sleeping.

By 8 a.m. the alcohol and drugs were leaving my system, and I started to hurt. The light coming through the curtains was pale and nauseating. The sheets were coarse and felt like stiff paper on my skin. I couldn't sleep, or even get comfortable, so I put on my old black suit, which now smelled like beer and other people's cigarettes, and walked to the train station.

I'd been hungover thousands and thousands of times. My hangovers in high school and college had been inconsequential, like soft California coastal fog that dissipated by noon. My hangovers in the late 1990s and early 2000s had seemed charming and even literary: physical connections to alcoholic heroes like Charles Bukowski and John Cheever. But now when I was hungover I felt like I had poisoned my DNA. Hangovers these days felt wrong, and not lower-case "wrong," like driving a few miles an hour over the speed limit, but upper-case "WRONG," like feeding gasoline to a newborn.

At the train station I bought two bottles of water and boarded the Amtrak train to Penn Station. The ride up had been calm and magical, but now I was hungover in my undertaker's suit, pressing my body against a windowless wall and getting as far away from the light as possible. I tried to distract myself by reading my *New Yorker*, but I couldn't follow the words.

I was so sick and tired. Again. And I'd been sick and tired and hungover most of this last week.

And the week before that.

And the month before that.

And the year before that.

And the years before that.

It was unrelenting, a tautological journey of damage and nausea, and whenever I drank I ended up this way. I'd tried cutting back on drinking more times than I could count, but every time I tried to drink like a normal person I ended up where I was now: ill, destroyed, and wanting to die.

The week before I'd tried to kill myself by tying a plastic bag over my head before going to sleep, but my atavistic survival mechanisms must have kicked in. Although I didn't remember pulling the bag off my head, it was lying next to my pillow when I woke up.

Nevertheless, I wanted to keep drinking, so I tried to think of times in my life when I'd been able to drink in moderation, evidence that I could brandish to prove to myself that I wasn't an alcoholic. And I remembered: one time in 1986 I went to a Christmas party and had only two glasses of champagne.

I'd been drinking for most of the last thirty-three years, since I was ten years old in 1975, and I could think of only one time that I had been able to drink like a normal human being.

I wasn't physically capable of reading, so I took out my CD player and listened to "Wait for Me" again. I'd recorded the demo vocals myself, but I knew at some point I'd have to get a real singer to do them:

> *I'm gonna ask you to look away*
> *I loathe my hands and it hurts to pray*
> *The life I have isn't what I'd seen*
> *The sky's not blue and the field's not green*
> *Wait for me*

> *I'm gonna ask you to look away*
> *This broken life I can never save*
> *I try so hard but I always lack*
> *Days are gray and the nights are black*
> *Wait for me*

The song ended and I sat quietly crying.

The train pulled into New York and I stumbled through the fluorescent horror of Penn Station. Once I got outside I saw that it was a beautiful day: not a cloud in the sky, the October air perfectly warm and cool.

I took a taxi to my apartment, dropped off my bag, and walked to the only AA meeting I knew of, on 1st Avenue and 1st Street.

I'd visited this meeting a few times before over the previous year, but each time I'd been convinced that I wasn't actually an addict. The other people I'd seen at the meeting had been the broken ones. They were the alcoholics whose lives were unmanageable. They were the people who needed this weird, old cult of Bill Wilson.

I'd always balked at the declaration required to take the first step: that I was an alcoholic and that my life was "unmanageable." I'd sold twenty million records and had stood onstage in front of millions of people. I'd met heads of state and dated movie stars. I'd collaborated with my heroes and owned penthouses and beachfront property I'd never even seen. So I scoffed: that was unmanageable?

But I knew other truths: I couldn't get close to women without having debilitating panic attacks; I couldn't go out and have fewer than fifteen drinks; most days I was too hungover to get out of bed; and every afternoon when I woke up I was sad that I hadn't died in my sleep. I finally admitted to myself: that was unmanageable.

A year ago I'd been at a party and had struck up a conversation with an old, well-known musician who was famously sober. I was hungover and sick, and he was calm and annoyingly healthy.

"So," I asked, "you're in AA?"

"Twenty years this month. Why, do you think you're an alcoholic?"

I paused, holding onto my belief that I was just an alcohol enthusiast.

"It's funny," he told me, "people think that being an alcoholic is about drinking. I mean, it is, but it isn't."

I looked at him, confused. I wanted to say, "Of course being an alcoholic is about drinking. What the fuck are you talking about?"

He continued, "Before I got sober I was so afraid, and I fucking hated myself. So much. But after I got sober I learned only the first step is about drinking – the others are about dealing with the fear and the brokenness that made me a drunk in the first place. To this day, when I say, 'I'm an alcoholic,' I'm saying, 'Left to my own devices I'm terrified of everything and want to die.'"

I didn't know what to say, so he smiled and wrote down his phone number on a napkin.

"Sorry for rambling on, man. Call me if you ever want to go to a meeting."

I was too embarrassed to call him, but I went to some AA meetings on my own. I'd seen people sitting with their heads bowed, unable to look at anything except the floor beneath them. I'd been smug and had pitied them in their brokenness. And now it was October 18, 2008, and I was one of them, sitting in a metal folding chair at an AA meeting and staring at the wooden floor. I wanted to look up, to see who else was in the room, but I was too ashamed.

Being a spectator at AA meetings had been surprisingly fun – a lot like being a cultural anthropologist. But now I was the person who couldn't make eye contact, the suicidal addict who didn't have even one day sober, the sick and broken man who still had beer and vodka and cocaine running through his veins.

I vainly searched for any shred of evidence that could get me to leave this room, to return to the world of bars and feral promiscuity. But I had nothing except panic and sickness. I had been a rock star. I had been a king. Fame and wealth were supposed to have protected me and given my life meaning. They were supposed to have healed everything. But I'd failed. Fame hadn't solved my problems, and even my last loves, alcohol and degeneracy, didn't work anymore.

new york city (2008)

I settled into my metal folding chair and thought, *I'm done.* The tension left me as I sank into my defeat, and I started crying. I raised my hand, still unable to look at the room or meet anyone's eyes. I didn't want to say it. But I knew, finally, that it was true.

"I'm Moby, and I'm an alcoholic."